Legal Weed

A COMPREHENSIVE GUIDE TO CALIFORNIA
CANNABIS LAW & REGULATION

MANZURI LAW

Since 2008, the attorneys of Manzuri Law have vigorously defended those accused of cannabis - related crimes and educated the public about cannabis laws. We are dedicated to education, law, and working to affect policy.

MEITAL MANZURI, ESQ

Meital Manzuri has dedicated her career to legalization and to social justice. She began with criminal defense as her primary focus and was involved in several headline federal cannabis cases, beginning in 2005. Ever since, she has worked hard to defend and protect cannabis businesses from prosecution. Armed with her courtroom knowledge and expertise, Meital is California's premier Cannabis Law Attorney. Throughout her career, she has successfully gotten hundreds of cases dismissed, repeatedly persuaded government officials to return funds and cannabis to her clients, and advised thousand of cannabis businesses on compliance.

ALEXA STEINBERG, ESQ

Alexa joined Manzuri Law in 2015 and has quickly become one of LA's premier Cannabis Law Attorneys. She has a passion for cannabis business legal solutions and advises businesses operating in every facet of the cannabis industry. With countless hours of research, writing, and courtroom experience, she is an expert. Prior to 2015, Alexa excelled as a civil litigator for six years and as an investigative journalist for FOX 11 and CBS 2 News before that.

MICHELLE MABUGAT, ESQ

Michelle joined Manzuri Law of counsel in 2013 and then fully joined the firm in 2016. Michelle is an experienced trial attorney whose powerful combination of intellect and charm has quickly earned her a reputation for being one of the most highly-gifted young litigators in Southern California. In addition to her criminal practice, Michelle is one of the brightest legal minds in L.A.'s cannabis industry. Through her vast experience defending medical marijuana clients in criminal courts throughout Southern California, Michelle developed, almost inadvertently, an expertise in the fields of cannabis business law and regulatory compliance.

Provided By:

MANZURI LAW
Criminal Defense & Cannabis Law

Legal Weed is the 5th edition to the Legally-Blunt series: *Cannabis Law 101, Cannabis Law 102, California's Year of Marijuana 2016, CA Legal Cannabis Markets (2016)*

For an up to date, comprehensive review of California Law, Federal law and what 2017 has in store for us.

Written, Edited, and Compiled By:
Meital Manzuri, Michelle Mabugat and Alexa Steinberg

Graphics By:
Martina Lund

Special thanks and recognition to:
Hon. (ret) Steven Lubell and An-Chi Tsou for all your research and insight.

Supported By:

Navigating the weeds of cannabis justice.

Meital Manzuri, Esq. and Alexa Steinberg, Esq. are two attorneys of Manzuri Law. Since 2008, our office has been focusing on the ever-evolving cannabis laws. As legal cannabis business counsel and criminal defense attorneys, we provide legal support for cannabis businesses and patients.

The best legal trip you'll ever take.
WWW.LEGALLY-BLUNT.COM

LEGALLY-BLUNT
A CANDID PODCAST ON CANNABIS LAW
Available on iTunes

After ten years of educating cannabis businesses and consumers alike, Manzuri Law has taken its legal discussions to the next level with Legally-Blunt, a Manzuri Law Podcast where we provide insight into legal cannabis issues in California and the Los Angeles area. Legally-Blunt is the most fun you'll have listening to legal cannabis issues.

Join Beverly Hills Attorneys Meital Manzuri and Alexa Steinberg as they blaze a trail with their candid discussions on cannabis reform, confusing or vague local laws, and breaking industry news. They'll cut through the haze of cannabis regulations in California with a full dose of facts, timely hits of perspective, and tons of special guests.

A MANZURI LAW PUBLICATION

LEGAL WEED
A COMPREHENSIVE GUIDE TO CALIFORNIA CANNABIS LAW AND REGULATION

TABLE OF CONTENTS

FOREWORD	**1**
INTRODUCTION	**2**
CHAPTER I. FEDERAL LAW & CANNABIS	**4**
A. FEDERAL ENFORCEMENT POLICY: UNDER THE TRUMP ADMINISTRATION	4
B. FEDERAL ENFORCEMENT POLICY: UNDER THE OBAMA ADMINISTRATION	6
1. THE OGDEN MEMO – 2009	7
2. THE COLE MEMO - 2013	7
3. CONGRESS BANS DEA INTERFERENCE - 2014	8
4. CONGRESS VS. DEPARTMENT OF JUSTICE	9
a. THE COURT'S INTERPRETATION OF CONGRESS'S ROHRBACHER-FARR AMENDMENT - 2014	9
5. NINTH CIRCUIT AFFIRMS ROHRBACHER-FARR AMENDMENT AND DENIES FUNDING FOR FEDERAL PROSECUTION OF STATE COMPLIANT MEDICAL CBs	11
C. CANNABIS PROHIBITION IN THE UNITED STATES	13
1. FEDERAL CONTROLLED SUBSTANCES ACT ("CSA")	13
D. CANNABIS AS A SCHEDULE I SUBSTANCE	14
1. EFFORTS TO DE-SCHEDULE & RE-SCHEDULE CANNABIS	14
a. IN 2016, DEA FAILS TO RESCHEDULE	15
b. OBAMA ALLOWS FOR CANNABIS EDUCATION RESEARCH FACILITIES	17
E. HEMP AND CBD	18
1. FEDERAL HEMP LAW	18
a. HEMP NOT LEGAL IN ALL 50 STATES	20
2. MANUFACTURING AND/OR SELLING CBD PRODUCTS	21
a. THE INTERPLAY WITH FEDERAL HEMP LAWS AND CBD	21
b. FDA RULES CBD CANNOT BE MARKETED AS A DIETARY SUPPLEMENT	23
3. DEA'S ATTEMPT TO RESCHEDULE CBD	24
F. FEDERAL CANNABIS CRIMINAL LAW AND PENALTIES	25
1. MANDATORY MINIMUM SENTENCING	25
2. HOLDER'S PUSH AGAINST MINIMUM SENTENCING	26
G. PREEMPTION AND THE INTERPLAY BETWEEN STATE AND FEDERAL LAWS	27
H. CANNABIS AT THE BORDER: CUSTOMS AND BORDER PROTECTION	29
I. TRIBAL LAW	30
J. LOOKING AHEAD: PENDING FEDERAL CANNABIS BILLS (2017-2018)	34

CHAPTER II. CALIFORNIA CANNABIS LAW — 36

A. COMPLYING WITH THE COLLECTIVE MODEL — 36
   1. COMPASSIONATE USE ACT OF 1996 ("CUA") — 37
   2. THE MEDICAL MARIJUANA PROGRAM ACT ("MMP") — 38
       a. VOLUNTARY IDENTIFICATION CARD PROGRAM — 39
       b. QUANTITY LIMITATIONS — 40
   3. THE 2008 ATTORNEY GENERAL GUIDELINES — 41
       a. BASIC DEFINITIONS OF THE A.G. GUIDELINES — 42
       b. DIFFERENCE BETWEEN A COOPERATIVE AND A COLLECTIVE — 43
   4. PRACTICAL APPLICATION - THE CUA, MMP AND AGG — 45
       a. CHOOSING AN ENTITY — **45**
       b. BYLAWS AND CORPORATE GOVERNANCE — 52
       c. REQUIREMENTS OF COLLECTIVE MEMBERSHIP UNDER THE ATTORNEY GENERAL GUIDELINES — 52
       d. SELLER'S PERMITS, BUSINESS LICENSES AND SALES TAX — 54
       e. REASONABLE COMPENSATION — 55
   5. PRACTICAL APPLICATION: BUSINESS MODELS — 56
       a. DISPENSARY — 56
       b. DELIVERY SERVICES — 56
       c. CULTIVATING CANNABIS FOR A DISPENSARY OR COLLECTIVE — 56
       d. SELLING AND/OR MANUFACTURING CANNABIS CONCENTRATES — 57
       e. MAKING AND/OR SELLING EDIBLES — 59

B. THE MEDICAL CANNABIS REGULATION AND SAFETY ACT 2015 ("MCRSA") — 62
   1. THE COMPONENTS OF THE MCRSA — 62
   2. LICENSING UNDER MCRSA — 63
   3. CULTIVATION LICENSE TYPES 1-4 — 67
       a. LARGE SCALE CULTIVATORS (TYPES 3, 3A, 3B) — 68
       b. MEDIUM SCALE CULTIVATORS (TYPES 2, 2A, AND 2B) AND SMALL SCALE CULTIVATORS (TYPES 1, 1A, AND 1B) — 68
       c. "COTTAGE" CULTIVATORS (TYPE 1C) — 69
       d. NURSERIES (TYPE 4) — 70
   4. MANUFACTURING AND DISTRIBUTION LICENSES — 70
       a. MANUFACTURERS (TYPES 6 AND 7) — 71
       b. DISTRIBUTORS (TYPE 11) — 72
       c. AB 2679: PROTECTION FOR MANUFACTURERS — 72
   5. TRANSPORTAION LICENSES (TYPE 12) — 74
   6. TESTING LICENSES (TYPE 8) — 74
   7. DISPENSARY LICENSES (TYPE 10 AND 10A) — 75
   8. ENTITY STRUCTURE — 76
   9. PATIENT RIGHTS — 77
   10. COSTS OF ENFORCEMENT — 77
   11. LOCAL POWER — 77
   12. "PRIORITY" LICENSURE — 78

C. PROP 64, THE ADULT USE OF MARIJUANA ACT ("AUMA") — 78
   1. AUMA AFFECT ON THE MCRSA — 81

2. LICENSING UNDER AUMA	83
a. MCRSA vs. AUMA LICENSING	*85*
3. WHO QUALIFIES FOR AUMA LICENSING?	86
4. CRIMINAL PENALTIES UNDER AUMA	87
5. DRIVING UNDER THE INFLUENCE OF CANNABIS	89
6. THE IMPORTANCE OF LOCAL ORDINANCES	91
7. SEPTEMBER 1, 2016 DEADLINE	92
8. VERTICAL INTEGRATION	93
a. MCRSA – LARGELY PROHIBITED	*93*
b. AUMA – MORE PERMISSIVE	*95*
9. AUMA: INDUSTRIAL HEMP	95
a. THE INTERPLAY WITH FEDERAL HEMP LAWS AND CBD	*96*
D. LOOKING AHEAD: PENDING CALIFORNIA CANNABIS BILLS (2017-2018)	**100**
1. PROPOSED LEGISLATION	100
a. CULTIVATION	*100*
b. DRIVING UNDER THE INFLUENCE	*101*
c. GOVERNMENT INVOLVEMENT	*102*
d. MARKETING AND ADVERTISING	*102*
e. EDIBLE PACKAGING AND LABELING	*103*
f. PATIENTS AND EDUCATION	*103*
g. COURT PROCEEDINGS	*103*
h. PENALTIES	*104*
i. REGULATION	*104*
j. RESEARCH	*105*
k. TAXES, GRANTS AND CASH COLLECTIONS	*105*
l. TESTING	*106*
m. BUDGET BILLS AND PROPOSALS	*106*
2. TIMELINE FOR PROPOSED BILLS	107
E. CURRENT UNKNOWNS UNDER THE MCRSA & AUMA	**107**
1. LOCAL LICENSING	107
2. RESIDENCY REQUIREMENTS	108
3. BANKING	109
4. FOR-PROFIT VS. NON-PROFIT	109
5. DISTRIBUTORS	110
6. DELIVERY SERVICES	110
7. "CANOPY SIZE" AND "ONE PREMISES"	110
8. PRIORITY LICENSING	111
9. NUMBER OF AVAILABLE LICENSES	111
10. LICENSING APPLICATIONS AND FEES	111
11. LICENSING AVAILABLITY	112
12. COMBINING MEDICAL AND NON-MEDICAL LICENSES	112
13. "GREATER ENFORCEMENT" BY THE TRUMP ADMINISTRATION	113
F. 6 KEY STEPS TO PREPARE YOUR BUSINESS FOR STATE LICENSING	**113**
1. PICKING THE APPROPRIATE LICENSE TYPE FOR YOUR BUSINESS	113
2. OBTAINING A SUITABLE STATE AND LOCAL LAW COMPLIANT LOCATION	116
3. ORGANIZE YOUR FINANCES	116

4. Clean Up Your Criminal Record	117
5. Understand Priority Licensing	117
6. Get In Compliance with Local Law	117
G. California's Criminal Justice System and Cannabis	**118**
1. Criminal Laws & Penalties for Cannabis	118
2. The Collective and Cooperative Medical Defense	119
a. MCRSA: Collective Defense Sunset Clause	*120*
3. MCRSA: Criminal activity	120
4. Return of Propery After Criminal Case	122
5. Immigration Consequences of Cannabis-Related Convictions	123
6. Does Having A Criminal Record Affect Chances of Getting a Sate License?	123
H. Prop 64 Felony Reductions	**125**
1. Why You should Reduce Your Felony Conviction Under Prop 64	125
I. City Compliance	**126**

CHAPTER III. LOCAL ORDINANCES   128

A. Importance of Local Ordinances Under Both MCRSA and AUMA (Prop 64)	**128**
B. Local Enforcement Power Under the Constitution	**129**
C. California Cities that Regulate CBs	**130**
1. Proposition M in Los Angeles	131

CHAPTER IV. REAL ESTATE   135

A. Land Use, Real Estate & Landlord/Tenant Issues	**135**
1. Location	135
2. Renting to a Medical Cannabis Business	135
a. Under Federal Law	*135*
b. Under California Law	*137*
c. Under City Law	*137*
3. How to Verify if a Dispensary is Legal	138

CHAPTER V. BANKING & TAXATION   139

A. Banking & Cannabis	**139**
1. The Problem	139
2. The "Solutions"	139
a. Some Banks Will Take the Risk	*139*
b. Operating in Cash	*139*
c. Form 8300	*141*
d. Alternative Banking	*143*
e. State Ballot Efforts May Help Motivate Congress to Act	*143*
f. Small Banks Face Challenges Serving Cannabis Businesses	*144*

  g. Bigger Banks Will Become More Interested   *145*
  h. Federal Regulators Will Remain Reluctant to Push Major Policy Changes   *145*
B. Taxation & Cannabis   **146**
 1. Reducing 280E Exposure   147
  a. Costs of Goods Sold   *147*
  b. Additional Revenue Streams   *148*

CHAPTER VI. INTELLECTUAL PROPERTY ISSUES   149

A. Trademarks   **149**
 1. Federal Protection   150
 2. State Protection   151
 3. Common Law Protection   152
B. Trademark Licensing   **152**
C. Patents   **152**
D. Copyrights   **153**
E. Trade Secrets   **154**

CHAPTER VII. ANCILLARY BUSINESSES & ADVERTISING   155

A. Definition of Paraphernalia   **155**
 1. Federal Law: Paraphernalia   155
 2. California Law: Paraphernalia   156
 3. Advertising and Primary Intent of the Product   156
  a. California vs. Federal Law   *157*
 4. Items With No Lawful Use = Paraphernalia   157
 5. Lawful Sales of Smoking Products   157
B. Interstate Advertising & Disclaimers   **158**
C. New Advertising Rules Under the AUMA   **158**
D. Advertising Online & Potential Conflicts   **160**
 1. Facebook   160
 2. Twitter   160
 3. Instagram   160
 4. App Store   161
 5. Google   161

CHAPTER VIII. KNOW YOUR RIGHTS & ENCOUNTERS WITH LAW ENFORCEMENT   162

1. Assert Your Right to Remain Silent   **162**
2. What to do if You are Being Detained   **162**
3. What to do if You are Being Arrested   **163**
4. What to do if You are Being Questioned   **164**
5. What to do if You are Being Searched   **164**

6. WHAT TO DO IF YOU ARE STOPPED IN YOUR CAR 165
7. WHAT TO DO IF AN OFFICER SHOWS UP AT YOUR DOOR 165
8. WHAT DO DO IF AN OFFICER HAS A SEARCH WARRANT 166

APPENDIX 167

APPENDIX I – FEDERAL LAW 168

OGDEN MEMO - MEMORANDUM FOR SELECTED UNITED STATES ATTORNEYS: INVESTIGATIONS AND PROSECUTIONS IN STATES. AUTHORIZING THE USE OF MEDICAL MARIJUANA 169

COLE MEMO - MEMORANDUM FOR SELECTED UNITED STATES ATTORNEYS: GUIDANCE INVOLVING MARIJUANA ENFORCEMENT 173

GUIDELINES FOR FEDERAL PROSECUTION OF MARIJUANA RELATED CASES - DEPARTMENT OF JUSTICE MEMORANDUM TO DEA, HIDTA, AND FEDERAL TASK FORCE PARTNERS IN CALIFORNIA 179

SIGNIFICANT FEDERAL CASE LAW 185

APPENDIX II – CALIFORNIA LAW 192

ATTORNEY GENERAL GUIDELINES FOR THE SECURITY AND NON-DIVERSION OF MARIJUANA GROWN FOR MEDICAL USE (2008) 193

SIGNIFICANT CALIFORNIA CASE LAW 209

APPENDIX III – LOCAL ORDINANCES, PROPOSITION D & PROPOSITION M 217

LOS ANGELES PRE- ICO DISPENSARY LIST 218

LA CITY ATTORNEY REPORT ON DISCONTINUING BTRCs 219

PROPOSITION M, MARCH 2017 220

SIGNIFICANT LOCAL CASE LAW 221

END NOTES 227

FOREWORD

A few years ago, my former boss, Assemblymember Rob Bonta, and his then chief-of-staff, Dean Grafilo, asked me to help staff a bill on medical cannabis. I was thrilled. Not only was it a hot topic, but also it was a new and exciting space in public policy where no one had ever successfully passed a law to regulate cannabis in California. The challenge - a mountain of research and few reliable resources. As the Legislative Director for the Medical Cannabis Regulation and Safety Act ("MCRSA"), I had to start from scratch. If there had been a resource like *Legal Weed – A Comprehensive Guide to California Cannabis Law & Regulation* three years ago, I probably would have gotten a lot more sleep.

While working on the MCRSA, I had the pleasure of meeting and working with the incredible attorneys of Manzuri Law. They actively participated in state and local policy, providing legislators with valuable feedback from their legal and business experiences having lawyered in the cannabis space for nearly 10 years.

Legal Weed is a comprehensive guide that covers <u>all</u> aspects of the cannabis industry. From walking readers through the history of cannabis prohibition to legalization and tips on how to deal with law enforcement, the authors leave no stone unturned for the curious reader. And, unlike other legal publications that threaten to bore readers to tears with complex "legalese," *Legal Weed* is written in a fresh, compelling tone with a style that readers can relate to and understand.

The political climate and cannabis policies in California continue to change rapidly. Unlike when I first worked on the MCRSA, the question is no longer where to find information, it's about what information is both valuable, authoritative and trustworthy. This is your reliable, comprehensive resource on the evolving landscape of cannabis law in California. Enjoy.

An-Chi Tsou, Ph.D.
Principal, Tsou Consulting, LLC
Former Lead Staffer of the MCRSA &
Former Senior Policy Advisor to the Bureau of Medical Cannabis Regulation

INTRODUCTION

Interested in an opportunity in legal cannabis markets in California? We don't blame you...it's a highly sought after industry. According to the Arcview group, in 2016 alone, the California legal market for cannabis was a $2.7 billion dollar industry. By 2020, the California market is slated to reach $22 billion. See Change Institute expects these markets to enjoy explosive growth in the next five years – and this doesn't include the 20-plus potential new markets predicted to open. Nor does it include yet-to-be-conceived markets that surely will be opened by creative entrepreneurs and savvy visionaries. It is clear to everyone involved-- Mary Jane is on her way to a major makeover.

The "green" makeover in California began in October 2015, when Governor Jerry Brown signed into law the Medical Cannabis Regulation and Safety Act ("MCRSA"). This new law represents a complete overhaul of the state's program, dragging with it different kinds of consequences and an obstacle of rules. The landscape will change dramatically with this law for many reasons, the most potent of which is the fact that State's medical cannabis industry will no longer be a purely non-profit endeavor. Since the MCRSA implicitly permits for-profit cannabis enterprises in California, it will open significant opportunities for investors to capitalize on the world's single-largest market for legalized medical cannabis.

Then, in a historic vote in November 2016, California voters threw their support behind the full legalization of cannabis. By a vote of about 56% to 44%, voters passed Proposition 64, also called the Adult Use of Marijuana Act ("AUMA"), making California the fifth state to legalize recreational pot, after Colorado, Washington, Oregon and Alaska. The AUMA's regulatory system for recreational pot is modeled much after the MCRSA. The AUMA legalizes the cultivation, possession and use of cannabis for adult-use purposes, and it provides for state licenses to be issued for commercial activities related to recreational pot.

In sum, the evolution of the law aims for the robust regulation of medical and recreational cannabis businesses in California, which will create jobs, increase tax revenue, and, in general, greatly boost the state's economy. Now that the MCRSA and AUMA have passed, California is poised to become the largest legal weed market in the entire world.

Combine the eye-popping numbers with the seemingly limitless opportunities bound to spring up, and it's easy to see why many outside business investors are rushing to get in. And getting in now (or at least soon), with the industry still in its relative infancy, may mean your best chance at realizing amazing profits.

However, if you want to get involved with this burgeoning industry, tread carefully. True, opportunities this new and great haven't existed in California in some time, but profit-turning comes with a price. In addition to the typical business owner problems – such as marketing, logistics, and capital –Cannabis Businesses ("CBs") have a myriad of other unique legal hurdles. For starters, they must navigate various federal, state, and local agencies and remain up-to-date with a host of ever-changing medical cannabis laws and regulations. To add to that, CBs require a substantial investment. Yet banks are not industry-friendly, and any CBs lucky enough to get a bank to take their money is subject to overinflated tax rates. Furthermore, without proper local permitting law enforcement could raid an operation and arrest everyone on site at any given time. Thus, anyone deciding to take the plunge into this industry must prepare for hurdles.

In light of the newly elected Trump Administration and Attorney General Jeff Sessions, some suggest that the state should put recreational licensing on hold until federal enforcement policies are made more clear with respect to recreational cannabis.

However, when asked whether state officials were worried about a possible shift in cannabis policy under the new Trump administration, Bureau chief Ajax stated that unless the feds announce a dramatic shift in federal policy, California is moving ahead as planned with state licensing for recreational pot.

Take heart, though. Despite the reams of red tape and uncertainty, the industry has nowhere to go but up. If you want to take advantage and get in before the industry really soars, do it now.

Disclaimer: Although not exhaustive, this book provides some of the tools and information needed to navigate the maze of legal requirements for operating a medical or recreational CB in California. It does not, however, constitute legal advice; thus, always consult an attorney before moving forward. By following these guidelines and consulting an attorney, you can set up your business more confidently.

CHAPTER I.
FEDERAL LAW & CANNABIS

The circumstances surrounding cannabis and Federal Law continue to keep us all scratching our heads. Below is a summary of Federal Cannabis Law, its progression, and where it is speculated to go.

Under the Obama administration, it was made clear that Federal policy "steadfastly oppose[d] legalization of marijuana," but it did not stand in the way of states such as Colorado, Oregon and Washington from legalizing cannabis within their own borders.[1]

The new Trump administration, however, appears ready to take a much tougher stance on legalized cannabis than the Obama administration ever did – at least when it comes to recreational pot. Therefore, any shifts in federal enforcement policy under the new administration could likely impact the California's recreational industry going forward.

A. FEDERAL ENFORCEMENT POLICY: UNDER THE TRUMP ADMINISTRATION

During his campaign, President Donald Trump pledged his support behind medical cannabis "100%," and suggested that recreational cannabis should remain an issue that's dealt with at the state level.

Then, in February 2017, White House press secretary Sean Spicer suggested otherwise. During a press briefing, Spicer told reporters at the White House that he expects states to be subject to "greater enforcement" of federal laws against cannabis use, a move that could potentially undercut the growing number of jurisdictions that have legalized the drug for recreational purposes.

Spicer explained that President Trump sees "a big difference" between use of cannabis for medical purposes and for recreational purposes. "The president understands the pain and suffering that many people go through who are facing, especially terminal diseases, and the comfort that some of these drugs, including medical marijuana, can bring to them," Spicer told reporters. "[But] that's very different than recreational use, which is something the Department of Justice, I think, will be further looking into."[2]

If there were any teeth to Spicer's statements, a renewed focus on recreational pot in weed-friendly states would present a departure from the Trump campaign's statements in favor of states' rights. "Greater enforcement" by the feds would also shift away from cannabis policy under the Obama administration, which said in the 2013 Cole Memo that it would not intervene in state's cannabis laws as long as they keep the drug from crossing state lines and away from children and drug cartels.

So far, Trump's pick for U.S. Attorney General – former Alabama senator Jeff Sessions – has stayed vague on the issue. It's no secret that the staunch Republican has been a long-time vocal opponent of cannabis legalization. In March 2017, the Attorney General reiterated his position on a conservative radio show, saying that the Justice Department will commit to enforcing federal laws on cannabis in an "appropriate way." "[M]arijuana is against federal law, and that applies in states where they may have repealed their own anti-marijuana laws," Sessions said. "And I'm not in favour of legalization of marijuana. I think it's a more dangerous drug than a lot of people realize."[3] Sessions also recently told reporters that the Cole Memo is under review.[4]

Unfortunately, the reality is – if Sessions wanted to start raiding recreational pot shops in California, there's nothing California could do to stop him because cannabis is still federally illegal.

Currently, medical cannabis in California is somewhat protected from the feds by the Rohrabacher-Farr Amendment. Passed in 2014, this amendment prohibits the DOJ from using federal funds to prosecute medical cannabis businesses that are "fully compliant" with state law. But while the amendment provides some comfort to those in the medical industry, the newly-legalized adult use industry will enjoy no such protection because the amendment only applies to medical cannabis.

At this point though, it's still too early to predict what Sessions may or may not do with respect to recreational pot in California. While Sessions technically wields the power to destroy the entire legal weed industry, the "nuclear option" would come with some serious economic and political backlash from the states. In fact, a Quinnipiac University poll released in February 2017 found that 71% of Americans would oppose efforts to enforce federal cannabis laws in legalized states. The poll also found that 93% of voters support allowing the use of cannabis for medical purposes and 59% support making it legal for all purposes.[5]

Before he was confirmed, Sessions reportedly gave some private assurances to senators that he was not considering a major shift in federal enforcement, despite his opposition to the use of cannabis. "He told me he would have some respect for states' rights on these things. Ando so I'll be very unhappy if the federal government decides to go into Colorado and Washington and all of these places. And that's not [what] my interpretation of my conversation with him was. That this wasn't his intention," said Senator Rand Paul (R-Kentucky) in an interview.[6]

Nonetheless, law enforcement leaders in L.A. seem to believe that the potential of "greater enforcement" is real. In a March interview with the Associated Press, Los Angeles County Sheriff Jim McDonnell said that he fully expects the DOJ to follow through on threats to crack down on recreational pot and that he wouldn't be surprised if the DOJ specifically targeted California just "to set the tone."[7]

If McConnell is right, does this mean that all the rec shops in California would get raided by the feds? Highly unlikely. From a practical standpoint, it just wouldn't be feasible. The DOJ simply doesn't have enough resources to shut down every single shop in the state. A more likely scenario would be the DOJ going after bigger players in the state's rec industry in hopes that the threat of prosecution would deter others from operating.

Again, however, no one can be sure yet how encompassing the federal government will be with its enforcement, but it clearly has the industry, and investors, on edge. State and federal officials from legalization states have asked the Justice Department for guidance but have received no clear answers.[8]

For now, the cannabis industry is moving forward with the assumption that it will be "business as usual"[9] and that cannabis is a low priority item on Trump's agenda. "We are going to focus on what we can control in our state," says Lori Ajax, California's chief of the Bureau of Cannabis Regulation. "Now we're operating under the federal guidelines (established by former President Obama). We will operate under these guidelines until we hear otherwise. That's the best way to move forward at this point."[10]

In other words, while the coming months could mean status quo or chaos for the legal cannabis industry, the broad approach seems to be: Until something changes federally, legal states (like California) are moving ahead as planned. The industry will continue to watch Sessions closely.

B. FEDERAL ENFORCEMENT POLICY UNDER: THE OBAMA ADMINISTRATION

When Barack Obama ran for President in 2008, he insisted that medical cannabis was an issue best left to state and local governments. During a March 22, 2008 interview with Gary Nelson, editorial page editor for the Oregon newspaper *Mail Tribune,* Obama promised: "I'm not going to be using Justice Department resources to try to circumvent state laws on this issue."[11] Shortly after Obama was elected, White House spokesman Nick Shapiro spoke in alignment with the President's promise stating:

> "The president believes that federal resources should not be used to circumvent state laws, and as he continues to appoint senior leadership to fill out the ranks of the federal government, he expects them to review their policies with that in mind."[12]

1. THE OGDEN MEMO – 2009

In October 2009, Holder recorded his stated policy in a memo written by then Deputy Attorney General David W. Ogden. (See Appendix I for complete text of the Ogden Memo) This memo was direct to United States attorneys in states with medical cannabis programs, and said that federal law enforcement efforts should not **"focus federal sources ... on individuals whose actions are in clear and unambiguous compliance with state laws providing for the medical use of marijuana."**[13] The Ogden Memo listed certain characteristics of "illegal drug trafficking activity of potential federal interest," which included, among other things, sales to minors, violence, unlawful possession of firearms and ties to criminal organizations.[14]

Although Obama's campaign statements in the Ogden memo sounded promising for medical cannabis, they specifically extended only to individual patient protection. Then, in 2010, Holder announced that federal authorities would continue to prosecute individuals for cannabis crimes, regardless of cannabis being legal in some states. In fact, according to CNN, Holder went so far as to say that the Department of Justice ("DOJ") would continue to "vigorously enforce"[15] the CSA in California even if state voters approved an initiative on the 2010 ballot to legalize the drug.[16] This extreme position was immediately reaffirmed by federal prosecutors in Oakland, California, when United States Attorney Melinda Haag warned the city that the federal government "[would] enforce the [CSA] vigorously against individuals and organizations that participate in unlawful manufacturing and distribution activity involving cannabis ... even if such activities are permitted under state law."[17]

2. THE COLE MEMO – 2013

But in August 2013, the DOJ backtracked. James Cole, who replaced Ogden as Deputy Attorney General, issued a memo stating that the DOJ's position to limit federal resources, as articulated in the Ogden Memorandum has not changed. Specifically, the Cole Memo stated "it is likely not an efficient use of federal resources to focus enforcement efforts on individuals with cancer or other serious illnesses who use cannabis as part of a recommended treatment regimen consistent with applicable state law, or their caregivers."[18] The Cole Memo, also established that caregivers were "not commercial operations cultivating, selling or distributing cannabis."[19] (*See* Appendix I for complete text of the Cole Memo) It went on to state that the Ogden Memo "was never intended to shield such activities from federal enforcement action and prosecution, even where those activities purport to comply with state law."[20] This meant that cannabis dispensaries, even those operating legally under state law, were still vulnerable to criminal prosecutions by federal action. For example, in California, "clear and unambiguous compliance with state law" thus referred to individual patients in possession of a personal amount of cannabis or cultivating a personal amount of cannabis. In California, commercial cultivation and distribution is still subject to Federal prosecution.

In April 2012, in a *Rolling Stone* interview, President Obama tried to explain his 2008 campaign comments regarding medical cannabis, claiming that the recent crackdown on dispensaries was in line with his intent. "What I specifically said was that we were not going to prioritize prosecutions of persons who are using medical marijuana," Obama said. "I never made a commitment that somehow we were going to give carte blanche to large-scale producers and operators of marijuana -- it's against federal law."

As will be discussed in more detail below, current U.S. Attorney General Jeff Sessions has indicated that the so-called Cole Memo is "under review."

3. CONGRESS BANS DEA INTERFERENCE – 2014

May 2014 marked a huge change in Federal cannabis policy when Congress approved the Rohrbacher-Farr Amendment ("the Amendment"), named after its lead proponents, Dana Rohrabacher (R-California) and Sam Farr (D-California).

Therein, by a vote of 219-189, Congress stripped the DEA and DOJ of its funds to interfere with states where medical cannabis has been legalized.

In a statement after the Amendment's passing, Farr said: "States with medical marijuana laws are no longer the outliers; they are the majority. This vote showed that Congress is ready to rethink how we treat medical marijuana patients in this country. This amendment gives states the right to determine their own laws for medical cannabis use; free of federal intervention. It also gives patients comfort knowing they will have safe access to the medical care legal in their state without the fear of federal prosecution."

Similarly, Congressman Ted Lieu from Los Angeles stated: "Spending one penny on cannabis criminalization or enforcement is a ridiculous waste of taxpayer dollars."

The Result? Exciting things. First, the DEA's budget for cannabis crackdowns, formerly a $23 million expenditure, has become a ransacked piggy bank. That cannabis crackdown money has now been reassigned to the fight against child abuse, deficit reduction, processing rap kits and paying for body cameras on police officers. Second, as discussed below, the Amendment proved to have real teeth here in California where an appellate court kicked the DEA out of a Dispensary prosecution case.

Since the Amendment was first passed in 2014, it has been renewed each year with increasing number of votes from Congress. We are thus happy to report that, although there is much progress to be made, Congress is finally making an attempt to catch up with the American Public. The most recent extension of the Amendment expires on April 28, 2017.

4. CONGRESS VS. DEPARTMENT OF JUSTICE

a. THE COURTS' INTERPRETATION OF CONGRESS'S ROHRBACHER-FARR AMENDMENT – 2014

The DOJ protested the Rohrabacher-Farr Amendment in several ways. First, the DOJ tried to dissuade Congress from renewing the Amendment. The DOJ circulated a 30+ page secret memo warning lawmakers of the threat that the Amendment posed to civilized society. The memo further revealed the DOJ position that, even if the Amendment passed, the DOJ was not bound by it at all. Specifically, the DOJ concluded in the memo that the Amendment doesn't actually prevent the federal government from pursuing prosecutions against anyone, even those who are operating strictly in accordance with state medical cannabis laws. The DOJ memo pushed the idea that the DEA can still raid, and U.S. attorneys can still prosecute, medical cannabis businesses who violate the CSA, whether in a legalized state or not.

The DOJ says the memo only narrowly applies to them - that the DOJ is only prohibited from actions against state officials for issuing licenses and collecting taxes, or lawsuits claiming state laws are preempted by federal ones. We now know that the DOJ's interpretation of the Amendment in this memo was completely wrong.

In October 2015, the Amendment beat the DOJ in a district federal court in California. In a case now spanning more than 17 years, U.S. District Court Judge Charles R. Breyer gave some real teeth to the Amendment by narrowing the scope of an injunction against a California dispensary called Marin Alliance for Medical Marijuana ("MAMM"), effectively allowing the dispensary to re-open for business, and prohibiting the DOJ from spending any more public money to enforce the CSA against California dispensaries.[21]

Some background to the case: In 1998, the DOJ filed suit against MAMM and several other California dispensaries on the grounds that they were distributing cannabis in violation of the CSA. In 2002, a permanent injunction was entered against MAMM prohibiting it from operation. MAMM ignored the injunction and continued operating for nine (9) more years. The DOJ did nothing in response and stayed mum the entire time. Then, in 2011, the DOJ issued a cease-and-desist letter to MAMM and initiated asset forfeiture proceedings, which ultimately forced MAMM to close its doors. Throughout the case, there was never a dispute that MAMM was operating in compliance with state law. In fact, the Fairfax mayor, in a letter to U.S. Attorney Melinda Haag and in court filings, described MAMM as a "model business" that carefully followed the conditions of its local use permit.[22]

Fast-forward to June 2015, MAMM filed a motion arguing that the newly-enacted Amendment warranted taking another look at the injunction entered against it. Judge Breyer agreed and revisited the injunction. Although he did not grant MAMM's request to lift the injunction entirely, he did order that the injunction could only be enforced against MAMM insofar as MAMM violated state law. Because MAMM's compliance with state law was never at issue, it effectively allowed MAMM to re-open its doors for business (although it does not appear that MAMM has any immediate plans to do so).[23]

In his 13-page order issued October 2015[24], Judge Breyer vehemently disagreed with the DOJ's interpretation of the Amendment, calling it "tortured" and "opportunistic." In his view, the DOJ was arguing that the injunction should be kept in place because the closure of one dispensary did not interfere with the implementation of state medical cannabis laws. "It defies language and logic for the Government to argue that it does not 'prevent' California from 'implementing' its medical marijuana laws by shutting down these same heavily-regulated medical cannabis dispensaries," Breyer wrote. "And contrary to the Government's representation, the record here does support a finding that Californians' access to legal medical cannabis has been substantively impeded by the closing of dispensaries, and the closing of MAMM in particular."[25] Based upon a plain reading of the Amendment, the judge held that the DOJ was prohibited from spending public money to enforce the CSA against medical cannabis dispensaries in California. The DOJ initially asked the United States Court of Appeals for the Ninth Circuit to reverse Judge Breyer's decision, but later changed its mind and abandoned the appeal. In other words, rather than continuing to prosecute MAMM in hopes of setting a landmark legal precedent, the feds just gave up on the case. MAMM, if it so chooses, is now free to operate as a dispensary in California without fear of federal prosecution.

With this decision, the cannabis industry won a major legal victory, as it stood for the argument that medical CBs should be shielded from federal raids and prosecution, so long as they comply with state law. Interestingly, it also coincided with California's passage of MCRSA. The need for state law to be clear-cut has never been more apparent.

5. NINTH CIRCUIT AFFIRMS ROHRBACHER-FARR AMENDMENT AND DENIES FUNDING FOR FEDERAL PROSECUTION OF STATE COMPLIANT MEDICAL CBs

On August 16, 2016, another federal appeals court agreed with Judge Breyer's reading of the Amendment, sending yet another strong message to the DOJ to "back off." In *United States v. McIntosh,* the U.S. Court of Appeals for the Ninth Circuit (which includes California) issued an opinion ruling that the Amendment prohibits the DOJ from prosecuting cannabis suppliers who "fully comply" with state laws allowing medical cannabis within their borders. The *McIntosh* case grouped together 10 separate appeals by medical cannabis growers and dispensary operators in California and Washington who were indicted on a variety of federal charges.

Like MAMM, the defendants in *McIntosh* argued that prosecuting them violated the Amendment, which states that "none of the funds made available in this Act to the Department of Justice" to "prevent [states] from implementing their own State laws that authorize the use, distribution, possession or cultivation of medical marijuana."[26] The Ninth Circuit agreed with the defendants, explaining that even though the Amendment is "not a model of clarity," it prohibited the DOJ from spending money on prosecuting people "who engaged in conduct permitted by the State Medical Marijuana Laws and who fully complied with such laws."[27] The Ninth Circuit stated that federal cannabis defendants are therefore entitled to evidentiary hearings at which they can try to show their actions were authorized by state law.[28]

While the *McIntosh* ruling is a tremendous victory for cannabis reform (and another huge setback for the DOJ), the *McIntosh* decision is actually very complicated and has several limitations. For one, the *McIntosh* case applies *only* to medical cannabis (and nothing else) in the specific geographic area covered by the Ninth Circuit: Alaska, Arizona, California, Hawaii, Idaho, Montana, Nevada, Oregon, Washington, Guam and the Northern Marianas Islands.[29] This means that the ruling doesn't technically cover medical cannabis markets in other states nor does it cover the recreational markets in Alaska, Washington and Oregon. Moreover, the *McIntosh* ruling firmly details that cannabis remains illegal under federal law: "To be clear, [the Rohrbacher Amendment] does not provide immunity from prosecution for federal marijuana offenses. Anyone in any state who possesses, distributes, or manufactures marijuana for medical or recreational purposes (or attempts or conspires to do so) is committing a federal crime."[30]

Secondly, it could prove difficult for these 10 defendants to ultimately pass the test under *McIntosh*. The ruling makes clear that there is *no guarantee* that any of the defendants' convictions will actually be thrown out. Instead, what the Ninth Circuit basically did is this: They remanded (i.e., sent back) the cases to the lower federal courts because "[defendants] are entitled to evidentiary hearings to determine whether their conduct was completely authorized by state law, by which we mean that they strictly complied with all relevant conditions imposed by state law …"[31] So, if a district court conducts a hearing and finds that a defendant operated in a manner that violated state cannabis laws (i.e., for profit in California[32]), the Amendment does not apply. If the Amendment does not apply, then the DOJ can continue to prosecute them using public funds. At the time of writing of this book, there have been no evidentiary hearings held yet for any defendants in *McIntosh*. As such, it still remains to be seen whether all or *any* of these dispensaries will be able to avoid prosecution.

Finally, and of certainly no small import, the *McIntosh* opinion hints that its ruling could only be temporary. The court notes that such prosecutions *could* happen in the future (if the DOJ wanted) because "Congress could appropriate funds for such prosecutions tomorrow."[33] The court continues: "The federal government can prosecute such offenses for up to five years after they occur … Congress currently restricts the government from spending certain funds to prosecute certain individuals. But Congress could restore funding tomorrow, a year from now, or four years from now, and the government could then prosecute individuals who committed offenses while the government lacked funding." In a footnote, the court also noted that "a new president will be elected soon, and a new administration could shift enforcement priorities to place greater emphasis on prosecuting marijuana offenses."[34] Translation – if the Amendment fails to be renewed in the next federal budget, the DOJ can pick up right where it left off and continue going after medical cannabis operators in any state, as early as the beginning of 2017.[35]

C. CANNABIS PROHIBITION IN THE UNITED STATES

1. FEDERAL CONTROLLED SUBSTANCES ACT ("CSA")

When President Nixon took office in 1970, he declared a national "war on drugs." Congress then enacted legislation that resulted in the Comprehensive Drug Abuse Prevention and Control Act of 1970.[36] Title II of the Act is known as the Controlled Substances Act ("CSA").[37] The CSA creates a statutory framework through which the federal government regulates the lawful production, possession and distribution of controlled substances.[38] The purpose of the CSA was to combat drug abuse, prevent the movement of drugs from legal to illegitimate channels, and eliminate "[t]he illegal importation, manufacture, distribution, and possession and improper use of controlled substances."[39] **To accomplish these purposes, the CSA places various "drugs" into one of five "schedules" based on the substance's medical use, potential for abuse, and safety or dependence liability.**[40]

Cannabis is currently classified under the CSA as a "Schedule I" drug. Drugs fall into Schedule I if the drug has: (1) "a high potential for abuse"; (2) "no currently accepted medical use in treatment in the United States"; and (3) "a lack of accepted safety for use under medical supervision."[41] This means that cannabis is subject to the most severe restrictions contained within the CSA.[42] No exceptions are made for cannabis used in the course of a recommended medical treatment.[43]

Though public opinion polls demonstrate that Americans today largely view cannabis as safer than all the drugs listed in Schedules I and II, the power to reschedule or de-schedule cannabis ultimately lies in the hands of Congress, either through new legislation specific to cannabis or through tailored amendments to the CSA.[44] In response to public sentiment, multiple bills have been introduced that, at minimum, propose to move cannabis from a Schedule I to a Schedule II drug. Unfortunately, all the proposed bills have died in committee. Should cannabis be successfully rescheduled or descheduled altogether in the future, it would be huge – that would mean that states could freely promulgate state-wide regulation without fear of federal intervention and CBs could operate without fear of federal prosecution.

D. CANNABIS AS A SCHEDULE I SUBSTANCE

The **Controlled Substance Act ("CSA")** puts known drugs into one of five (5) schedules. Under the CSA requirements, the government must consider eight (8) factors when deciding how to schedule an illicit substance. These factors include the drug's potential for abuse, the state of current scientific knowledge about the substance and the drug's psychic or physiological dependence liability.[45]

Schedule I drugs are those that are the most restricted by the law while Schedule V are the least restricted. The Drug Enforcement Administration (DEA) defines Schedule I drugs, amongst other criteria, as substances "with no currently accepted medical use and a high potential for abuse."[46] They are "the most dangerous drugs of all the drug schedules with potentially severe psychological or physical dependence."[47] Schedule I drugs are heroin, LSD, ecstasy and, yes, cannabis.[48]

Schedule II drugs have "less abuse potential than Schedule I drugs," but "are also considered dangerous," these include methamphetamine, Oxycodone, Adderall, Cocaine and others.[49]

1. EFFORTS TO DE-SCHEDULE & RE-SCHEDULE CANNABIS

Public opinion polls demonstrate that Americans today largely view cannabis as safer than all the drugs listed in Schedules I and II. Furthermore, many believe that cannabis doesn't belong in the DEA schedule, period. However, there is still a minority of Americans who agree with the DEA that cannabis has "no currently accepted medical use" or that it has "a high potential for abuse."[50]

In response to public sentiment, multiple bills have been introduced that propose to move cannabis from Schedule I to Schedule II. The first of which was introduced in 1981. Subsequently, similar bills were introduced, all of which died in committee. Most recently, in 2011, Senators Rand Paul, Cory Booker and Kirsten Gillibrand introduced a Senate bill to legalize medical cannabis under federal law. Most importantly, the bill required the DEA to not only reschedule cannabis, but also to remove cannabis from the schedules entirely ("de-scheduling").[51]

The power to reschedule or de-schedule cannabis lies in the hands of Congress, either through new legislation specific to cannabis or through tailored amendments to the CSA.[52] Furthermore, the Obama administration is fully willing to work with Congress if lawmakers want to take cannabis off the list of what the federal government considers the most dangerous drugs.[53] Even more notable is that the DEA has the power to reschedule cannabis on its own, but has thus far refused to do so.[54]

The DEA is the federal agency that is primarily responsible for regulating controlled substances like cannabis. But the Food and Drug Administration, along with the National Institute on Drug Abuse, provides the DEA with recommendations about the appropriate level of restriction for illicit substances which translates to the drug Scheduling statuses.[55] Per DEA request, the FDA is currently engaged in a review of the medical evidence concerning the safety and effectiveness of cannabis. This evaluation was a request from the DEA, following a number of citizens' petitions asking for a review.

Rescheduling cannabis from Schedule I to Schedule II or de-scheduling cannabis altogether would mean that the current or future medical cannabis states could freely promulgate statewide regulation without fear of federal intervention. Furthermore, businesses that are now operating in the black market or gray area would have an avenue to legitimize themselves without fear of federal prosecution.[56] Rescheduling will serve to reduce the black market for cannabis, scale back enforcement expenditure, and rationalizes current law, all while freeing many cannabis users from ill-advised legal threats and penalties.[57] Furthermore, the rescheduling or de-scheduling will lend an avenue to allow for medical research of cannabis.

That is exactly what was argued for in *United States v Pickard*,[58] in 2015. Much to our dismay, in *Pickard*, the federal district court judge in Sacramento held that Congress acted rationally in classifying cannabis as a Schedule I substance.

a. IN 2016, DEA FAILS TO RESCHEDULE

As expected, in August 2016, the DEA formally denied a petition to reschedule cannabis, meaning that in the eyes of the feds, cannabis continues on as a Schedule I narcotic with no medical value, akin to drugs like heroin and LSD.[59] DEA Chief, Chuck Rosenberg, claims the decision was rooted in science, and they gave "enormous weight" to conclusions by the Food and Drug Administration (FDA) that cannabis has "no currently accepted medical use in treatment in the United States."[60] Rosenberg added that the decision wasn't based on "danger," but only whether cannabis "is a safe and effective medicine … and it's not."[61]

Although expected, the DEA's failure to reschedule clashed with cannabis advocates across the country. Representative Early Blumenauer (D-OR) described the decision as "further evidence that the DEA doesn't get it."[62] According to Beverly Hills attorney, Alexa Steinberg, who regularly represents clients in California's medical cannabis industry, "The DEA has tried to do this three times already. So I think that people were hopeful, but they weren't surprised when it ended up not being rescheduled."[63]

Though Steinberg "sees the DEA's decisions as a lost opportunity,"[64] some believe that even if the DEA had chosen to reschedule cannabis, it would have been a "nightmare scenario"[65] for medical cannabis businesses from a legal standpoint. "It's not really clear that rescheduling would do a whole lot to solve the conflict between federal marijuana laws," law professor Alex Kreit explains. "If marijuana were moved into Schedule II, the conflict between state medical marijuana laws and federal drug law would really remain, to a large degree. Because Schedule II drugs can't just be distributed in the way that state medical marijuana laws permit them to be distributed."[66]

Take, for instance, other Schedule II drugs such as Adderall and OxyContin. Though these drugs have widely accepted medical value, they are among the most tightly regulated drugs that U.S. pharmacies are allowed to dispense due to strict regulations from the Food and Drug Administration (FDA). Because cannabis is currently prohibited as an illegal Schedule I drug with no medical benefit, its manufacture, distribution, sale and use is policed by federal law enforcement agencies, such as the DEA. But experts say that if cannabis is reclassified as a Schedule II drug, the FDA will have to step in and subject it to the same kind of scrutiny typically reserved for drugs like Adderall and OxyContin.[67]

Many worry that keeping up with FDA compliance could ultimately prove too costly for smaller players in the cannabis industry.[68] Not only would cannabis companies be subject to intense inspections and testing, they would also need to get their packaging and labeling approved by the FDA, and their manufacturing facilities would have to be up to FDA standards. If, for example, a small brand says its cannabidiol (CBD) oil cures seizures, the product would be targeted for testing.[69] If the claim that the product "cures" seizures is unproven, the small company could be charged with criminal misbranding, subjecting its operators to huge fines and/or potential prison time.[70] Simply put, today's cannabis industry may not be prepared to hang with the pharmaceutical big boys who already have the necessary know-how and deep pockets to manufacture Schedule II drugs. Indeed, "this is the red carpet for Purdue Pharma and Pfizer to enter the industry."[71] As such, some people in the cannabis industry believe that the DEA's recent refusal to reschedule could actually be a blessing in disguise.[72]

With that said, the DEA's decision to deny rescheduling still stung for those in the reform community because it repeated a statement about cannabis: that it has *no* medical value.

b. OBAMA ALLOWS FOR CANNABIS EDUCATION RESEARCH FACILITIES

The DEA did, however, toss a meaningful bone to the industry in August 2016 by making a parallel announcement that it would expand the amount of cannabis grown for medical research.[73] For almost 50 years, the University of Mississippi has been the *only* site in the U.S. that can legally manufacture cannabis for scientific purposes. This is due to a DEA-mandated monopoly on the growth of cannabis for research, which is administered through the National Institutes on Drug Abuse (NIDA).[74] Under the NIDA monopoly, researchers have long complained about the inability to access sufficient quality cannabis to conduct comprehensive research.

For instance, researcher Dr. Sue Sisley, who was awarded millions by the state of Colorado to research the medical use of cannabis as a treatment for PTSD, said in recent weeks that her team had yet to receive the study plant for the trial despite having requested it over twenty months prior.[75] According to NIDA, the specific strain she requested can't be provided because Ole Miss hasn't been able to create it yet, which means that Dr. Sisley's research will continue to be delayed until NIDA learns how to grow better cannabis.[76] These bureaucratic barriers created by the NIDA are "really the final hurdle that continue to impede cannabis research in this country," says Dr. Sisley.[77]

The DEA plans to change all that. The DEA's new policy proposes to not only allow new registrants to grow cannabis for federally funded research, but also for privately funded commercial endeavors.[78] "As long as folks abide by the rules, and we're going to regulate that, we want to expand the availability, the variety, the type of cannabis available to legitimate researchers," DEA Chief Rosenberg said in comments published by National Public Radio. "If our understanding of the science changes, that could very well drive a new decision."[79]

This is positive news, says Steinberg: "I think the denial to reschedule and the expansion of access to research opens a lot more doors."[80] The end of the NIDA monopoly will lead to the expansion of federal grow sites, which will mean higher-grade and more diverse cannabis for better scientific research. This, in turn, will allow researchers an opportunity to more convincingly answer the multi-billion dollar question: does cannabis have medical value??? So, although cannabis remains a Schedule I drug, at least for now, the end of the NIDA monopoly could facilitate rescheduling (or maybe even descheduling!) in the future.

E. HEMP AND CBD

Before we discuss the federal laws surrounding hemp, it's important to understand the scientific differences between hemp and cannabis. Though the terms hemp and cannabis are often used interchangeably, these two plants have very different characteristics. This is why the law treats hemp differently than it treats cannabis.

Both hemp and cannabis are derived from the plant species *Cannabis sativa L.,* which is one of the world's oldest domesticated crops. [Fun Fact: George Washington and Thomas Jefferson both used to grow hemp![81]] Ancient cultivators grew one variety of the cannabis plant to be tall and durable – which is what we now call industrial hemp. Upon later discovering that the flower buds of the cannabis plant had psychoactive effects, cultivators then began breeding and manipulating the flowering plants in order to isolate their "medicinal characteristics" – which has evolved into what we call cannabis plants today.[82]

While hemp only contains trace amounts of THC (less than 1%), cannabis typically contains around 20% THC. Cannabis is usually grown to produce the maximum amount of female flowering plants (which contain the highest concentration of THC), while hemp is primarily cultivated to produce male plants and thus does not produce flowers.

But THC is not the only chemical compound produced by hemp and cannabis. After THC, cannabidiol (CBD) is the second major cannabinoid found in both hemp and cannabis. Because CBD doesn't have psychoactive, mind-altering affects, it has become a popular choice for medical users. However, as will be discussed below, the law essentially states that the legality of CBD depends on whether it was sourced from either hemp or cannabis. We know – it's a weird state of affairs. But that's simply how the federal hemp laws have evolved to date.

1. FEDERAL HEMP LAW

Hemp was outlawed in 1937 under the Prohibitive Marihuana Tax law. Under current U.S. drug policy, all cannabis varieties, including hemp, are considered Schedule I controlled substances under the Controlled

Substances Act. (CSA, 21 U.S.C. §§801 et seq.; Title 21 CFR Part 1308.11). Hemp production is therefore controlled and regulated by the U.S. Drug Enforcement Administration (DEA).[83]

But if growing hemp is federally illegal in the U.S., then why do we see hemp everywhere? We use hemp lotion, eat hemp cereal, wear clothing made out of hemp, use reusable hemp shopping bags ... etc. In fact, the U.S. is the world's largest consumer of hemp products, but is the only major industrialized country that outlaws commercial hemp production.[84] Confused yet?

The conundrum exists due to a few legal loopholes. In 2003, the Ninth Circuit Court of Appeals ruled that although it is federally illegal to cultivate hemp *inside the U.S.*, it is technically not illegal to *import* hemp if it contains less than .3% THC. This federal court case was called *Hemp Industries Association ("HIA"), et al. v. Drug Enforcement Administration*.[85] In that case, manufacturers of hemp products were challenging some of the DEA's rules regarding hemp and THC. One of these DEA rules purported to ban *all naturally-*occurring THC (including the trace amounts of THC found in hemp) thus making it illegal for hemp manufacturers to produce and sell their products.

The Ninth Circuit Court struck this DEA rule down. In doing so, the court found that the DEA had exceeded its authority in enacting the rule.[86] The Ninth Circuit basically said that the DEA can't regulate hemp products that only contain trace amounts of THC because Congress didn't regulate non-psychoactive hemp when drafting the CSA. But ... the court also ruled that *growing* hemp is prohibited without a permit from the DEA because at some point in the lifecycle of the *Cannabis sativa L.* plant, the plant will inevitably produce cannabis. Thus, a loophole was created. When taken together, the *HIA* court's rulings opened the door for companies to import hemp from countries that allow it and to sell it throughout the U.S.

With respect to domestically-grown hemp, it's no big surprise here that the DEA issues very few permits for hemp cultivation in the U.S. Over ten years after the *HIA* case, President Obama signed the Agricultural Act of 2014 (or the "Farm Bill") into law. The Farm Bill featured Section 7606, allowing for universities and state departments of agriculture to begin cultivating hemp for limited research purposes. The law also requires that hemp grow sites be certified by – and registered with – their state.

In August 2016, the U.S. Department of Agriculture (USDA), the U.S. Drug Enforcement Administration (DEA) and the U.S. Food and Drug Administration (FDA) released a "Statement of Principles on Industrial Hemp" to clarify the Farm Bill, which legalized the cultivation of industrial hemp for research purposes. The Statement reiterates that hemp growing "may only take place in accordance with an agricultural pilot program to study the growth, cultivation, or marketing of industrial hemp established by a State department of agriculture or State agency responsible for agriculture in a State where the production of industrial hemp is otherwise legal under State law."[87]

In other words, only "institutions of higher learning, State departments of agriculture, or persons licensed by State departments of agriculture" in hemp-friendly states are free to cultivate hemp under federal law. The Statement makes clear industrial hemp products may *not* be grown or sold for commercial purposes. Moreover, industrial hemp plants and seeds may *not* be transported across State lines.

While the Farm Bill benefits hemp research, it does little to help commercial farmers in hemp-friendly states. This stems from the fact that although many states (such as California) have legalized industrial hemp, its production remains illegal under federal law for non-research purposes.

[Some, however, have taken the view that that a state can comply with the Farm Bill by enacting laws that allow the private commercial sector to grow and cultivate hemp for *economic* research purposes. The idea being that if a state is conducting research on the *economic* impact of a hemp industry within its borders, it only makes sense to involve the commercial private sector. That way, the state can obtain actual financial data from the hemp industry, rather than base research on speculative economic models.]

a. HEMP NOT LEGAL IN ALL 50 STATES

Several states have legalized the cultivation and research of industrial hemp, including Colorado, Hawaii, Kentucky, Maine, Maryland, Montana, North Dakota, Oregon, Vermont, Washington, West Virginia, and, most recently, California. However, as aforementioned, a grower still must get permission from the DEA in order to grow hemp, or face the possibility of federal charges or property confiscation, even if he or she has a state-issued permit.[88]

2. Manufacturing and/or Selling CBD Products

CBD is all the buzz right now. Some studies have shown that CBD can be used to treat anxiety, epilepsy, psychosis, diabetes, various neurodegenerative and inflammatory disorders, and cancer. And this only seems to scratch the surface of the boundless list of medicinal attributes that CBD has to offer.

Unlike THC, however, CBD can't get you "stoned" because it doesn't have psychoactive, mind-altering affects. While this makes CBD a less popular choice for recreational users, it gives the compound a significant advantage in the medical field because it confers the same medical benefits as THC, but without the "high" that some patients do not desire. This is the reason why CBD – which is primarily taken in liquid oil form – has so quickly become the rock star of the medical cannabis industry today.

Due to the increasing demand for CBD and the legal gray area in which it exists, there is much debate about whether the production and/or sale of CBD is legal. The answer to this question revolves in large part around whether the CBD was sourced from either hemp or cannabis.

a. The Interplay With Federal Hemp Laws and CBD

For reasons that none of us can comprehend, industrial hemp – with THC levels below 0.3% – is still classified as a Schedule I drug.

As we know, however, the *HIA* case created a legal loophole for *imported* industrial hemp. CBD companies have been able to use this loophole to their advantage. By claiming that their CBD is sourced from imported industrial hemp (rather than cannabis), CBD companies have been able to side-step the CSA's definition of "marijuana." The argument essentially being – if CBD is sourced from cannabis, then the CBD is 100% illegal. But if the CBD is sourced from imported industrial hemp, then the CBD is legal to use, sell, manufacture and even to ship across state lines.

But in December 2016, the DEA issued regulations that effectively put a stop to attempts to dance around the CSA's definition of "marijuana" when it comes to hemp-derived CBD. The new rule creates a new "Controlled Substances Code Number" for "Marihuana Extract" and extends that classification to all forms of CBD. In response to public comment on its initially proposed rule, the DEA stated that "[f]or practical purposes, all extracts that contain CBD will also contain at least small amounts of other cannabinoids. However, if it were possible to produce from the cannabis plant an extract that contained only CBD ... such an abstract would fall within the new drug code," and would thus be federally illegal.[89]

So what does this mean for CBD sellers in weed-friendly states like California? It means that the DEA is explicitly saying that it considers your product to be federally illegal under the CSA, despite it being *technically* legal under state law. Importantly, it also means that CBD cannot be shipped or transported across state lines, even if it's to another state where cannabis is legal. According to the DEA, these rules apply regardless of whether the CBD is sourced from either hemp or cannabis.

The hemp industry has since filed a legal challenge against the DEA's new "marihuana extract" rule, citing its seeming inconsistency with the Farm Bill. In a December 2016 press release, the Hemp Industries Association said: "The DEA final rule is concerning to the industry, as it creates confusion in the marketplace among consumers and legitimate businesses alike, and may potentially result in federal agencies improperly treating legal products such as CBD oils, body balms and supplements as controlled substances."[90]

Intelligent attorneys across the country disagree as to whether the new DEA rules pass legal muster when it comes to hemp-derived CBD (For a more in-depth discussion on the DEA's Attempt to Reschedule CBD, Section E3 below). But as unhappy as we are with the DEA's statement, we must advise everyone to heed this warning: the DEA has apparently taken the position that using, producing and selling CBD is illegal under federal law. Whether the new DEA rule is ultimately enforced, however, is a whole other story.

Currently, there are temporary safeguards in place that protect individuals in many states (including California) from prosecution for violations of federal hemp and CBD laws.

The Rohrabacher-Farr Amendment (the "Amendment") is the most important of those protections. Originally passed in 2014, the Amendment prohibits the DOJ from spending federal funds to interfere with the implementation of state medical cannabis laws.

(Note: The Amendment is silent on recreational use laws and therefore does not apply to recreational cannabis.) This spending ban does not legalize cannabis – it merely states that the DOJ cannot prosecute individuals for cannabis crimes when they are in compliance with state laws.

The Amendment must be renewed every year in order for the safeguards to stay in place. The Amendment was mostly renewed in December 2016, as part of the continuing House resolution known as H.R. 2028, which funds the federal government through April 28, 2017. But unless the Amendment is renewed again, the protections afforded by the Amendment will expire on April 28th.

Many, however, are confident that the Amendment will be renewed again. During a January 11th speech on the floor of the House of Representatives praising the appointment of Jeff Session as Attorney General, Rep. Rohrabacher said: "The [Amendment] currently remains in effect through April 28, though I expect it to be renewed moving forward. With the House and Senate both on record, and Mr. Trump's stated position that the issue should be left to the states, I am confident that the [Amendment] will be renewed."[91]

With regard to hemp, Congress has similarly banned the feds from using federal funds to interfere with industrial hemp. Specifically, the Massie Amendment states that: "None of the funds made available by this act or any other act may be used… to prohibit the transportation, processing, sale or use of industrial hemp that is grown or cultivated in accordance with section 7606 of the Agricultural Act of 2014, *within or outside the State in which the industrial hemp is grown or cultivated.*"[92]

Long story short, it is currently debatable whether industrial hemp and hemp-derived CBD is legal under federal law. In Colorado, some companies are manufacturing CBD derived from industrial hemp grown in the US and shipping across state lines. Clearly, these businesses are taking a risk and it is up to each CB to decide how risky they want their business model to be. At a bare minimum, however, the DEA simply has no funds to enforce its anti-hemp CBD rule. For now.

b. FDA RULES CBD CANNOT BE MARKETED AS A DIETARY SUPPLEMENT

Recently, the FDA issued an opinion that CBD cannot be marketed as a dietary supplement.[93] Although the FDA was clear about its current position, it left the door wide open for the future and wavered in its reasoning by essentially explaining that no one has succeeded in persuading them otherwise.[94]

A spokeswoman for the FDA's Center for Drug Evaluation and Research stated: "CBD meets the definition of Schedule I under the Controlled Substances Act. *The DEA is the regulatory agency.*" Therefore, the agencies are starting to play responsibility ping-pong.

3. DEA'S ATTEMPT TO RESCHEDULE CBD

In December of 2016, the U.S. Drug Enforcement Administration ("DEA") decided to reclassify CBD as a Schedule I Drug stirring up the nation in a panic. But did the DEA have the power to unilaterally reclassify a drug?

Here's the scoop - When Congress passes a law, it is recorded in the United States Code, or U.S.C. Within the U.S.C. is the Federal Controlled Substances Act ("CSA"). The CSA defines drug policies for the federal government under which the manufacture, importation, possession, use and distribution of certain drugs is regulated. CBD, derived from hemp, is not specifically defined under the CSA.[95]

The DEA attempted to reschedule CBD by amending the Code of Federal Regulations (CFR). The CFR, unlike the CSA, is written by government agencies, not Congress, and does not stand on its own as law unless it is based upon actual acts of Congress. When the DEA acted to amend the classification of CBD, Congress made no acts to incorporate the rescheduling into the U.S.C. or CSA. Thus, the U.S.C. and CSA remained unchanged. Therefore CBD was not effectively rescheduled as a Schedule I Substance.

When the DEA, in 2003, attempted to initiate rules and interpretations concerning cannabinoid constituents of marijuana that were not expressly set forth under the CSA or the DEA's own regulations, the Ninth Circuit Court of Appeals struck down its efforts, stating that "an agency is not allowed to change a legislative rule retroactively through the process of disingenuous interpretation of the rule to mean something other than its original meaning.

Then, in another case in 2004, the court stated:

"In keeping with the definitions of drugs controlled under Schedule I of the CSA, the DEA Final Rules can

regulate foodstuffs containing natural THC if it is contained within marijuana, and can regulate synthetic THC of any kind. But they cannot regulate naturally-occurring THC not contained within or derived from marijuana -- i.e., non-psychoactive hemp products -- because non-psychoactive hemp is not included in Schedule I. The DEA has no authority to regulate drugs that are not scheduled, and it has not followed procedures required to schedule a substance."

In sum, the CSA, as found in the United States Code, remains unchanged. CBD derived from hemp is not a Schedule I substance as found in the CSA. This is the law and the DEA has no authority to change Congress' interpretations or make laws.

F. FEDERAL CANNABIS CRIMINAL LAW AND PENALTIES

Although many states have legalized cannabis in some form, the cultivation, distribution or possession of cannabis remains a federal crime under the CSA and the federal government continues to issue harsh sentences for those convicted of these crimes. Various factors contribute to the ultimate sentence received, but standard sentences can include federal prison and up to millions of dollars in fines.

The Cole Memo and internal documents between U.S. Attorneys (discussed below and included in the appendix), indicate that the federal government appears mostly concerned with large-scale operations. If you are not operating a large-scale cultivation or distribution, is it likely that you will be prosecuted under federal law? **No.** Is it possible? **Yes.** The key is recognize that the larger an operation, the greater the risk of Federal involvement. The Feds, then, seem to send the message: *don't grow thousands of plants in your backyard unless you are prepared to attract the attention of federal authorities.* Most importantly, the Feds clearly say *do not cross state lines.*

1. MANDATORY MINIMUM SENTENCING

Under federal law, certain cannabis crimes have a mandatory minimum sentence. This means that the judge has *no power* to sentence the defendant to less time than the mandatory minimum. E.g., see chart below, more than 1,000 plants carries a 10-year minimum. In certain situations, where the defendant provides "substantial assistance" in the investigation or prosecution of another person, the federal prosecutor can recommend a lower sentence.[96] Despite the mandatory minimums, a defendant convicted of a federal offense with a mandatory minimum can sometimes qualify for the safety valve exception. Under the safety valve exception, a judge may go below the mandatory minimum if the defendant did not possess a firearm, was a first offender and he/she expressed acceptance of responsibility. However, the judge does have the ability to give a higher sentence if he/she deems it appropriate.

Below is a chart that outlines the stiff federal penalties and mandatory minimums for cannabis crimes:

Offense	Type of Penalty	Incarceration	Max Fine[97]
Possession (21 U.S.C. § 844)			
Any amount (1st offense)	Misdemeanor	Up to one year	$1,000
Any amount (2nd offense)	Misdemeanor	15 days*	$2,500
Any amount (later offense)	Misdemeanor or Felony	90 days* to 3 years	$5,000
Sale or Trafficking[98] (21 U.S. § 841)			
< 50 kg	Felony	Up to 5 years	$250,000
50 - 99 kg	Felony	Up to 20 years	$1,000,000
100 - 999 kg	Felony	5 to 40 years*	$5,000,000
> 1,000 kg	Felony	10 years to life*	$10,000,000
Cultivation[99] (21 U.S.C. § 841)			
< 50 plants	Felony	Up to 5 years	$250,000
50 - 99 plants	Felony	Up to 20 years	$1,000,000
100 - 999 plants	Felony	5 to 40 years*	$5,000,000
> 1,000 plants	Felony	10 years to life*	$10,000,000
Paraphernalia (21 U.S.C. § 863)			
Sale of paraphernalia	Felony	Up to 3 years	None

*Indicates a Mandatory Minimum Sentence

2. HOLDER'S PUSH AGAINST MINIMUM SENTENCING

The problem with mandatory minimum sentences is that some non-violent drug cases result in sentencing that is "inappropriate and inconsistent with the spirit of the policy."[100] The tough sentencing laws lead to both high incarceration rates and high prison costs.[101]

As a result, Attorney General Eric Holder issued a memo in September 2014, prohibiting prosecutors from threatening enhanced mandatory minimum sentences for the sole purpose of forcing criminal defendants to plead guilty in drug cases.[102]

The push to soften mandatory sentences for non-violent drug crimes has gained support from both political parties, but the move to phase out mandatory minimums still faces an uphill battle.[103] Despite the adversity, Holder's efforts are reflected in practice. Federal prosecutors are bringing fewer prosecutions for illegal drugs and less often seeking mandatory minimum sentences. Holder cites new data showing that prosecutors are pursuing mandatory minimums in just over 51% of drug cases in 2014, down from nearly 64% of such cases in fiscal 2013.[104] "These numbers show that a dramatic shift is underway in the mindset of prosecutors handling nonviolent drug offenses…"[105] to institutionalize this fairer, more practical approach.

G. Preemption and the Interplay Between State and Federal Laws

Although cannabis is forbidden under federal law, many states – including California – and the District of Columbia have enacted laws to legalize the use of cannabis in some form. Thus, while the commercialization and use of cannabis is authorized under California law; cannabis-related activities are still prohibited and individuals can still face federal criminal prosecution.

So why are people in California permitted to legally use cannabis when it's illegal under federal law? This is where the doctrine of "preemption" comes into play. The idea of preemption comes from the Supremacy Clause of the United States Constitution. The Supremacy Clause says, in essence, that where a state law is in conflict with a federal law, the federal law generally "preempts" or "trumps" state law and prevails.

There is one requirement however - the CSA expressly limits preemption to situations where the state laws are in "positive conflict" with federal law such that "the two cannot stand together" because they have a direct conflict.[106] While most people tend to think that a state law allowing the medical or recreational use of cannabis is in direct conflict with a federal law that criminalizes the use of cannabis for any reason, this is not necessarily the case. **Courts have generally established that a state cannabis law is only in "positive conflict" with the CSA if it is *"physically impossible"* to comply with both the state and federal law,** or where the state law *"stands as an obstacle to the accomplishment and execution"* **of the CSA.**[107]

Generally speaking, state legalization of the possession and use of cannabis does nothing to change the fact cannabis remains illegal under federal law – therefore, there is no direct conflict. Though the state law prevents the prosecution of these individuals under *state* law, the federal authorities are still free, legally speaking, to enforce the CSA by prosecuting these individuals under *federal law*.[108] Therefore, state law is not preempted by federal law, at least when it comes to prosecuting (or not prosecuting) cannabis-related crimes.

Further, the CSA does not prevent all state laws associated with cannabis because the act leaves room for states to use what is called the "historic police powers of the States."[109] This means that, although the federal government can criminalize cannabis, the states can ultimately make their own choices when it comes to regulating controlled substances within their borders. States are allowed to enact medical cannabis laws because states are provided with police powers in defining criminal conduct and regulating drugs and medical practices.[110]

Sometimes, however, a state law *is* found to be in direct conflict with federal law. For example, in 2011, in the case of *Pack v. Superior Court*, a California appellate court determined that provisions of the City of Long Beach's medical cannabis ordinance were preempted by the Federal CSA.[111] The *Pack* court held that cities were preempted under the CSA from enacting affirmative regulations to permit or authorize medical cannabis businesses, which led other California cities (such as Los Angeles[112]) to believe that it would be in violation of federal law if it permitted or authorized medical cannabis businesses. The California Supreme Court, however, dismissed review of the *Pack* case, so the appellate opinion is unpublished and technically of no legal consequence. But it serves as an example of a situation where a court finds federal preemption in cannabis law.

With the emergence of cannabis legalization and decriminalization at the state level, the question of preemption is undoubtedly going to remain a hot topic in the future. As of right now, however, it appears that the federal government is more focused on the wide-scale distribution and trafficking of cannabis, rather than the personal use of cannabis in states where it has been medically and/or recreationally legalized. As former President Obama previously told ABC News: "We've got bigger fish to fry."[113]

H. CANNABIS AT THE BORDER: CUSTOMS AND BORDER PROTECTION

Thinking about packing your bathing suit, sunscreen and medical cannabis and heading to San Diego…or anywhere else in the United States where there is an international border for that matter? Maybe you should think again…. So what exactly does happen when a medical cannabis patient carrying state-legal cannabis passes through a federal border patrol checkpoint?

The answer appears to be "it depends." Generally speaking, once a patient crosses state lines with medical cannabis in possession, they are in federal territory and thus federal jurisdiction where cannabis, whether medical or not, is illegal.

This is where we are faced with yet another wrinkle in the interplay of state and federal cannabis laws. If a qualified medical cannabis patient were attempting to cross between the U.S. and Mexico, it would be clear he was engaging in interstate drug trafficking which is a definite no-no under the Cole Memo would fall into the hands of federal prosecution. But, what happens when a border checkpoint is along the interstate and *is completely within the State's territory*?

This is the exact issue at the heart of a suit out of New Mexico against the U.S. Customs and Border Protection ("CBP") in which a qualified medical cannabis patient is seeking to enforce his right to possess cannabis.

Interaction with CBP agents in a situation like this falls into a legal gray area. Assuming that the patient's use and possession of medical cannabis falls within the permissible limits, the Cole Memo (discussed above) should control. Thereunder, a patient should be able to disclose that he is in possession of medical cannabis without fearing arrest. Problem is - the Cole Memo issues directives to the U.S. Attorneys, and the U.S. Attorneys are part of the DOJ. CBP, however, is a part of the Department of Homeland Security, not the DOJ. Long story short, CBP didn't get the memo, which means that CBP agents may feel they are at liberty to detain medical cannabis patients.[114]

The Rohrabacher-Farr Amendment supports an argument that CBP cannot interfere with a qualified patient's right to possess medical cannabis. This is because the Rohrabacher-Farr Amendment purports to prevent federal prosecution of medical cannabis patients and businesses by eliminating funding to go after such businesses and activities in states where it has been legalized or decriminalized. However, herein lies that problem - that provision, like the Cole Memo, was aimed directly at the

DOJ. So again, border patrol agents may be justified in their inquiries, even where they potentially reach activity lawful under the Compassionate Use Act.[115]

The situation really gets silly when you consider that any federal prosecution would actually be brought by the U.S. attorneys and assistant U.S. attorneys – the very same individuals who, under the Cole Memo and Rohrabacher-Farr, are supposed to be occupying themselves with other, more pressing matters.[116] In the case currently being prosecuted in New Mexico, local federal officials are tip-toeing around regulations. When asked how these checkpoint cases would be handled, the U.S. Attorney's office in Albuquerque responded that it follows the Cole Memo and does not prosecute MMJ patients with "small amounts" of cannabis.[117] Despite those statements, agents have indeed stopped MMJ patients and seized their medicine.[118]

Still, what patients really need is assurances from the powers that be within the Department of Homeland Security that CBP will not make an issue out of state-legal medical cannabis possession.

I. TRIBAL LAW

In December 2014, the DOJ issued an enforcement memo indicating that it would not prosecute federal cannabis laws on Native American tribal lands, even in states where cannabis remains illegal.[119] The memo was authored by Monty Wilkonson, Director of the Executive Office for U.S. Attorneys, and it appeared to give Native American tribes ("Tribes") a pass, like states, to legalize cannabis due to their unique sovereign status.[120] Specifically, the Wilkonson Memo provides:

> *"Indian Country includes numerous reservations and tribal lands with diverse sovereign governments, many of which traverse state borders and federal districts. Given this, the United States Attorneys recognize that effective federal law enforcement in Indian Country, including marijuana enforcement, requires consultation with our tribal partners in the districts and flexibility to confront the particular, yet sometimes divergent, public safety issues that can exist on any single reservation."*

> *"The eight priorities in the Cole Memorandum will guide United States Attorneys' marijuana enforcement efforts in Indian country, including in the event that sovereign Indian Nations to seek to legalize the cultivation or use of marijuana in Indian County. Consistent with the Attorney General's 2010 Indian Country*

Initiative, in evaluating marijuana enforcement activities in Indian Country, each United States Attorney should consult with the affected tribes on a government-to-government basis."[121]

Though the Wilkonson Memo neither legalized cannabis for Tribes nor made any changes to federal drug laws, it essentially instructed all U.S. attorneys to no longer prevent Tribes from growing or selling cannabis on reservation land.[122] It also appeared like the DOJ was open to working with Tribes to legalize cannabis in their native lands, under the same guidelines as states. As explained by business lawyer Hilary Bricken: "In other words, so long as a Tribe first consults with the appropriate U.S. attorneys regarding its plans for legalization or decriminalization and so long as that Tribe's plans include the 'robust regulations' required by the Cole Memo, one ought to be able to assume that the DOJ would allow that Tribe to legalize, just as so many states have done with both recreational and medical marijuana."[123] Unfortunately, however, this hasn't seemed to be the case so far.

"In the early part of 2015 there was chaos," said Timonthy Purdon, who was U.S. attorney for North Dakota at the time. "People in the cannabis industry were putting the full-court press on tribes."[124] Robert Williams, an University of Arizona law professor and Indian law expert, similarly observed: "Tribal leaders went to conferences, boutique law firms popped up and consultants were telling (tribal leaders) in a couple of months you'll be making millions of dollars."[125] This DOJ's apparent "green light" to legalize was exciting news for Tribes who had been trying to figure out for a long time how to cash in on the booming cannabis industry. Despite the $28 billion in revenue that Indian gaming pulled in the previous year, nearly one in four Native Americans still lived in poverty in 2014.[126] So, needless to say, the Tribes and the cannabis industry alike were ecstatic at the hope of the astronomical profits that could be made from selling cannabis. "We had a lot of individuals and companies coming forward to be our consultants," said Gary Besaw, chairman of the Wisconsin tribe Menominee. "Some were legit and others were taking a shot in the dark trying to jump in on a potential gold mine."[127]

But as the year progressed, reality began to set in. In July 2015, federal law enforcement authorities, including the DEA and special agents with the Bureau of Indian Affairs (BIA), raided two large grow operations run by the Alturas and Pit River Indian tribes in Northern California and seized 12,000 cannabis plants and 100 pounds of processed cannabis, crumbling their entire operation.[128] According to a statement by the regional U.S. Attorney's office, the two neighboring tribes planned to distribute the cannabis off tribal lands and the large-scale operations may have been inappropriately financed by a third-party foreign investor.[129]

Then, three months later in October 2015, the DEA raided an even more massive grow belonging to the Menominee tribe in Wisconsin, wherein the DEA seized more than 30,000 cannabis plants that were being cultivated for industrial hemp.[130] What made the Menominee raid so infuriating though for tribal leaders was that the Menominee tribe (unlike the two California tribes that were raided three months earlier) had actually been engaged in active and ongoing dialogue with the BIA, state law enforcement, and an assistant U.S. attorney.[131] And yet, despite the Menominee's attempts to be open and transparent with government officials, the feds still raided them.

Evidently, these two raids were enough to instill intense fear in the Flandreau Santee Sioux tribe of South Dakota, a tribe which had earlier made national headlines when it announced plans to open the country's first cannabis-friendly "resort" on its lands.[132] In November 2015, shortly after the Menominee raid, the Sioux tribe made the decision to suspend its grow operation and then burned its entire first crop, citing concerns about criminal prosecution. Apparently, the Sioux tribe was feeling the heat from state officials who had reviewed the Tribe's business plans and determined that "any changes in tribal law would only affect tribal members, therefore, non-tribal members ingesting cannabis on the reservation risked prosecution under state law ... [a]lso according to state officials, any non-tribal member returning to state land with marijuana in their system were violating state law, and thus, also subject to prosecution."[133] After consulting with the feds, the Tribe ultimately decided that it would be "in the best interest of both tribal and non-tribal members" to temporarily suspend its operations.[134]

South Dakota Attorney General Marty Jackley stated that tribal leadership wanted more "clarification" from the DOJ before continuing with its plans, and that next time it would use a more "calculated approach" to cannabis.[135] On the decision to burn all their crops, the Tribe's president Anthony Reider says: "We just felt it would be best to go in with a clean slate to look for answers on how to proceed so that all sides are comfortable with it."[136] [Note: Sources say that tribal officials knew that the feds were planning on raiding the Sioux operation in approx. two weeks.[137] So, it's highly likely that the Tribe panicked and burned its crops in order to remain on good terms with the feds. It has been reported that the Tribe destroyed an estimated $1 million worth of crops. Ouch!![138]]

In yet another interesting turn of events, less than a year after the Sioux tribe halted its grow operation, Jackley announced that two executives of a Colorado-based cannabis company, Monarch America, Inc., were being charged with conspiracy to grow cannabis for their efforts in assisting the Sioux tribe with growing the very same crops that they had destroyed.[139] According to the investigation, the cannabis seeds were obtained illegally and concealed during shipment, in violation of state and federal law. Jackley states that the Sioux tribe "is, to some degree, a victim in this case."[140] "There has been a considerable amount of funds that could have gone to better reasons and should have gone to better reasons," said Jackley. "My position as the Attorney General is those should be tribal funds, and should be returned, whether it be a restitutionary reward or otherwise."[141] No criminal charges have been filed against the Sioux tribe.

Against this backdrop, many people are asking: What's up with the mixed signals? Why are the feds raiding tribal grows and why did the Sioux burn their crops after the Wilkonson Memo was just issued? What gives? Well, there are a number of long, possible legal explanations, but the key takeaway is this: the federal raids have shown tribal leaders that "there may be more red tape for tribes to negotiate when it comes to legalizing cannabis than states have faced."[142] In other words, contrary to initial thinking, the Wilkonson Memo wasn't really a green light for Tribes to legalize, but more of a yellow one – i.e., an instruction to proceed with caution. In some ways, tribal leaders have to be *more* careful than the states in deciding how to move forward with legalizing and growing cannabis because (1) it remains illegal under federal law, and (2) there is a complex tangle of state, federal *and* tribal law enforcement oversight on Native American reservations, making it extra tricky.[143] This is especially the case for Tribes that are within states where cannabis remains illegal, such as Wisconsin or South Dakota.

"Everybody who is smart is pausing to look at the feasibility and risks of growing hemp and marijuana," said Lance Gumbs, a former chairman of the Shinnecock Tribe in New York and regional vice president of the National Congress of American Indians. "But are we giving up on it? Absolutely not."[144] Legal experts estimate that, as of December 2015, no more than a dozen tribes nationwide have legalized medical or recreational cannabis on their reservations.[145] So, the legal and economic impact of cannabis on Native American land still largely remains to be seen. "When [the Wilkonson Memo] appeared, everyone was like, 'Marijuana is legal! Marijuana is legal in Indian Country!'" said Lael Echo-Hawk, an attorney at Garvey Schubert Barer and member of the National Indian Cannabis Coalition. "It absolutely is not."[146] What we know now is that the secret to success for Native Americans in the cannabis industry will ultimately depend upon "the relationship between the federal government and the tribe, not the tribe and the state." Duke Rodriguez, founder and CEO of an Arizona-based medical cannabis company that works with Native

American tribes, says: "If we respect the rules of the federal government, the federal government will respect the role of the sovereign nation."[147]

J. LOOKING AHEAD: PENDING FEDERAL CANNABIS BILLS (2017-2018)

2016 was a watershed year for weed. After a historic election cycle in November 2016, cannabis was fully legalized via ballot measure in four (4) states (California, Nevada, Massachusetts and Maine), thus joining the ranks with the other 5 states where recreational pot is already legal (Alaska, D.C., Colorado, Oregon and Washington). In addition, three (3) more states – Arkansas, Florida and South Dakota – legalized cannabis for medical purposes, making the grand total of medical cannabis states in the U.S. now 28.

Although huge advances were made in 2016 for the legalization of cannabis, 2017 looks to be an even more exciting year. Though it still remains to be seen whether there will be any drastic changes in federal enforcement policy under the current Trump administration, there has already been a big ramp up in legislation with several pot bills already being discussed by Congress.

In February 2017, a bipartisan group of congressmen – including Rep. Early Blumenauer (D-Oregon), Rep. Ed Perlmutter (D-Colorado), Rep. Jared Polis (D-Colorado), Rep. Dana Rohrabacher (R-California) and Rep. Don Young (R-Alaska) – launched a group called the "Congressional Cannabis Caucus" to form a united front for purposes of advancing sensible cannabis policy reform. Members of the Cannabis Caucus say they plan to further congressional action on cannabis by introducing a slew of legislation and resurrecting bills from sessions' past. The formation of the Cannabis Caucus has created a lot of optimism on Capitol Hill that Congress could still maintain (or even accelerate) the momentum of cannabis legalization – even in the face of rising concerns that the growing industry could be snuffed out by "greater enforcement" of federal drug laws. Needless to say, we are very excited to see what these cannabis lawmakers have in store for us ahead!

For now, here's a breakdown of the weed bills currently pending before the 115th U.S. Congress:

H.R. 975 (Rep. Rohrabacher) (R - California): Among other things, this bill amends the Controlled Substances Act to provide for a new rule regarding the application of the act to cannabis.

H.R. 714 (Rep. Griffith) (R – Virginia): This bill provides for the legitimate use of medical cannabis in accordance with the laws of various states.

H.R. 715 (Rep. Griffith) (R – Virginia): Among other things, this bill provides for the rescheduling of cannabis, the legitimate medical use of cannabis in accordance with state law, and the exclusion of CBD from the definition of "marihuana."

H.R. 1227 (Rep. Garrett) (R-Virginia): This bill limits the application of federal laws to the distribution and consumption of marijuana. It also calls for the deregulation of cannabis and prohibits inter-state shipping of cannabis.

H.R. 331 (Rep. Lee) (D-California): This bill prevents civil asset forfeiture for property owners of state-sanctioned medical cannabis facilities.

After the November election, a quarter of the U.S. population now lives in places where adult use is legal.[148] Given all this momentum towards widespread legalization, cannabis clearly has a ton of wind in its sails this year – perhaps even enough to change cannabis history forever.

CHAPTER II.
CALIFORNIA CANNABIS LAW

2016 was a remarkable year for California and cannabis, especially compared to the 20 years' stagnation since the passage of Proposition 215, commonly known as the Compassionate Use Act of 1996 ("CUA") that made medical cannabis legal in California. Subsequently, the Medical Marijuana Program Act ("MMP") passed qualifying the CUA and defining the rights of patients.

Thereafter, in 2008, our then Attorney General, now Governor, Jerry Brown wrote the Attorney General Guidelines for Security and Non-Diversion of Medical Marijuana ("AGG") that set forth an unofficial framework for businesses to operate within. The Attorney General Guidelines, along with the CUA and MMP, until recently, exclusively governed medical cannabis and medical CBs in a gray area.

Now, the game has changed for medical CBs in California. On October 9, 2015, Gov. Jerry Brown signed into law the Medical Cannabis Regulation and Safety Act ("MCRSA"). For the first time California's multi-billion dollar medical cannabis industry got a regulatory structure. In other words, California is officially moving away from an unregulated gray cannabis market under the MMP and AGG, to a state law regulated medical cannabis industry with the creation of Bureau of Marijuana Control.

Continuing the progression, in November 2016, California voters approved Proposition 64, the Adult Use of Marijuana Act "AUMA", legalizing and governing the recreational or "adult use" market.

Below, we dive deeply into each of these laws, their implications, their progeny, and our speculation in to California

A. COMPLYING WITH THE COLLECTIVE MODEL

While it has been well-settled in California that patients may use medical cannabis, there is still confusion as to exactly how and where patients can actually obtain their cannabis. This, in turn, has created an unregulated, ambiguously gray cannabis market that has loomed over patients, law enforcement, medical CBs, and state courts for the past 20 (twenty) years. Medical CBs that comply with the CUA, MMP and AGG are armed with what is called the collective defense, in essence, a legal defense that protects compliant collectives.

Though the MCRSA is a huge step forward for California cannabis reform, the legislation is by no means complete, or perfect for that matter.

Not all of the regulations of the MCRSA are clearly spelled out, and there will assuredly be more details to be worked out in the future. The MCRSA is in for many growing pains. Fortunately, however, legislators are already in the process of actively engaging with the broader community and proposing (and passing) legislative corrections.

Despite its flaws, the implementation of the MCRSA has already been influential in determining the shape of future cannabis legalization efforts in California and will hopefully mean less federal intervention going forward. Lets review quickly with a brief legal history of medical cannabis in California.

1. THE COMPASSIONATE USE ACT OF 1996 ("CUA")

The history of legalizing medical cannabis in California begins with the CUA, which was passed by statewide initiative in 1996. The CUA is codified as Health & Safety Code § 11362.5. The CUA was enacted "[t]o ensure seriously ill Californians have the right to obtain and use medical cannabis for medical purposes," when their use of medical cannabis has been recommended by a physician as treatment for illness.[149] Its purpose is to provide such patients and their primary caregivers a defense to criminal prosecution for obtaining and using cannabis for medical purposes.[150]

Specifically, the CUA provides that:

> "Section 11357, relating to the possession of cannabis, and Section 11358, relating to the cultivation of cannabis, shall not apply to a patient or to a patient's primary caregiver, who possesses or cultivates cannabis for the personal medical purposes of the patient upon the written or oral recommendation or approval of a physician."[151]

Essentially, CUA grants a **_limited immunity from state prosecution_** (also called an "affirmative defense") to qualified patients and their primary caregivers for the crimes of possession and cultivation of cannabis.[152] Qualified patients and their primary caregivers are not only armed with a defense to possession and cultivation, but they are also provided with a defense with regard to the transportation of cannabis. A qualified patient has a defense to prosecution for transportation of cannabis if the "quantity transported and the method, timing and distance of the transportation are _reasonably related_ to the patient's current medical needs."[153] At trial, a criminal defendant need only raise a reasonable doubt as to whether the cannabis was possessed, cultivated or transported legally under the CUA.[154]

But be careful, **the CUA does <u>not</u> grant immunity from *arrest*.**[155] This means that so long as law enforcement officers have probable cause[156] to believe that possession or cultivation of cannabis has occurred, they may arrest a person *regardless* of whether or not the arrestee has a physician's recommendation or approval.[157]

Contrary to popular opinion, individuals who distribute cannabis to large quantities of people, as opposed to caregivers who provide for another individual (singular), cannot claim the protection of the CUA – even if they are distributing cannabis to those who are considered to be "qualified patients." While these actions are not protected under the CUA, there may be a defense for this type of action based on a "cooperative" or "collective" theory under the MMP.

Established by case law, "a cooperative where two people grow, stockpile and distribute marijuana to hundreds of qualified patients or their primary caregivers, while receiving reimbursement for these expenses, does not fall within the scope of the language of the CUA or the cases that construe it"[158] - what most people identify as a medical cannabis business. Therefore, in criminal cases involving collectives, cooperatives or dispensaries, the defendants cannot raise a defense under the CUA but must rely instead on the MMP.

2. THE MEDICAL MARIJUANA PROGRAM ACT ("MMP")

In 2003, the California Legislature enacted Senate Bill 420, otherwise known as the Medical Marijuana Program Act ("MMP"). The MMP, enacted to "address issues not included in the CUA,"[159] added eighteen new sections to the Health & Safety Code. The MMP is now codified and enforced as Health & Safety Code § 11362.7, *et seq.*

In effect, the MMP served to expand the scope of the CUA by, among other things, extending the CUA's affirmative defense. In other words, the MMP extends protection to cover prosecutions for the following crimes:

- possession for sale[160];
- transportation[161];
- maintaining a place for the sale, giving away or use of cannabis[162];
- making available a premises for the manufacture, storage or distribution of cannabis[163]; and
- abatement of nuisance created by a premises used for the manufacture, storage or distribution of cannabis.[164]

For the very first time, the MMP provided for immunity from criminal prosecution for the collective and cooperative cultivation and distribution of cannabis.[165] In order to raise the collective or cooperative defense in court, the following elements must be proven[166]: (1) the defendant is a qualified patient or caregiver; and (2) the collective or cooperative was being operated within the scope of those acts immunized by the CUA and MMP.[167]

This expansion of protected activities "represent[ed] a dramatic change in the prohibition on the use, distribution and cultivation of cannabis for persons who are qualified patients or primary caregivers ..."[168] **In enacting the MMP, the Legislature quite clearly intended to broaden the scope of the CUA in order to "enhance the access of patients and caregivers to medical cannabis through collective, cooperative cultivation projects.**[169]

Most importantly, the MMP specifically required the Attorney General's Office to "develop and adopt guidelines" for the enforcement of the CUA and MMP provisions.[170] To fulfill this mandate, on August 25, 2008, California Attorney General Edmund Brown, Jr. issued "Guidelines for the Security and Non-Diversion of Marijuana Grown for Medical Use" ("A.G. Guidelines").[171] (See Appendix for complete text of the Attorney General Guidelines.) Although the A.G. Guidelines are not strictly binding as law, they hold considerable weight in court determination[172] and they provide a good indication as to what criteria (if any) law enforcement look for in determining whether someone is in compliance with state law.[173] Anyone interested in operating a medical cannabis business, should be familiar with the A.G. Guidelines.

[Note: As will be discussed in the Medical Cannabis Regulation and Safety Act, the MCRSA has created an "SB 420 collective defense sunset," which will essentially abolish the "collective defense" provided by the MMP. To be exempt from prosecution, all CBs will have to be licensed in the near future, except for individual patient and caregiver gardens serving no more than five patients.]

a. VOLUNTARY IDENTIFICATION CARD PROGRAM

At the heart of the MMP is the voluntary "identification card" program. Unlike the CUA – which, as noted, provides only an *affirmative defense* to a charge of possession or cultivation of cannabis – the MMP's identification card program provides *protection against arrest* for those and other related crimes. The identification card program is *voluntary* – meaning a qualified patient does not need to obtain an identification card in order to be entitled to the protections of the CUA and MMP.[174] Only a qualified patient or caregiver can choose to obtain an identification card to protect from unlawful arrest.

As required by the MMP, the California Department of Health Services established and maintains a program under which qualified applicants may apply for a renewable state-issued identification card that identifies them as qualified for the exemptions of CUA and MMP. The program is also in place to provide law enforcement with a 24-hour telephone number to verify the validity of the state identification card.[175]

The purpose of the MMP's identification card program is to protect qualified patients and primary caregivers from *unnecessary arrest*. "Participation in the identification card program, although not mandatory, provides a significant benefit to its participants: they are not subject to arrest for violating California's laws relating to the possession, transportation, delivery or cultivation of cannabis, [if] they meet the conditions outlined in the MMP,"[176] specifically possession of no more than six (6) mature or 12 immature plants and 8 oz. of dried cannabis. Absent probable cause to believe that the card was obtained or being used fraudulently, a law enforcement officer must accept the identification card.[177] In other words, according to the A.G. Guidelines, if an identification card is valid and not being used fraudulently, there is no other evidence of illegal activity (e.g., weapons, illicit drugs or large amounts of cash), and the person is within the state and local possession guidelines, the person should not be arrested. However should an arrest occur, the identification card holder must be released and any cannabis seized must be returned.[178]

b. QUANTITY LIMITATIONS

Unlike the CUA, which does not specify any amount of cannabis that a patient may legally possess or cultivate, the MMP establishes quantity limitations for qualified patients and primary caregivers. The MMP states that individuals may possess no more than "eight (8) ounces of dried marijuana" and "maintain no more than six (6) mature or 12 immature plants."[179] This "safe harbor" provision applies to "[a] qualified patient or person holding a valid identification card, or the designated primary caregiver of that qualified patient or person."[180]

If a person is acting as primary caregiver for more than one patient under Health & Code § 11362.7(d)(2), he/she may combine the possession and cultivation limits for each patient to provide them the ability to legally possess amounts for more than one patient at a time.[181] For example, if a caregiver is responsible for three patients, he/she may possess up to 24 ounces of cannabis (8 ounces per patient) and may grow up to 18 mature or 36 immature plants (6 mature or 12 immature plants per patient). Similarly, collectives and cooperatives may cultivate and transport cannabis in aggregate amounts tied to its membership numbers.[182]

In 2010, however, the *Kelly* court struck down the quantity restrictions imposed by the MMP by finding them unconstitutional.[183] In a unanimous decision, it was determined that the CUA's only limit on the amount of cannabis someone may possess is that it must be "reasonably related to the patient's current medical needs,"[184] thus eliminating the quantity limitations imposed by the MMP and the Attorney General Guidelines. Therefore, any numerical values associated with possession were eliminated. Thus, patients can possess and grow as much as they want, so long as it is reasonably related to their medical need.

Legally, however, the police are still permitted to arrest anyone who exceeds the MMP's limits. In effect, the significant change of the law is the lack of an *automatic quantity limit for guilt*. This means, a criminal conviction cannot be *solely* based upon a defendant exceeding the MMP's limits because there are no longer exact limits in place. With that said, it is still a good rule of thumb to abide by the original MMP limits that were set even though they are no longer "current" law. In other words, one can simply avoid the hassle of being arrested and dragged into court for a felony trial if they simply abide by the MMP and its quantity limitations.

3. THE 2008 ATTORNEY GENERAL GUIDELINES

In 2008, for the first time since California's Proposition 215 was passed in 1996, the A.G. Guidelines served to clarify the state's laws governing medical cannabis and provide clear guidelines for patients and law enforcement to ensure that medical cannabis is not diverted to illicit markets. (See Appendix II for complete text of the Attorney General Guidelines) Although the A.G. Guidelines are not strictly binding as law, they hold considerable weight in court determination[185] and they provide a good indication as to what criteria (if any) law enforcement look for in determining whether someone is in compliance with state law.[186] Anyone interested in operating a medical cannabis business, should be familiar with the A.G. Guidelines. (See full copy of the A.G. Guidelines in the Appendix).

Once California decided to remove the use and cultivation of "physician recommended" cannabis from the scope of the state's drug laws, the A.G. Guidelines sets forth that state and local law enforcement officers not arrest individuals or seize cannabis under federal law when the officer determines that the cultivation, possession, or transportation is permitted under California law.[187]

a. BASIC DEFINITIONS OF THE A.G. GUIDELINES

Physician's recommendation: A recommendation by a licensed physician stating that cannabis is a beneficial treatment for some serious condition that the patient is suffering from.[188] Such recommendation can be oral or in writing.

Qualified patient: A person whose physician has recommended the use of cannabis to treat a serious illness, including, but not limited to, cancer, anorexia, AIDS, chronic pain, spasticity, glaucoma, arthritis, migraines, or any other illness for which cannabis provides relief.[189]

Primary Caregiver: A person who "consistently assum[es] responsibility for the housing, health, or safety" of the patient. This individual is usually designated by a qualified patient.[190] California courts have emphasized the requirement of consistency in the patient-caregiver relationship. Although a "primary caregiver who consistently grows and supplies . . . medicinal marijuana for a section 11362.5 patient is serving a health need of the patient," someone who merely maintains as a source of cannabis to a patient does not automatically become the party "who has consistently assumed responsibility for the housing, health, or safety" of that purchaser.[191] A person may serve as primary caregiver to "more than one" patient, provided that the patients and caregiver all reside in the same city or county.[192]

Recommending Physician: A physician who: (1) possesses a license in good standing to practice medicine in California; (2) has taken responsibility for an aspect of the medical care, treatment, diagnosis, counseling, or referral of the patient; and (3) has conducted a medical examination of that patient before recording in the patient's medical record the physician's assessment as to whether he/she suffers from a serious medical condition and whether the use of medical cannabis is appropriate.[193]

Business Forms: Any group that is collectively or cooperatively cultivating and distributing cannabis for medical purposes should be organized and operated in a manner that ensures the security of the crop and safeguards against diversion for non-medical purposes. The following are guidelines to help cooperatives and collectives operate within the law, and to help law enforcement determine whether they are doing so.

Statutory Cooperatives: Defined by California Law. A cooperative must file articles of incorporation with the state and conduct its business for the mutual benefit of its members.[194] No business may call itself a "cooperative" (or "co-op") unless it is properly organized and registered as such a corporation under the Corporations or Food and Agricultural Code.[195] Cooperative corporations are "democratically controlled and are not organized to make a profit for themselves, as such, or for their members, as such, but primarily for their members as patrons."[196] The earnings and savings of the business must be used for the general welfare of its members or equitably distributed to members in the form of cash, property, credits, or services.[197]

Cooperatives must follow strict rules on organization, articles, elections, and distribution of earnings, and must report individual transactions from individual members each year.[198] Agricultural cooperatives are likewise nonprofit corporate entities "since they are not organized to make profit for themselves, as such, or for their members, as such, but only for their members as producers."[199] Agricultural cooperatives share many characteristics with consumer cooperatives.[200] Cooperatives should not purchase cannabis from, or sell to, non-members; instead, they should only provide a means for facilitating or coordinating transactions between members.[201]

Collectives: California law *does not* define collectives, but the dictionary defines them as "a business, farm, etc., jointly owned and operated by the members of a group."[202] Applying this definition, a collective should be an organization that merely facilitates the collaborative efforts of patient and caregiver members – including the allocation of costs and revenues. As such, a collective is not a statutory entity, but as a practical matter it might have to organize as some form of business to carry out its activities. The collective should not purchase cannabis from, or sell to, non-members; instead, it should only provide a means for facilitating or coordinating transactions between members.[203]

b. DIFFERENCE BETWEEN A COOPERATIVE AND A COLLECTIVE

While these two entities have very similar purposes, they do share a few differences.

"Cooperatives" are explicitly defined in California law. A cooperative must file articles of incorporation with the state and be organized in strict accordance with certain provisions spelled out in the Corporations or Food and Agricultural Code.[204] A cooperative must be "democratically controlled" and conduct its business for the mutual benefit of its members.[205] It cannot be organized to make a profit[206] and should not purchase cannabis from, or sell to, non-members; it should only provide a means for facilitating or coordinating transactions between members.[207] Because cooperatives must organize in a specific way, register with the state, and follow strict rules on operating and reporting on their activities, some CBs in California choose not to operate as a cooperative but rather as a collective.

Although California law does not explicitly define a "collective," the A.G. Guidelines apply the following definition: "a business, farm, etc., jointly owned and operated by the members of a group."[208] The purpose of a collective is merely to facilitate the collaborative efforts of patients and primary caregivers – including the allocation of costs and revenues. Similar to a cooperative, a collective must be a non-profit enterprise and it should only provide a means for facilitating or coordinating transactions between members.[209] Unlike a cooperative, however, a collective does not have to follow strict rules on organization and reporting because it is not technically defined in the law. Thus, collectives have a greater degree of flexibility in their establishment and operations.

"Storefront dispensaries," are not specifically recognized under state law either, but court cases have shown that the operation of a medical cannabis storefront dispensary is legal so long as the dispensary qualifies as a "collective" or "cooperative" under the CUA and MMP.[210] The A.G. Guidelines, however, state that "dispensaries that merely require patients to complete a form summarily designating the business owner as their primary caregiver – and then offering marijuana in exchange for cash 'donations' – are likely unlawful."[211]

REQUIREMENTS	COOPERATIVE	COLLECTIVE
File articles of incorporation	Yes, must file articles of incorporation and report activities and register with the state.	No, but as a practical matter, encouraged to do so.
Organize according to state Corporations Code	Yes, must organize according to California Corporations Code governing statutory cooperatives.[212]	Not defined by Corporations Code, but must substantially comply with A.G. Guidelines.
Must run for mutual benefit of members	Yes	Yes
Non-profit entity	Yes	Yes

May buy/sell to non-members	No	No
Purpose of operation	Facilitate transactions between members	Facilitate collaborative efforts of patient and primary care givers (who are members) and allocate costs and revenues

4. PRACTICAL APPLICATION – THE CUA, MMP AND AGG

a. CHOOSING AN ENTITY

Many businesses fail to take the correct steps when choosing and creating their business entity – the same applies, even more so, to CBs. Depending on the business's specific needs, one business entity may make sense over the other. Relevant factors in making this decision may include: who runs the business; who controls the business; expected size of the business; number of board members; limitation of liability; and financing requirements. Additionally, there are tax consequences specific to each entity that should be considered.

Each for-profit entity option described below has its own advantages and disadvantages, so it is important to discuss these matters with an experienced medical cannabis attorney and a CPA who can guide you in deciding which entity works best for your situation.

An additional determination CBs must now make is whether to operate as a for-profit or non-profit entity. The passage of the MCRSA not only created the licensing structure for CBs, but also marked a significant change in how CBs do business in that it allows for for-profit entities.

Hold your horses though! Remember, the MCRSA will not begin issuing licenses until 2018, at the earliest, and in the mean time the current law still prevails, which requires non-profit operation. If that doesn't make your head spin, I don't know what will!

1. STOCK CORPORATION ("C-CORP OR S-CORP")

A stock corporation is an independent legal entity with shareholders (or "stockholders"). The shareholders contribute capital, which is then divided into shares represented by certificates. This allows for the ownership of the corporation to be readily determined because shares are property and are transferable just like any other property, subject to certain conditions. Shares are used for voting on matters of corporate policy or to elect directors, at the corporation's meetings. If a stockholder owns at least 50% of a corporation's voting shares, plus one share (51%), he/she has a controlling interest in the corporation, because he/she possesses more votes than all other owners combined. Corporations may also be non-stock and may switch back and forth between stock and non-stock status.

> **Advantages:**

- **Asset protection**: Corporations are entitled to "limited liability," which ensures that owners cannot be held personally liable for the debts and liabilities of the corporation.
- **Simple structure**: A corporation is a separate legal entity owned by shareholders and ruled by directors who elect officers to do day-to-day management.
- **Privacy**: The corporate shell is a great way to keep your personal identity and business affairs private and confidential. If you were operating as a sole proprietor or partnership, your name would be public record.
- **Transferability**: Corporations are easier to sell and are more attractive to buyers due to their limitation of liability.
- **Increased credibility**: People and other businesses tend to feel more secure when they are dealing with a corporation as opposed to an individual.

> **Disadvantages:**

- **Higher costs:** Corporations pay a number of state filing fees and, often times, dealing with corporate rules and regulations require the professional expense of an attorney or accountant.
- **More paperwork:** Increased regulations and complex rules require a corporation to file a number of documents, including Articles of Incorporation, corporate bylaws, corporate minutes, certificates of good standing, and more.
- **Double taxation:** All corporations are considered C-Corporations (under subchapter "C" of the Tax Code) unless they file for "S" status (under subchapter "S" of the Tax Code). A corporation must file to become an S-Corp for tax purposes within 75 days of incorporation. If you take no action, your corporation is a C-Corp. When a C-corp makes a profit, it pays a federal corporate income tax on that profit. If the corporation also declares a dividend, the stockholders must report the dividend as personal income and pay more taxes. So taxation occurs twice, once at the corporate level and again at the personal level. S-Corps, however, avoid this double taxation because all income or loss is reported

only once on the personal tax returns of the stockholders. For tax reasons, however, electing S status is not usually advisable for cannabis businesses so it is recommended to maintain C status.

2. COOPERATIVE CORPORATION

A cooperative corporation (or "co-op") is an enterprise owned and run by the people who use it, i.e., its members. Cooperatives are "democratically controlled" and operated to meet the *mutual need* of its members. To operate as a cannabis cooperative in California, you must organize as a "Consumer Cooperative Corporation" pursuant to the California Corporations Code. A co-op cannot be organized to make a profit – its earnings and savings must be used for the general welfare of its members.

i. FORMING A CONSUMER COOPERATIVE CORPORATION

As with all corporations in California, to create a consumer cooperative corporation, you must file Articles of Incorporation with the Secretary of State's office. The statutory requirements for the articles are set forth in California Corporations Code section 12310, which states that the articles must include the corporation's name and address, as well as a special statement that the corporation is formed under the Consumer Corporation Law and whether member voting will be equal or based on ownership interest. The corporation's name must include the word "cooperative" and an indication of its corporate status by use of a designation such as "Inc." or "Corp."

ii. MEMBERSHIPS

Consumer cooperative corporations can have an unlimited number of members or no members at all. If neither the corporation's articles or bylaws state whether it will have members, the corporation shall have no members. A consumer cooperative cooperation without members vests all voting rights in its board of directors. The directors are authorized to issue memberships for no payment or to set the amount of payment required per membership, unless otherwise prohibited by the corporation's articles or bylaws. If the directors set the membership payment at $300 or less, the memberships are exempt from registration with the Department of Corporations.

iii. USES

A consumer cooperative corporation is one of the preferred forms of incorporation to ensure compliance with the 2008 the California Attorney

General Guidelines. Because California law prohibits diversion of cannabis for non-medical purposes, qualified persons can work cooperatively regarding the handling of the cannabis for the members' benefit and safeguard it from improper diversion.

Although many attorneys used to use this as the exclusive entity type for CBs, more and more people are moving away from this type of business structure.

> ➢ **Advantages:**

- **Asset protection:** Co-op members are entitled to "limited liability," which ensures that members cannot be held personally liable for the debts and liabilities of the co-op.
- **Compensation:** Co-ops may distribute surplus income to its members. Although co-ops are rarely tax exempt, surplus income may be distributed to members in such a way as to minimize corporate taxes.
- **Favorable tax treatment:** Cooperatives can receive special tax treatment under Subchapter T of the Internal Revenue Code. Subchapter T allows a cooperative to avoid double-taxation on some earnings, if those earnings are paid out as "patronage refunds." This is because patronage refunds are considered a tax-deductible business expense for the cooperative.

> ➢ **Disadvantages:**

- **Strict rules of organization and reporting:** Co-ops must file articles of incorporation, report activities, and register with the state.
- **Decision-making and control:** Because co-ops must be democratically controlled, decision-making can be cumbersome and the original "founders" could eventually lose "control" of the cooperative. Furthermore, because voting power is not related to capital contribution (as in "regular" for-profit corporations), potential large investors are discouraged from participating in a co-op.

3. LIMITED LIABILITY COMPANY ("LLC")

An LLC has the limited liability features of a corporation along with the tax efficiencies and operational flexibility of a partnership. Similar to a shareholder of a corporation, the liability of LLC owners for the debts and obligations of the LLC is limited to their financial investment. However, like a general partnership, members of an LLC have the right to participate in the management of the LLC, unless the LLC's articles of incorporation provide that the LLC is to be managed in another way. An LLC may have one or more owners, and may have different classes of owners. In addition, an LLC may be a combination of individuals or business entities.

Since LLCs are not non-profit entities, they are not usually used for the formation of a collective. They can, however, be used in conjunction with a collective in many ways. For example, if the collective requires management or help with management, that can be outsourced to an LLC. Moreover, because an LLC can have both entities and individuals as members, a collective can own part of an LLC.

The potential relationship between an LLC and a Collective Corporation can be quite complicated and consulting a legal expert is a must!

Although, once licensing is available under the MCRSA, this may be the preferred corporate entity structure for smaller CBs.

➢ **Advantages:**

• **Asset protection:** LLC owners are entitled to "limited liability," which ensures that owners cannot be held personally liable for the debts and liabilities of the corporation beyond their initial investment in the LLC.
• **Simpler and faster than forming and maintaining a corporation:** LLC's do not issue stock and are not required to hold annual meetings or keep written minutes, which a corporation must do in order to preserve the liability shield for its owners. With less stringent requirements for compliance and less necessary paperwork, LLCs are easier to form and easier to keep in good legal standing.
• **Tax flexibility:** LLC's are normally established to be taxed as if they *were* a partnership which is considered an advantage because of the flexibility and single level (i.e., "pass-through") of taxation it offers. Generally, members of an LLC that are taxed as a partnership may agree to share the profits and losses in any manner. If the LLC chooses to be taxed as a corporation, members receive profits and losses in the same manner as shareholders of a corporation.

➢ **Disadvantages:**

• **Higher fees:** LLC's must typically pay more fees to file with the state as compared to other business entities.
• **Higher taxes:** The favored tax flexibility of LLC's can also result in complex accounting and tax issues. Unless you choose to be taxed like a corporation, LLC's are usually subject to self-employment taxes. This means that the profits of the LLC won't be taxed at the corporate level, but

will pass through to its members who will account for those profits on their personal federal tax returns. Often times, these taxes are higher than they would be at the corporate level. However, if an LLC is taxed as a partnership, they are subject to both an $800 California "minimum" tax and a California "fee" on gross receipts in excess of $250,000.

- **Confusion about roles:** Whereas corporations have specific roles (like directors, managers, and employees), LLC's generally do not. This can make it difficult for the company and especially investors to know who's in charge, who can sign certain contracts, etc. Some of this confusion can be avoided by creating an LLC Operating Agreement.

4. NON-PROFIT CORPORATION

A non-profit corporation is a legal entity, which incorporates under the law for purposes *other than* making profits for its owners. A non-profit corporation is much like a regular corporation except that non-profits have to take the extra steps of applying for tax-exempt status with the IRS and the Franchise Tax Board. The most common type of tax-exempt non-profit organization falls under section 501(c)(3) of the Internal Revenue Code. A not-for-profit qualifies for 501(c)(3) status, and is thus exempt from federal income tax, if it is organized and operated exclusively for one or more exempt purposes. Note, although it is advisable that CBs incorporate hereunder, they do not currently qualify as a 501(c)(3).

> ➤ **Advantages:**

- **Legitimacy to law enforcement:** If you are a non-profit corporation, it will help establish that your organization is operated on a purely non-profit basis. This will help shield your business from raids by law enforcement.
- **Asset protection:** Non-profits are entitled to "limited liability," which ensures that members and officers cannot be held personally liable for the debts and liabilities of the corporation.
- **Eligibility to receive tax-deductible charitable contributions:** Non-profit status encourages donations by providing donors with tax deductions.
- **Tax consequences:** Non-profit corporations are eligible for state and federal tax exemptions from corporate income taxes.

> ➤ **Disadvantages:**

- **Very difficult to achieve:** Due to current state law, it is highly unlikely that a CB will qualify for tax-exempt status.

- **Recordkeeping:** Non-profits are required to keep detailed books and records detailing the organization's activities, both financial and non-financial.
- **Regulatory demands:** Non-profits must comply with numerous regulatory requirements, including submitting annual reports to federal and state agencies.
- **Compensation:** Managers and employees can only be paid "reasonable salaries" and the Board of Directors cannot be paid at all. Furthermore, there are no dividends for shareholders and no sales of shares.
- **Higher costs:** Non-profits pay a number of state and federal filing fees. Often, dealing with various non-profits rules and regulations require the professional expense of an attorney or accountant.

Non-Profit corporations however, are not all created equal. It is important to note the three types of non-profit corporations – 1. non-profit religious corporations, 2. non-profit public benefit corporations, and 3. non-profit mutual benefit corporations.

Religious corporations, just as the name indicates, are meant for religious purposes and are subject to less rigorous state and federal filing and reporting requirements than many other tax-exempt organizations. A **non-profit public-benefit corporation** is chartered by a state government, and organized primarily for social, educational, recreational or charitable purposes. Non-profit public-benefit corporations are organized for the general public benefit, rather than for the interest of its members. Neither of these non-profit corporations are necessarily suitable, however, for a CB. A very common way to structure a CB is as a **non-profit mutual benefit corporation**.

5. NON-PROFIT MUTUAL BENEFIT CORPORATION ("NPMB")

This is another common and widely used entity for California CBs. Like a traditional corporation, a non-profit mutual benefit corporation ("NPMB") has members, a board of directors, and officers. What sets the NPMB apart from usual for-profit corporations is that the purpose of a NPMB is to provide only for the benefit of its members, and not to make a profit. There is no one owner and all of the members are in effect owners. Though an NPMB is technically a "non-profit," it is a non-profit in spirit only but acts as a regular business for all other intents and purposes because CBs are still illegal federally, they are unlikely to qualify for 501(c) tax-exempt status.

➢ **Advantages:**

- **Limited liability:** NPMB owners are entitled to "limited liability," which ensures that owners cannot be held personally liable for the debts and liabilities of the corporation.
- **Compensation:** Since there are no owners with this type of business, the "owners" or those that start the business are actually going to be employees that work for the business. If you are an "owner," you can take a salary for wearing multiple hats within the business. For example, you may receive a salary for sitting on the Board of Directors and another salary for managing the day-to-day operations. Your salaries, however, must be "reasonable" given your personal qualifications and the industry standard.

> **Disadvantages:**

- **Tax consequences:** An NPMB captures the essence of a non-profit but acts as a regular business for all other business, paying taxes like a regular for-profit C-Corp.
- **Higher costs:** NPMB's pay a number of state filing fees and, often times, dealing with NPMB rules and regulations require the professional expense of an attorney or accountant.
- **Non-Profit:** Because it is a non-profit, the NPMB should show no profits at the end of the year. Any leftover profits will need to be reinvested in the business – they cannot be redistributed to the organization's members, directors or officers.

b. BYLAWS AND CORPORATE GOVERNANCE

All corporations, whether "for-profit" or "non-profit," are guided by bylaws or some other type of operating agreement under which the entity, its board, officers, and members function. Operating rules help establish the responsibilities of, for example, officers and members. Most corporate entities are also required to hold membership/shareholder meeting where issues of the CB are discussed and officers are voted for. Records of corporate meetings are critical to the maintenance of the entity and it is important to make sure that members are aware of their status as members/shareholders and their right to be present and to vote at these meetings.

c. REQUIREMENTS OF COLLECTIVE MEMBERSHIP UNDER ATTORNEY GENERAL GUIDELINES

In 2009, the California Court of Appeal addressed the question of whether the operation of a medical cannabis storefront dispensary was legal under existing law.²¹³ The court concluded that storefront dispensaries that qualify as a "collective" or "cooperative" under the CUA and the MMP are legal operations. To qualify as a valid collective or cooperative under the CUA and MMP, storefront dispensaries must adhere to the following guidelines:

1. NON-PROFIT ENTERPRISE

An entity," both collectives and cooperatives are required to be established and operated for the sole purpose of benefiting its members and must not be established or operated for profit.²¹⁴ Indeed, nothing in the CUA or the MMP authorizes collectives, cooperatives or individuals to profit from the sale or distribution of cannabis.²¹⁵ ("Nothing in this section shall authorize … any individual or group to cultivate or distribute cannabis for profit."). It is important to note that this not-for-profit model changed with the signing of the Medical Cannabis Regulation and Safety Act by Governor Brown. This new legislation redefines "'Cannabis Business" as a for profit or nonprofit entity that cultivates, concentrates, processes, wholesales, or retails Cannabis."²¹⁶ This is a significant change from the past when dispensary owners could be prosecuted and jailed for being in the shadows, even accidentally.

2. CLOSED-CIRCUIT MEMBERSHIP

"Collectives and cooperatives should acquire cannabis only from their constituent members, because only cannabis grown by a qualified patient or his/her primary caregiver may lawfully be transported by, and/or distributed to other members."²¹⁷ "Nothing allows marijuana to be purchased from outside the collective or cooperative for distribution to its members."²¹⁸ Similarly, "nothing allows individuals or groups to sell or distribute marijuana to non-members."²¹⁹ "Instead, the cycle should be a closed-circuit of marijuana cultivation and consumption with no purchases or sales to or from non-members."²²⁰

Given the above, CBs should pursue reasonable measures to prevent the diversion of cannabis to non-members. **To ensure that this goal is met, CBs should:**

(1) Verify an individual's status as a qualified patient or primary caregiver before distributing cannabis to them;
(2) Have members agree not to distribute cannabis to non-members;
(3) Maintain membership records on-site;
(4) Track when members' physician recommendations expire; and
(5) Exclude members whose recommendations have expired or who are caught diverting cannabis to non-members.²²¹

3. SIZE OF MEMBERSHIP

California courts have found that there are no limitations on cooperative and collective membership numbers under the CUA or MMP.[222] To ensure compliance with state law, make sure that cannabis amounts at the business correspond to membership numbers. For example, if the MCB has 1,000 qualified patient-members, the business should only have the amount of cannabis that is "reasonably related" to the medical needs of those patients, and nothing more. As a practical matter, it is generally recommended to use the MMP's quantity limitations of 8 ounces per patient.

4. MEMBER RESPONSIBILITIES

Collective and cooperative members do not have to be directly involved in the cultivation of cannabis or the day-to-day operation of the business. This means that it is permissible for a member's involvement to be limited to the purchasing of cannabis. Nevertheless, it is still recommended that a MCB's membership agreement contain provisions clarifying the scope of a member's duties. Law enforcement authorities tend to believe that collectives or cooperatives are more "legitimate" when they require its members to provide more than just money for cannabis – e.g., donate time or goods to the collective.

d. SELLER'S PERMITS, BUSINESS LICENSES AND SALES TAX

There are a number of different licenses or permits required by California and local governments to lawfully operate as a CB in California.

First, all sales of medical cannabis are subject to sales tax even when there is no profit and CBs must obtain a seller's permit from the State Board of Equalization ("BOE"). Prior to October 2005, the BOE did not issue seller's permits to sellers of items that could be considered illegal – e.g., cannabis. However, a policy change was issued in October 2005, which requires the BOE to issue seller's permits regardless of whether the property sold is illegal, or not indicated.[223] Therefore, if money is *ever* exchanged for the cultivation and/or distribution of cannabis, a CB must obtain a seller's permit or a resale certificate. If a CB sells medical cannabis without a seller's permit, it may be audited and subject to back taxes, heavy penalties, and interest.

Second, most cities require a business license from the city or county to operate any business, including a CB. The catch here though, is that local municipalities will not issue business licenses to CBs, and, most cities have laws banning the use of land for the purpose of operating a CB, medicinal or recreational. Under current law, those municipalities may therefore reject a CB application for a business license.[224] A CB however, may be able to obtain a Business Tax Registration Certificate, which would at least allow it to pay local taxes. Depending on the zoning and tax laws in the CBs' city it may be available for varying level of licenses and it is important to obtain as many of those license as possible to ensure legal operation.

e. REASONABLE COMPENSATION

A common question that people in the cannabis industry ask is: "How do I pay myself?" The short answer to this is that CB officers and employees are entitled to reasonable compensation: a salary commensurate with what other people, with similar experiences and qualifications would earn who provide a similar service.

The longer answer requires some additional background information. A CB may pay "reasonable compensation" to its owners, directors, managers and employees, but the term "reasonable" is not defined in any California law or regulation. Typically, for non-profit organizations, "reasonable compensation" as defined by the IRS, is set by standard industry practices. With the medical cannabis industry, however, there is no real standard industry practice. Moreover, just as with any other job, compensation should also depend on the individual's specific qualifications and experience. In short, you must use your best judgment. The best way to establish compensation is to: (1) compare similar pay rates of similar positions in similar industries; and (2) take into consideration the type of job, level of education and experience of the employee, and hours worked.

If an officer or employee wear multiple hats within the CB – e.g., she sits on the Board of Directors and manages the day-to-day operations – she may be paid for each function, but both salaries must be "reasonable." Remember, each person acts on behalf of a non-profit company, so she must always act in the best interests of the *company* and not herself – meaning she should not bleed the company dry with her salary.

Similarly, if a collective opts to contract with a for-profit corporation for any service, the contract fee must be reasonable. Whatever the route, make sure that the corporation bylaws document and explain the reasoning for anything related to compensation.

5. PRACTICAL APPLICATION - BUSINESS MODELS

a. DISPENSARIES

Dispensaries were the first formal CBs in California to sell marijuana in a retail fashion. Currently, CBs who operate as a retail dispensary must abide by the same rules as any other CB collective. Dispensaries may also deliver to patients under a delivery service model (discussed below).

Under the MCRSA, when licenses are issued, cannabis can be dispensed to qualified patients by dispensaries in cities or counties where not prohibited by local ordinance. All sales and operations will need to be documented. Dispensaries can also be taxed by the local county where they operate.

b. DELIVERY SERVICES

Currently, CBs who operate as a delivery service must abide by the same rules as any other CB collective.

Under the MCRSA, when licenses are issued, cannabis can be delivered to qualified patients only by dispensaries and only in cities or counties where not prohibited by local ordinance. All deliveries need to be documented. No locality can bar transport of delivered products through its territory. Deliveries can be taxed by the local county where they operate.

c. CULTIVATING CANNABIS FOR A DISPENSARY OR COLLECTIVE

Under current California law, qualified patients and primary caregivers can collectively cultivate as much cannabis as needed for their patients' personal medical use. Although growing a personal amount of cannabis requires no business formation, cultivating large quantities to sell to a collective or dispensary, requires organization, preparation and extra precautions be taken. Moreover, several local cities and counties have disallowed collective grows for more than 2 or 3 people so operating a large-scale grow could potentially lead you to local prosecution as well.

Currently, under the Compassionate Use Act and the Attorney General Guidelines, to legally grow cannabis and sell it to a collective or dispensary, you must: (1) be a qualified patient; (2) be a member of that collective; and (3) sell the cannabis to the collective on a non-profit basis. It is also recommended that you enter into a formal written agreement with the collective verifying that you are responsible for cultivating cannabis for a certain number of the collective's patients.

Some doctors charge clients extra money for so-called "growers licenses," which supposedly increase a person's individual grow limit to 99 plants. Please beware, there is no such thing as a "growers license" under the CUA or MMP. These grower's licenses are essentially medical cannabis recommendations that state the doctor's opinion that a specific amount of cannabis is reasonable for the patient's medical needs. The license does *not* authorize you to grow 99 plants for a collective and it does *not* license you to sell your surplus cannabis to other patients or collectives. Unless a doctor can plausibly testify in court that you need 99 plants for your medical condition, you could be prosecuted for illegal cultivation even if you have one of these doctor's recommendations. Again, available law tells us that the best way to cultivate cannabis legally in California is to join a collective and then obtain written authorization from that collective to grow for other members.

As we inch closer to licensing under the MCRSA, AUMA, and local ordinances, the collective model will likely become obsolete and you will be able to grow for multiple dispensaries and not be required to maintain a closed circuit patient group.

d. SELLING AND/OR MANUFACTURING CANNABIS CONCENTRATES

In December 2014, a state appellate court in Sacramento ruled that "concentrated cannabis" qualifies as cannabis for purposes of medical use under the CUA[225]. Thus, concentrated cannabis – e.g. wax, shatter, hash oil, dabs etc. – is legal to use and possess, and for dispensaries to sell in California. In dispensaries throughout California, concentrates have become best-sellers. Oddly enough, even though possession and sales of concentrates can be legal, the production of some concentrates remains illegal.

We say "some" concentrates because there are different methods of manufacturing, each of which carry a different legal implication. Concentrates can be manufactured via cold-water extract, CO2 or butane (BHO). The cold-water method of making hash oils is held to be 100% legal. The use of CO2, while not specifically addressed by lawmakers as illegal, is probably defensible in court because CO2, a safe, non-flammable substance, poses no public threat. BHO, on the other hand, is a hazardous, toxic, and flammable chemical. "Chemical extraction," through use of butane remains **illegal** under the landmark case in 2008 called *People v. Bergen*.[226]

Before the *Bergen* case, it was arguably legal in California to make concentrated cannabis by using butane as a solvent (as is common practice). For years, prosecutors tried to charge butane hash oil producers with operating a drug lab under Health & Safety Code § 11379.6.[227] Defense attorneys were typically successful in arguing that these defendants should instead be charged with the more specific "marijuana processing" statute listed in Health & Safety Code § 11358[228]. In *Bergen,* however, the court ruled that the "drug lab" statute – which was created to address methamphetamine and PCP labs – appropriately applied to making concentrated cannabis using butane as a solvent.[229]

California Health and Safety Code §11379.6, also known as the "drug lab statute", prohibits illegal production of drugs, narcotics or controlled substances. As written, Health and Safety Code §11379.6 does not specifically state producing BHO is illegal. Rather, the statute prohibits engaging in manufacturing illegal substances and punishes those who endanger the public using toxic chemicals in production. The *Bergen* case, specifically, ruled that because butane is highly combustible and dangerous, Health and Safety Code §11379.6, now makes the production of BHO medical cannabis concentrates illegal. The *Bergen* court, however, went on to suggest that manufacture by means of pressure, screening, ice water and dissolving the plant in a non-chemical lipid extractor, such as butter would not violate the "drug lab" statute.[230]

Currently, using butane to extract cannabis concentrates is a felony, punishable by three (3), five (5) or seven (7) years in county jail and a $50,000 maximum fine. In addition, if children live, are present or are harmed where BHO is manufactured, AN ADDITIONAL TERM of up to five years may be added. Now, as of January 1, 2016, a new bill authored by Cal. Sen. Tony Mendoza of Southeast L.A. makes producing concentrates at home very risky. His bill, SB 212, unanimously approved by the Senate on June 3, 2015 and signed by Gov. Brown on August 7, 2015, adds an "aggravating factor" to cases of those convicted of making concentrates in their homes.

Mendoza's bill was drafted after multiple instances in which drug laboratories were found in residential neighbourhoods throughout California. Mendoza said state and federal law-enforcement officers located more than 800 illicit drug labs on private and public property and in close proximity to schools. To combat this unregulated BHO production, Mendoza's bill presses judges to lean toward seven years when sentencing home production. Additionally, the bill gives judges the power to impose an additional prison sentence for persons convicted of manufacturing BHO within 300 feet of an occupied residence.

Currently, we see two types of facilities where BHO is produced. There are regulated, safe and highly controlled labs in industrial warehouses that employ state certified extraction machines, and take every precautionary measure possible. These machines are completely legal in the state of California to extract anything from a legal substance, i.e. making rose water from rose petals! Conversely, due to the ease of access to online videos and inexpensive supplies, a highly dangerous, unregulated production of BHO in homes has become a new trend.

In the face of this new dichotomy, the "drug lab statute" seems to be overbroad, failing to differentiate between the two production conditions. The extraction-lab explosions that make a spectacle in news headlines, more often than not, are productions of BHO in homes under less than safe conditions. In an overgeneralization, the extraction-lab explosions are now named the new "meth-lab explosion" in the Golden State, further blurring any distinction between two facility types that produce BHO.

The real problem here stems from the vague and ambiguous set of laws that govern cannabis in California. The unclear regulations not only prohibit the unsafe and hazardous conditions in which BHO is produced at home, but also prohibit professional labs that employ the utmost safety precautions and regulations. The MCRSA and AUMA, however, have cleared up some of the ambiguity. Within the next couple of years, the MCRSA and AUMA will result in state-issued licenses for manufacturers of concentrated cannabis who use volatile solvents, i.e. butane, with a local permit. Once these licenses are available, licensed cannabis concentrates manufacturers who follow all applicable rules and regulations – which are yet to be set – will not be criminally prosecuted. For now, however, the manufacture of BHO remains illegal.

In fact, a recent raid in San Diego should serve as a cautionary tale for all those interested in the concentrate business here in California.[231] Recently, in January 2016, police raided MedWest Distribution, a California manufacturer of concentrated cannabis extracts such as "hash oil," "honey," "wax," and "shatter." As one of the reasons for the raid, police claim that the process used by the company to manufacture the concentrates was both dangerous and illegal.[232] The key takeaway here is that even though it is legal in California to possess and distribute medical cannabis extracts produced under any method, it is still illegal (at least for now) to manufacture them using BHO.

e. MAKING AND/OR SELLING EDIBLES

The MCRSA is the first statewide legislation to address edibles. The law calls for the California State Department of Public Health to develop standards for producing, testing and labeling all edible medical cannabis products. The Department of Public Health is in charge of regulating the edible potencies as well.

The MCRSA defines an edible cannabis product as follows:

"Edible cannabis product" means manufactured cannabis that is intended to be used, in whole or in part, for human consumption, including, but not limited to, chewing gum. An edible medical cannabis product is not considered food as defined by Section 109935 of the Health and Safety Code or a drug as defined by Section 109925 of the Health and Safety Code.

Though this language appears to exempt edibles from California's food safety laws and regulations governing conventional foods, it is still advisable that California manufacturers and producers of edible products educate themselves regarding the federal laws that apply to conventional forms of food now being used as vehicles for the consumption of cannabis and apply those standards to their production process. This will reduce the risk that cannabis edibles will cause foodborne illnesses – and will hopefully keep the U.S. FDA off your backs. Strict compliance with food safety standards will, of course, also help protect the legitimacy of cannabis edibles as medical treatments.

Because the Department of Public Health rules regarding edibles have yet to be set, we don't yet know exactly how edibles will be regulated under the MCRSA. However, the AUMA sets forth a more comprehensive list of labeling requirements. Specifically, the AUMA states, in pertinent part, the following:

All marijuana and marijuana product labels and inserts shall include the following information prominently displayed in a clear and legible fashion in accordance with the requirements, including font size, prescribed by the bureau or the Department of Public Health:

(1) Manufacture date and source.

(2) For marijuana: "GOVERNMENT WARNING: THIS PACKAGE CONTAINS MARIJUANA, A SCHEDULE I CONTROLLED SUBSTANCE. KEEP OUT OF REACH OF CHILDREN AND ANIMALS. MARIJUANA MAY ONLY BE POSSESSED OR CONSUMED BY PERSONS 21 YEARS OF AGE OR OLDER UNLESS THE PERSON IS A QUALIFIED PATIENT. MARIJUANA USE WHILE PREGNANT OR BREASTFEEDING MAY BE HARMFUL. CONSUMPTION OF MARIJUANA IMPAIRS YOUR ABILITY TO DRIVE AND OPERATE MACHINERY. PLEASE USE EXTREME CAUTION."

(3) For marijuana products: "GOVERNMENT WARNING: THIS PRODUCT CONTAINS MARIJUANA, A SCHEDULE I CONTROLLED SUBSTANCE. KEEP OUT OF REACH OF CHILDREN AND ANIMALS. MARIJUANA PRODUCTS MAY ONLY BE POSSESSED OR CONSUMED BY PERSONS 21 YEARS OF AGE OR OLDER UNLESS THE PERSON IS A QUALIFIED PATIENT. THE INTOXICATING EFFECTS OF MARIJUANA PRODUCTS MAY BE DELAYED UP TO TWO HOURS. MARIJUANA USE WHILE PREGNANT OR BREASTFEEDING MAY BE HARMFUL. CONSUMPTION OF MARIJUANA PRODUCTS IMPAIRS YOUR ABILITY TO DRIVE AND OPERATE MACHINERY. PLEASE USE EXTREME CAUTION."

(4) For packages containing only dried flower, the net weight of marijuana in the package.

(5) Identification of the source and date of cultivation, the type of marijuana or marijuana product and the date of manufacturing and packaging.

(6) The appellation of origin, if any.

(7) List of pharmacologically active ingredients, including, but not limited to, tetrahydrocannabinol (THC), cannabidiol (CBD), and other cannabinoid content, the THC and other cannabinoid amount in milligrams per serving, servings per package, and the THC and other cannabinoid amount in milligrams for the package total, and the potency of the marijuana or marijuana product by reference to the amount of tetrahydrocannabinol and cannabidiol in each serving.

(8) For marijuana products, a list of all ingredients and disclosure of nutritional information in the same manner as the federal nutritional labeling requirements in 21 C.F.R. section 101.9.

(9) A list of any solvents, nonorganic pesticides, herbicides, and fertilizers that were used in the cultivation, production, and manufacture of such marijuana or marijuana product.

(10) A warning if nuts or other known allergens are used.

This issue, in addition to others, will be addressed through state agency rule making that will take place until at least January 2018.

B. THE MEDICAL CANNABIS REGULATION AND SAFETY ACT 2015 ("MCRSA")

Composed of three separate bills – AB 266, AB 243 and SB 643 – the MCRSA[233] creates a comprehensive **state licensing system** for the **commercial** cultivation, manufacture, retail sale, transport, distribution, delivery, and testing of medical cannabis. This means that new and existing CBs must comply with the state's licensing system *in addition to* local government permitting, effective **January 1, 2016**.

Under the MCRSA, a new state agency was established within the Department of Consumer Affairs – The Bureau of Medical Cannabis Regulation (BMCR) - for the purpose of enforcing the MCRSA under the direction of Cannabis Czar Lori Ajax. Several other state agencies are creating departments to oversee and be responsible for different aspects of regulation.

Because California needs some time to set up the necessary agencies, information systems, and regulations to actually begin issuing licenses, state licenses under the MCRSA are not currently available. It is anticipated that the application process will tentatively begin no earlier than January 1, 2018. [Note: Awet Kidane, Director of the Department of Consumer Affairs, has already commented that a January 1, 2018 implementation date is an ambitious deadline.[234]]

In the interim, local governments may choose to adopt new ordinances to permit or license local businesses in preparation for the MCRSA state licensing. Facilities currently operating in accordance with California and local laws may continue to do so until their license applications are approved or denied. In the meantime, prospective applicants are strongly advised to apply to the state Board of Equalization (BOE) for the applicable sales permit, and to prepare for seeking approval from their local governments. If a local government does not have land use regulations or ordinances in place prohibiting cannabis cultivation, then the State will be the *sole* licensing authority for licensing applicants in that local jurisdiction. Medical CBs permitted by **both a state license and local government will be deemed lawful and are protected from arrest, prosecution, or other legal sanctions**.

1. THE COMPONENTS OF THE MCRSA

AB 243, AB 266, and SB 643, collectively, make up the MCRSA. Each bill deals with different aspects of licensing and regulating commercial medical cannabis cultivation, manufacturing, distribution, transportation, sales, and testing.

AB 243, among other things, establishes standards for a physician prescribing medical cannabis. The bill requires the Department of Consumer Affairs to have the sole authority to create, issue, renew, discipline, suspend, or revoke licenses for the transportation and storage of medical cannabis.

SB 643 and AB266 (discussed in depth below) work together to create a licensing scheme. Specifically, SB643 engages the following governmental agencies to oversee regulations or standards relating to medical cannabis and its cultivation:

- The Dept. of Food and Agriculture is responsible for regulating cultivation;
- The Dept. of Public Health is responsible for developing standards for the manufacture, testing, production and labeling of edibles;
- The Dept. of Pesticide Regulation is responsible for Developing pesticide standards; and
- The Depts. of Fish and Wildlife and State Water Board are responsible for protecting water quality.

These agencies are incorporated to mitigate the impact that cannabis cultivation has on the environment. This portion of the collaborative Act requires cities, counties, and their local law enforcement agencies to coordinate with state agencies to enforce laws addressing the environmental impacts.

Finally, AB 266 establishes a new **Bureau of Medical Cannabis Regulation** ("BMCR") under the Department of Consumer Affairs. The BMCR must establish a comprehensive Internet system for keeping track of licensees and reporting the movement of commercial cannabis and cannabis products. AB266 further creates fines and civil penalties for specified violations of the Act, and would require money be collected as a result of these fines and civil penalties to be deposited into the Medical Cannabis Fines and Penalties Account.

2. LICENSING UNDER THE MCRSA

Effective January 1, 2016, the following is California law for collective and cooperative operations.

AB266 in connection with SB643, creates a multitude of licenses to be issued. Generally, licensees can have **at most two separate kinds of licenses.** Below are the list of license types established under AB 266

(19300.7)) and SB 643 (19331(g)):

Type 1	**Cultivation;** Specialty outdoor. Up to 5,000 sq. ft. of canopy, or up to 5 noncontiguous plants
Type 1A	**Cultivation;** Specialty indoor. Up to 5000 sq ft
Type 1B	**Cultivation**; Specialty mixed-light. Using exclusively artificial lighting.
Type 2	**Cultivation**; Outdoor. Up to 5000 sq ft, using a combination of artificial and natural lighting
Type 2A	**Cultivation**; Indoor. 5001 -10,000 sq ft.
Type 2B	**Cultivation**; Mixed-light. 5001 -10,000 sq ft
Type 3	**Cultivation**; Outdoor. 10,001 sq ft - 1 Acre
Type 3A	**Cultivation**; Indoor.. 10,001 - 22,000 sq ft
Type 3B	**Cultivation**; Mixed-light. 10,001 - 22,000 sq ft
Type 4	**Cultivation**; Nursery.
Type 6	**Manufacturer** 1 for products not using volatile solvents.
Type 7	**Manufacturer** 2 for products using volatile solvents.
Type 8	**Testing**
Type 10	**Dispensary**; General
Type 10A	**Dispensary**; No more than three retail sites
Type 11	**Distribution**
Type 12	**Transporter**

A licensee may only hold a state license in **up to two separate license** categories, as follows:

- **Type 1, 1A, 1B, 2, 2A, and 2B licensees**, or a combination thereof, may apply for a Type 6 or 7 state license, or a combination thereof.

- **Type 6 and 7 licensees**, or a combination thereof, may apply for a Type 1, 1A, 1B, 2, 2A, and 2B state license, or a combination thereof.

- **Type 6 and 7 licensees**, or a combination thereof, may apply for a Type 10A state license.

- **Type 10A licensees** may apply for a Type 6 and 7 state license, or a combination thereof.

- **Type 1, 1A, 1B, 2, 2A, and 2B licensees**, or a combination thereof, may apply for a Type 10A state license.

- **Type 10A licensees**, may apply for Type 1, 1A, 1B, 2, 2A, and 2B state license, or a combination thereof.

- **Type 11 licensees** may apply for a Type 12 state license.

- **Type 12 licensees** may apply for a Type 11 state license.

As of right now, it is unclear how many licenses will actually be issued under the MCRSA. The Assembly Committee for the implementation of the MCRSA has indicated that the state-wide regulations are intended to protect the small and medium-sized cultivators so the provision of large-scale cultivation licenses will be limited in number. According to Hon. Steven K. Lubell, Commissioner of the Superior Court of the State of California (Ret.), the actual number of licenses is currently unknown but the market will adjust to itself based upon the amount of plant canopy that eventually is going to be the amount sufficient to provide a supply in the state of California.[235]

For medical CB owners, knowing how to navigate the complexities of the MCRSA's licensing restrictions will quickly become the key to maximizing business potential. In general, licensees can only hold licenses in up to two separate license categories (i.e., cultivators, manufacturers, distributors/transporters, dispensaries, etc.).[236] But it's not as simple as it sounds – the current licensing restrictions are actually quite complicated and deciphering all the "legalese" in the MCRSA is not the easiest of tasks.

If you (like most people) are unclear about how many licenses you can or cannot hold – all while staying compliant with the MCRSA – this simple "road map" will hopefully provide some clarity and serve as a good starting point for planning the future of your cannabusiness.

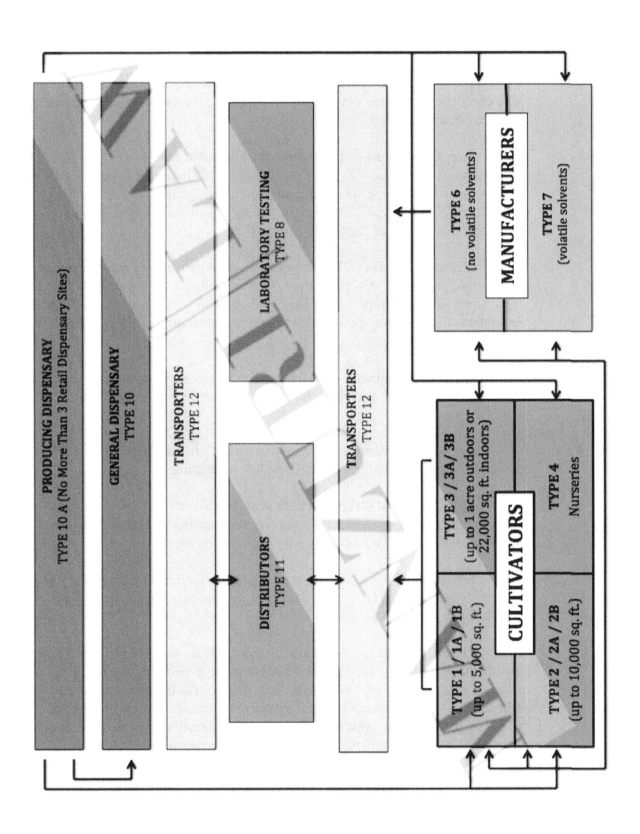

3. CULTIVATORS LICENSE TYPES 1-4

The MCRSA treats cultivator licensees differently based upon the size of their cultivation. For simplicity purposes, we will refer to them as large, medium and small.

Size Limitations - The maximum allowable size is (1) one acre (43,560 sq. ft.) outdoors (Type 3) or 22,000 sq. ft. indoors (Type 3A and 3B licenses). The Dept. of Food and Agriculture ("DFA") is directed to limit the number of Type 3, 3A and 3B licenses. Cultivation licensees have to declare themselves as "agricultural employers."

Licensing - The DFA is going to establish a medical cannabis cultivation program. All cultivation will be subject to local land use regulations and permits. In cities and counties without cultivation regulations of their own, the state is the sole licensing authority as of March 1, 2016.

Pesticide Standards - Standards for pesticides will be publicized by DFA and Dept. of Pesticide Regulation. The standards have not been released yet.

Organic Certification - Organic certifications will be made available by DFA by Jan 1, 2020, federal law permitting.

Appellations of Origin - The Bureau MAY establish designation of origin for cannabis grown in California. This means that no product may be marketed as coming from a county where it was not grown.

School Zones - Cultivation and dispensary facilities must be at least 600 ft. from schools (with grandfathered exceptions specified in HSC 11362.768).

Track & Trace Program - The DFA will implement an identification program for all cannabis plants at a cultivation site, to be attached at the base of each plant. The information will be incorporated into a "track and trace" program for each product and transaction. Cultivation in violation of these provisions is subject to civil penalties up to twice the amount of the license fee, plus applicable criminal penalties.

Here is how the MCRSA treats each cultivation license, respectively:

[Note: While the MCRSA generally only allows licensees to hold licenses in up to two separate license categories, there does not appear to be any restrictions on obtaining more than one type of license within one specific category. For example, you could have multiple cultivator licenses of any type or combination, if you so choose.]

a. LARGE-SCALE CULTIVATORS (TYPES 3, 3A, 3B)

The licenses for large-scale cultivators are as follows:

Type 3 = Outdoor (No Artificial Lighting) (10,001 sq ft - 1 Acre)
Type 3A = Indoor (Artificial Lighting Only) (10,001 - 22,000 sq ft)
Type 3B = Mixed-Light (Combo of Natural and Artificial Lighting) (10,001 – 22,000 sq ft)

Note that the above size limitations are limited to one premises only.[237] Premises is currently being defined by the BMCR. Also, keep in mind that the Department of Food and Agriculture ("DFA") will be limiting the number of Type 3 licenses[238], though it is still unclear right now what that limit will be.

- **No Manufacturing License for Large-Scale Cultivators Unless Part of a Type 10A Dispensary:** Unlike the smaller cultivators (see Types 1-2 below), Type 3 cultivators will not be allowed to obtain manufacturing licenses (Types 6-7) at all. However, Type 10A dispensaries could apply for both manufacturing and cultivation licenses, including Type 3, provided that their total cultivation area doesn't exceed 4 acres.[239]

- **May Hold a Transporter License:** Type 3 cultivators may hold a Type 12 transporter license provided that they only transport medical cannabis from a cultivation site to either a manufacturer or distributor. In other words, even if it has a Type 12 license, a Type 3 cultivator cannot transport cannabis directly to a dispensary. This rule applies to *all* cultivators, big or small.[240]

b. MEDIUM-SCALE CULTIVATORS (TYPES 2, 2A, AND 2B) AND SMALL-SCALE CULTIVATORS (TYPES 1, 1A, AND 1B)

The MCRSA treats medium and small-scale cultivator licensees identically.

The licenses for medium-scale cultivators are as follows:

Type 2 = Outdoor (No Artificial Lighting) (5,001 -10,000 sq ft.)

Type 2A = Indoor (Artificial Lighting Only) (5,001 -10,000 sq ft.)

Type 2B = Mixed-Light (Combo of Natural and Artificial Lighting) (5,001 –10,000 sq ft.)

The licenses for small-scale cultivators are as follows:

Type 1 = Outdoor (No Artificial Lighting) (Up to 5,000 sq ft of canopy *or* up to 50 noncontiguous plants)

Type 1A = Indoor (Artificial Lighting Only) (Up to 5000 sq ft)

Type 1B = Mixed-Light (Combo of Natural and Artificial Lighting) (Up to 5,000 sq ft)

Note that the above size limitations are limited to one premises only.[241] The MCRSA doesn't specify whether there will be a limit on the number of Type 1 or 2 licenses.

- **Both May Hold a Manufacturing License:** Type 1 and 2 cultivators may also hold either a Type 6 or 7 manufacturing license.[242]

- **Both May Hold a Transporter License:** Type 1 and 2 cultivators may also hold a Type 12 transporter license provided that they only transport medical cannabis from a cultivation site to either a manufacturer or distributor. In other words, even if it has a Type 12 license, a Type 1 or 2 cultivator cannot transport cannabis directly to a dispensary. This rule applies to *all* cultivators, big or small.[243]

- **Both May Hold a Type 10A Dispensary License:** Type 1, 1A, 1B, 2, 2A, or 2B licensees, or a combination thereof, may also hold a Type 10A dispensary license.[244]

c. *"Cottage" Cultivators (Type 1C)*

With the passage of AB 2516, a new cultivator license (Type 1C) was added for "micro farmers." This new license – dubbed the "specialty cottage" license – would be as follows:

Type 1C = Mixed-Light (Combo of Natural and Artificial Lighting) (Up to 2,500 sq ft) *or* Outdoor (No Artificial Lighting) (Up to 25 plants) *or* Indoor (Artificial Lighting Only) (Up to 500 sq ft)

Again, the above size limitations would be limited to one premises only.[245] The proposed bill doesn't specify whether there will be a limit on the number of Type 1C licenses.

- **Cottage Cultivators Will Probably Be Treated Like Types 1 and 2:** AB 2516 doesn't directly address the licensing restrictions for Type 1C cultivators, but it would be safe to assume that they would be treated identically to Type 1 and 2 cultivators (see above).

d. NURSERIES (TYPE 4)

Nurseries, which are given Type 4 licenses, can only cultivate "clones, immature plants, seeds, and other agricultural products used specifically for the planting, propagation, and cultivation of medical cannabis."[246] The MCRSA doesn't specify whether there will be a limit on the number of Type 4 licenses.

- **No Manufacturing License for Nurseries Unless Part of a Type 10A Dispensary:** Like Type 3 cultivators, it does not appear that Type 4 nurseries will be allowed to obtain manufacturing licenses (Types 6-7) at all. However, Type 10A dispensaries could apply for both manufacturing and cultivation licenses, including Type 4, provided that their total cultivation area doesn't exceed 4 acres.[247]

- **May Hold a Transporter License:** Like the other cultivators, Type 4 nurseries may hold Type 12 transporter licenses. If it has a Type 12 license, the Type 4 nursery may transport live plants from the nursery site to either a manufacturer or distributor.[248]

4. MANUFACTURING AND DISTRIBUTION LICENSES

Manufacturers - Manufacturers are to be licensed by the Dept. of Public Health. The DPH shall limit the number of Type 7 licenses that produce products using volatile solvents.

Testing - The DPH will now make sure that all cannabis is tested prior to delivery to dispensaries or other businesses, and specify how often such testing shall be conducted. Although it is unclear because 19346(c) says the costs of testing are to be paid by cultivators, whereas 19326(c)(3) states that distributors shall charge for the costs of testing; since distributors serve manufacturers as well as cultivators, it doesn't make sense that testing costs for the former should be charged to the latter.

Licensees will use standard methods established by International Organization for Standardization approved by an accrediting body that is signatory to the International Laboratory Accreditation Cooperation Mutual Recognition Arrangement. Licensees must test for cannabinoids, contaminants, microbiological impurities, and other compounds spelled out in Section 19344. Licensees may conduct tests for individual qualified patients, but not certify them for resale or transfer to other licensees.

Packaging - Products have to be labeled in tamper-evident packages with warning statements & information specified in Section 19347.

Distributors Required - Type 11 distributors are a new kind of entity that has been created to regulate the flow of products. ALL cultivation and manufacturing licensees are required to send their products to a Type 11 licensee for quality insurance and inspection before passing them to the next stage of manufacturing or retailing. The Type 11 licensee in turn submits the product to a Type 8 laboratory for batch testing and certification. Afterwards, the sample returns to the Type 11 distributor for final inspection and execution of the contract between the cultivator and manufacturer or manufacturer and retailer. The Type 11 distributor charges a fee that covers the testing plus any applicable taxes (the act doesn't impose any new taxes, but anticipates that could happen in the near future). Type 11 distributors and Type 8 testing facilities can't hold any other kind of licenses (however, licensees may have their own labs for in-house testing).

Deliveries - Cannabis may be delivered to qualified patients only by dispensaries and only in cities or counties where not prohibited by local ordinance. All deliveries need to be documented. No locality can bar transport of delivered products through its territory. Deliveries may be taxed by the local county where they operate.

Transportation - Only licensed transporters can transport cannabis or cannabis products between licensees. The bill doesn't specify whether cultivators, manufacturers, or retailers can also have transport licenses, but 19328 (a) states they can generally have at most two separate kinds of licenses. Licensed transporters shall transmit an electronic shipping manifest to the state and carry a physical copy with each shipment.

a. MANUFACTURERS (TYPES 6 AND 7)

The licenses for manufacturers are as follows:

Type 6 = Manufacturer level 1 for products not using volatile

solvents
Type 7 = Manufacturer level 2 for products using volatile solvents

Like Type 3 licenses, the DFA will be limiting the number of Type 7 licenses[249], though it is still unclear right now what that limit will be.

- **May Hold a Type 1 or 2 Cultivator License:** Type 6 or 7 licensees, or a combination thereof, may also hold either a small or medium-scale cultivator license (Type 1, 1A, 1B, 2, 2A, or 2B).[250]

- **May Hold a Transporter License:** Manufacturers (Types 6 or 7) may hold a Type 12 transporter license so long as they only transport medical cannabis and medical cannabis products as follows:
    (1) between a cultivation site and a manufacturing site;
    (2) between a manufacturing site and a manufacturing site; or
    (3) between a manufacturing site and a distributor.[251]

b. DISTRIBUTORS (TYPE 11)

Type 11 distributors *must* hold a Type 12 transporter license, but they cannot hold any other type of license.[252] Type 11 distributors are prohibited from having an ownership interest in any other licensee's entity or premises, unless it is a security interest, lien or encumbrance on property that is being used by a licensee.[253]

c. AB: 2679 PROTECTION FOR MANUFACTURERS

AB 2679, signed by Governor Brown, is a bi-partisan bill that establishes key standards for medical cannabis manufacturers, and protects them from raids and criminal prosecution – at least until the state begins issuing licenses in 2018. For all you manufacturers out there, this is a game changer!!!

Health & Safety Code ("H&S") § 11379.6, also known as the "drug lab" statute, prohibits illegal production of drugs, narcotics or controlled substances. As written, H&S § 11379.6 does not specifically state that producing concentrated cannabis with the use of butane (as is common practice) is illegal. Rather, the statute prohibits engaging in manufacturing illegal substances and punishes those who *endanger the public using toxic chemicals in production.*

However, due to landmark case called *People v. Bergen*[254], chemical extraction using butane is considered illegal under H&S § 11379. In *Bergen*, the court ruled that the "drug lab" statute – which was created to address meth and PCP labs – appropriately applied to those who make concentrated cannabis using butane as a solvent. This is due to the reasoning in *Bergen* that butane extraction poses a threat to the public because butane is both toxic and flammable. Since *Bergen* came down in 2008, law enforcement authorities have been going hard on cannabis manufacturers who use butane as a solvent. And because these cannabis manufacturers get convicted of H&S § 11379.6, many of them end up getting state prison sentences because they are treated the same way as those who run meth labs.

Now that AB 2679 has become law, H&S § 11379.6 will be amended to read that a "collective or cooperative" that "manufactures medical cannabis products" **shall not** be subject to criminal sanctions under H&S § 11379.6 so long as it meets specified requirements. These requirements include, among others, using specified manufacturing processes such as the utilization of a self-contained "close-loop" system, obtaining independent certification by a licensed engineer, complying with all applicable fire, safety and building codes, and possessing a valid local license, permit or other authorization.[255] These standards are designed to ensure the safety of the extraction process. AB 2679 is set to expire one year after the state starts issuing licenses.

"Last year, California took a historic step by regulating medical cannabis to protect patients, businesses, our communities, and the environment. But across the state, locally authorized medical cannabis manufacturers continue to be targeted by municipal law enforcement. As we await full implementation of medical cannabis regulations, manufacturers cannot continue to operate in a legal grey area," explained Assemblymember Rob Bonta (D-Oakland). "Under AB 2679, local governments will be given guidance and manufacturers will be protected in preparation for state licenses in 2018."[256]

So what does this mean for cannabis manufacturers who use butane extraction? It means that from now until 2019, manufacturers will be shielded from criminal prosecution so long as they have local approval and abide by strict safety standards. AB 2679 allows manufacturers to use volatile solvents, such as butane, so long as the solvent is generally recognized by the FDA as safe. In order to legally manufacture concentrated cannabis using butane, the manufacturer must be a "collective or cooperative" with a valid seller's permit issued by the BOE. The manufacturer must also have a valid local license or permit which specifically authorizes the manufacture of medical cannabis products. Because most local governments don't yet have any rules or regulations (much less licensing systems) specific to manufacturing, this will probably be the toughest requirement to meet because you'll have to first wait and see if your local government will be giving out manufacturing licenses. On top of all that, the manufacturer must also comply with various safety and certification requirements.

If you're a cannabis manufacturer currently facing criminal charges, AB 2679 probably won't be your saving grace. Unless, at the time of your arrest, you had a local permit to manufacture medical cannabis products *and* you utilized all the various safety and certification protocols outlined in AB 2679 (which few, if any, cannabis manufacturers did), then technically it can't be said that you were operating "legally" under the newly-amended version of H&S § 11379.6. However, an experienced criminal defense attorney *could* make an argument that because AB 2679 was passed, it is very clear that the legislature believes that cannabis manufacturers should be treated differently than meth lab operators, and thus the strict criminal penalties of H&S § 11369.6 shouldn't apply "in the interests of justice." While this novel legal argument isn't guaranteed to win, it is certainly an interesting and very logical one to make and it will undoubtedly be raised in hundreds of cannabis manufacturing cases currently pending in the state.

5. TRANSPORTATION LICENSES (LICENSE TYPE 12)

Type 12 transporters only need to obtain licenses for each physical location where the Type 12 transporter conducts business while not in transport or where any transporting equipment (i.e., truck or car) permanently resides.[257]

- **May Hold a Distributor License:** Type 12 transporters may hold a Type 11 distributor license, but it is not mandatory.[258]

- **Cultivators, Manufacturers and Type 10A Dispensaries May Transport:** As already explained above, cultivators, manufacturers and Type 10A dispensaries may have Type 12 transporter licenses subject to certain restrictions.[259]

6. TESTING LICENSES (TYPE 8)

Type 8 testing laboratories cannot hold any other type of license and are prohibited from having an ownership interest in any other licensee's entity or premises.[260]

7. DISPENSARY LICENSES (TYPES 10 AND 10A)

The licenses for dispensaries are as follows:

Type 10 = General Dispensary
Type 10A = Producing Dispensary; No more than three retail sites

To be given a Type 10A license, the "producing dispensary" must have no more than three individually licensed Type 10 dispensaries and must wish to hold either a cultivation or manufacturing license, or both.[261] The MCRSA doesn't specify whether there will be a limit on the number of Type 10 or 10A dispensaries.

As you will see below, there is tons of opportunity for a Type 10A dispensary to maximize its licensing structure because Type 10A dispensaries can pretty much hold all the other types of licenses *except* Type 8 (laboratory testing) and Type 11 (distributor) licenses.

- **Type 10 Dispensaries Cannot Obtain Any Other License Unless Part of a Type 10A Dispensary – Grandfathering OK for Vertical Integration:** Single, stand-alone Type 10 dispensaries cannot obtain any other type of license unless it is part of a Type 10A producing dispensary (see below). However, if the Type 10 dispensary is in a local jurisdiction that *requires* vertical integration – i.e., all cultivation, manufacturing and distribution must be conducted by the dispensary – then the Type 10 dispensary may continue to operate that way until January 1, 2026.[262]

- **Type 10A Dispensaries May Hold a Cultivator and Transporter License:** Type 10A dispensaries may hold a small or medium cultivator license (Types 1, 1A, 1B, 2, 2A, or 2B), or a combination thereof. If a Type 10A dispensary has a Type 1 or 2 cultivator license, then it may also hold a Type 12 transporter license (see above).[263]

- **Type 10A Dispensaries May Hold a Manufacturing and Transporter License:** Type 10A dispensaries may hold either a Type 6 or Type 7 manufacturing license, or a combination of both. If a Type 10A dispensary has a manufacturing license, then it may also hold a Type 12 transporter license (see above).[264]

- **Type 10A Dispensaries May Hold a Manufacturing, Cultivator, and Transporter License:** Type 10A dispensaries may hold a manufacturing license and *any* cultivator license (including Type 3!), or combination thereof, if their total cultivation area doesn't exceed 4 acres.[265] If a Type 10A dispensary has a manufacturing or cultivator license, then it may also hold a Type 12 transporter license (see above).[266] This, however, will only last until January 1, 2016.[267] After then, Type 10A dispensaries will no longer be able to have Type 3 licenses and they will not be able to simultaneously have both manufacturing and cultivation licenses.

8. ENTITY STRUCTURE

Vertical Integration - In general, licensees can only hold licenses in up to two (2) separate categories. Small cultivation licensee Types 1 -2 may hold manufacturing or Type 10A retail licenses (limited to three dispensaries). It appears that Types 3-4 licensees can't apply for manufacturing licenses at all. However, Type 10A licensees can apply for both manufacturing and cultivation licenses, provided their total cultivation area doesn't exceed 4 acres. Also, facilities in jurisdictions that require or permit cultivation, manufacture and distribution to be integrated as of July 1, 2015, may continue to operate that way until Jan 1, 2026.

For-Profit Entities - Under the MCRSA, "for profit entities" are implicitly allowed. New licensing provisions extend to individuals, partnerships, corporations, business trusts, etc. under the definition of "person" in AB266. This also means that applicants no longer need to be patients.

Licensing - The MCRSA sets up 17 different types of medical cannabis operational license types and limits vertical integration – meaning that licensees can only hold licenses in no more than two separate license categories. For example, testing and distribution licensees will not be able to hold any other class of license. Essentially, the MCRSA breaks up the current vertical integration model of a closed loop of patient members from seed to distribution and instead replaces it with a multi-tiered model consisting of:

Cultivation → Distribution → Transportation → Testing → Manufacturing → Dispensing

There are a few exceptions, however. Businesses operating in local jurisdictions that require or allow full vertical integration of their supply chain (cultivation, manufacturing and dispensing) will be allowed to continue operating as they do now. There is also a specialty dispensary license modeled after a "brew pub" license, which allows for a licensee to be vertically integrated if they operate no more than 3 retail sites, hold only

1 manufacturing license, and own no more than 4 acres of licensed cultivation sites in the State. Both the above exemptions are only valid until January 1, 2026, unless extended by the State legislature.

9. PATIENT RIGHTS

Privacy - Names of patients, caregivers, and medical conditions must be kept confidential.

Physician Recommendations - There are several new provisions clarifying the duties of medical cannabis physicians. However, they don't substantially affect or impair patients' current access to medical recommendations. The Med Board's enforcement priorities are amended to include "Repeated acts of clearly excessive recommending of cannabis for medical purposes, or repeated acts of recommending without a good faith prior exam." This is identical to existing language regarding controlled substances, which has generally been assumed to apply to medical cannabis heretofore. The Med Board must consult with the California Center for Medicinal Cannabis Research in developing medical guidelines for cannabis recs. These actions have not been taken yet.

10. COSTS OF ENFORCEMENT

Fees and Funding - Each licensing authority will establish a scale of application, licensing and renewal fees, based upon the cost of enforcement. Fees will be scaled dependent on the size of the business. A Medical Cannabis Regulation and Safety Act Fund is established in the state treasury to receive fees and penalties assessed under the act. $10 million is allocated to DCA (Department of Consumer Affairs) to begin operations, with the possibility of an additional operating loan of $10 million from the General Fund. The Bureau will use the fund for a grant program to assist in state and local agencies in enforcement and remediation of environmental impacts from cultivation.

County Taxation - Counties may levy a tax on the cultivating, dispensing, producing, processing, distributing, etc…of medical cannabis subject to standard voter approval requirements.

11. LOCAL POWER

The MCRSA permits local cities and counties to regulate medical CBs beyond the requirements set forth under the MCRSA, and the bill (AB 243) also allows them to *ban* medical CBs within their borders. The law also states that cities and counties that do not have ordinances prohibiting cannabis cultivation will be governed by state law only. Absent a local ordinance, state law will allow 100 square feet of medical cannabis per patient, and allow caregivers to grow 500 square feet for up to five patients.

12. "PRIORITY" LICENSURE

Facilities in operation before January 1, 2016, get priority in the licensing requests. Medical cannabis businesses applying for a license have to provide proof of local approval and evidence of legal right to occupy the location in which they intend to open business. Fingerprinting for the DOJ background checks will also be part of the application process.

Facilities already operating in compliance with local ordinances and current California law (MMP, CUA and A.G. Guidelines) on or before January 1, 2018, can continue to operate until their license is approved or denied. The licensing authority MAY deny an application if the applicant has been convicted of an offense substantially related to qualifications, including ANY felony controlled substance offense, violent or serious felonies, or felonies involving fraud, deceit or embezzlement, or any sanctions by a local licensing authority in the past 3 years.

To have a shot at priority licensing under the MCRSA, medical CB owners should prepare in advance by completing a criminal background check on all employees; make sure their businesses are compliant with all local laws; and make sure their taxes are squared away with the BOE, including all local, state and federal taxes.

C. ADULT USE OF MARIJUANA ACT ("AUMA") OR (PROP 64)

When California voters passed Proposition 215 in 1996 to legalize medical cannabis, the Golden State appeared poised to be the one to set the stage for cannabis legalization in the rest of the country. Since 1996, however, several states – Colorado, Oregon, Alaska, and Washington – and the District of Columbia have beaten California in the cannabis race towards legalization.

Like similar initiatives in Colorado, Washington, Oregon and Alaska, the AUMA sets the stage for the road towards legalization. Although it's not perfect, the 62-page initiative still represents the best practices to-date and has the best chance to replace a failed system of prohibition with an effective, legal and regulated system. With the passage of Prop 64, California now joins the ranks of states that have legalized recreational cannabis.

The AUMA, however, is an extremely lengthy and complex initiative. Its stated purpose is to establish a comprehensive system to "legalize, control and regulate … *nonmedical* marijuana"[268] activity for adult use, while also consolidating and streamlining it with the current regulations for *medical* cannabis activity. The AUMA writes *hundreds* of new restrictions and regulations into state law, but the general gist of the initiative is to:

(1)   "semi-legalize" recreational cannabis by allowing adults 21+ to possess up to one ounce of cannabis and cultivate up to six plants for personal use;

(2)   regulate and tax the production, manufacture and sale of nonmedical cannabis for adult use (which would be largely patterned on existing MCRSA regulations for state licensing); and

(3)   reduce criminal penalties for common cannabis crimes and allow prior cannabis offenders to petition for reduced charges.

In short, the AUMA's biggest change to existing law would be the legalization and regulation of cannabis for nonmedical adult use, leaving all the hard work surrounding medical cannabis intact. Other changes include:

Cannabis Cafés – California is the second state to host Amsterdam-style cannabis cafés, right behind Alaska. The AUMA sidesteps the hassle associated with allowing public consumption by instead allowing localities to permit places for on-site smoking, vaping and edible-ing.

Larger Cultivation Licenses Available in 5 years – Under the AUMA, an additional category of Type 5 cultivation licenses were created for large farms that exceed the MCRSA's current limit of 22,000 sq. ft. indoors or 1-acre outdoors.[269] This would make Type 5 licenses the largest cultivation licenses available. However, in order to encourage small business growth, no Type 5 licenses will be issued before January 1, 2023.[270] This is consistent with the AUMA's policy statement related to existing growers: "The [AUMA] ensures the nonmedical marijuana industry in California will be built around small and medium sized businesses by prohibiting large-scale cultivation licenses for the first five years."[271]

"Microbusiness" Licenses – The AUMA creates an additional category of Type 12 licenses for "microbusinesses,"[272] which are basically vertically-integrated small farm operations not exceeding 10,000 sq. ft. Basically, think of a craft beer microbrewery or a vineyard tasting room, but for cannabis.

Vertical Integration – Unlike the MCRSA, the AUMA doesn't prohibit vertical integration of licenses. Instead of being limited to only having up two different license types under the MCRSA, the AUMA instead allows a licensee to hold any number or combination of licenses: cultivator, manufacturer, retailer, distributor and tester. There will be one exception: large-scale growers (Type 5) will be prohibited from holding certain other licenses.

Higher Taxes – The AUMA imposes a 15% excise tax on retail cannabis sales (in addition to state and local taxes already in place).[273] There will also be a cultivation tax imposed on all harvested cannabis that enters the commercial market, at a rate of $9.25 per oz. of dried flowers and $2.75 per oz. of dried leaves. Only medical cannabis patients with a state ID card would be exempt from the existing 7.5+% state sales taxes, but not the other taxes.

Lifting Bans on Personal Indoor Grows – Under the AUMA, adults 21+ will be able to lawfully grow up to six cannabis plants for personal use. Local governments will be allowed to enact local ordinances to *reasonably regulate* personal cannabis grow. While local governments will be allowed to totally prohibit outdoor grows if they so choose, they cannot totally prohibit personal indoor grows.

Eliminates Mandatory "Distributors" and "Transporters" – Unlike the MCRSA, the AUMA allows, but does not require, that cultivators send their product to Type 11 distributors for transportation to other licensees. This mandatory requirement, modeled on the alcohol industry, is one of the most controversial features of the MCRSA, as it interjects a whole new costly distribution layer between the grower and distributor. The AUMA, however, removes this mandatory "middle-man" from the weed supply chain. Only large-scale growers (Type 5) will be required to use Type 11 distributors under the AUMA. The remaining licensees will be eligible to distribute for themselves.

Small-business friendly – The AUMA will restrain big business by withholding Type 5 licenses for large-scale growers for a period of five years.[274] The AUMA also throws a lot of obstacles in the way of big business and adds several anti-monopoly sections – e.g. no price fixing, no red lining, no undercutting the competition, no selling at a loss or giving away cannabis to hurt competitors, etc...

The AUMA is far from perfect – it is still a work in progress and there will be a lot of work needed to be done in the future (by the courts and the legislature) to iron out all the inconsistencies, ambiguities and glitches that are currently in the initiative. Nevertheless, it is still a big step (albeit partial) towards complete legalization. Not to mention the huge economic impact that adult use would have on the industry, as a whole, in California. "The market's going to go crazy," predicts Chris Lindsey, senior legislative analyst for the Marijuana Policy Project. "You'll get this whole new wave of business."[275] At the end of the day though, the key to success in the next green rush will be about who can get their act together.

1. AUMA AFFECT ON THE MCRSA

Now that the AUMA passed, many are wondering what this means for the MCRSA. Namely, for business owners, it all boils down to one question: how will the AUMA impact them going forward? The short answer is that unless you're a large-scale grower hoping to secure a Type 5 license, the AUMA does not significantly alter your road to state licensing because the AUMA bases most of its regulations on the MCRSA. For the most part, the AUMA serves as a mere overlay to the MCRSA. The AUMA builds on the current infrastructure of the MCRSA by (1) adding regulations for nonmedical ("adult use") cannabis, and (2) making other small changes to the existing regulations for medical cannabis.

Though the MCRSA and AUMA overlap in many respects, they also differ in others. To simplify things, here is a comparative breakdown of the key provisions of each:

MCRSA	AUMA
Regulatory structure: Establishes the Bureau of Medical Cannabis Regulation (BMCR) under the Department of Consumer Affairs to implement and enforce the MCRSA. Several other state agencies would be responsible for different aspects of regulation.	**Regulatory structure:** Establishes the Bureau of Cannabis Control (BCC) under the Department of Consumer Affairs to replace the BMCR. About a half-dozen state agencies would handle different aspects of regulation, exactly like the MCRSA.
Allows "For Profit" Operation: Allows medical cannabis businesses to operate "for profit". Repeals the existing Medical Marijuana Program Act, and the non-profit mandate with it.	**Semi-Legalization:** Legalizes possession of one ounce of cannabis and cultivation of six plants by adults 21 and over.
Licensing System: Sets up 17 different kinds of medical cannabis	**Licensing System:** Sets up 21 different kinds of medical cannabis operational license types.

operational license types. **Prioritizes Licensing for Certain Businesses:** Gives priority to applicants that can demonstrate to the state's "satisfaction" that it was "in operation and in good standing with [its] local jurisdiction by January 1, 2016." Also permits "grandfathering" – i.e., applicants operating in compliance with local law may continue to operate until their license is approved or denied. **Limits Vertical integration:** A licensee may only hold a state license in up to two separate license categories and only certain combinations of licenses are permitted. There are a few exceptions, however. **Local Government Power is Broad:** Permits cities and counties to regulate medical cannabis businesses, and also allows them to *ban* medical cannabis businesses within their borders. Also gives local jurisdictions the power to tax and assess fees against medical cannabis businesses. **Testing and Labeling Required:** Mandates testing of cannabis prior to delivery to dispensaries or other businesses. Also establishes labeling and packaging requirements for cannabis products. **Seed-to Sale-Tracking:** Requires a "track and trace" management system, which tracks cannabis from cultivation to sale.	**Prioritizes Licensing for Certain Businesses:** Gives priority to existing, licensed applicants who can demonstrate to the state's "satisfaction" that the applicant operated in compliance with existing state and local laws, similar to the MCRSA. **State Taxation**: Imposes 15 percent taxes on retail sales of recreational cannabis in addition to state and local sales taxes. Imposes taxes on cultivation as well, at a rate of $9.25 for every ounce of dried buds and $2.75 an ounce for leaves. **Local Government Power is Slightly Less Broad:** No local bans on personal indoor grows. Gives cities and counties wide latitude on allowing cannabis commerce and what types. But it takes a local majority vote to completely ban medical cannabis businesses. **Testing and Labeling Required**: Imposes testing, labeling and packaging requirements like the MCRSA, but also limits edibles to 10mg THC per serving. **Seed-to Sale-Tracking:** Requires a "track and trace" system like the MCRSA. **"Cannabis Cafes":** Allows localities to license places for on-site consumption. **Lessens Criminal Penalties for Past and Present Cannabis Crimes:** Reduces certain cannabis crimes to infractions and

Carves Out an Exception for Los Angeles: Allows the City to continue to prosecute violations of Proposition D.	misdemeanors. Allows people with past convictions for cannabis offenses to petition to have their charges reduced.

2. LICENSING UNDER AUMA

The AUMA provides for 19 different types of licenses – most of which mirror the 17 licenses already created by the MCRSA. Here's a brief breakdown:

MCRSA LICENSE TYPES	**AUMA LICENSE TYPES****
Type 1 = Cultivation; Specialty outdoor; Small. (*Up to 5,000 sf. of canopy, or up to 50 non-contiguous plants*)	Type 1 = Cultivation; Specialty outdoor; Small (*Same as MCRSA*)
Type 1A = Cultivation; Specialty indoor; Small (*Up to 5,000 sf.*)	Type 1A = Cultivation; Specialty indoor; Small (*Same as MCRSA*)
Type 1B = Cultivation; Specialty mixed-light; Small (*Up to 5,000 sf. using exclusively artificial lighting*)	Type 1B = Cultivation; Specialty mixed-light; Small (*Same as MCRSA*)
Type 1C** = Cultivation; Specialty Cottage; Mixed-Light (*Up to 2,500 sf. using a combo of natural and artificial lighting*); Outdoor (*Up to 25 plants*); Indoor (*Up to 500 sf.*)	Type 2 = Cultivation; Outdoor; Small (*Same as MCRSA*)
	Type 2A = Cultivation; Indoor; Small (*Same as MCRSA*)
Type 2 = Cultivation; Outdoor; Small (*Up to 5,000 sf. using a combination of artificial and natural lighting*)	Type 2B = Cultivation; Mixed-light; Small (*Same as MCRSA*)
Type 2A = Cultivation; Indoor; Small. (*5,001 -10,000 sf.*)	Type 3 = Cultivation; Outdoor; Medium (*Same as MCRSA*)
Type 2B = Cultivation; Mixed-light; Small (*5,001 -10,000 sf.*)	Type 3A = Cultivation; Indoor; Medium (*Same as MCRSA*)
Type 3 = Cultivation; Outdoor; Medium (*10,001 sf. - 1 Acre*)	Type 3B = Cultivation; Mixed-light; Medium (*Same as MCRSA*)
Type 3A = Cultivation; Indoor; Medium (*10,001 - 22,000 sf.*)	
Type 3B = Cultivation; Mixed-light.	Type 4 = Cultivation; Nursery (*Same*

Medium (*10,001 - 22,000 sf.*) Type 4 = Cultivation; Nursery Type 6 = Manufacturer 1 (*Using non-volatile solvents*) Type 7 = Manufacturer 2 (*Using volatile solvents*) Type 8 = Testing Type 10 = Dispensary; General Type 10A = Dispensary; No more than three retail sites Type 11 = Distribution Type 12 = Transporter ****Only available if AB2516 passes, which it likely will.**	as MCRSA) Type 5 = Cultivation; Outdoor; Large (*No artificial lighting greater than 1 Acre*) Type 5A =Cultivation; Indoor; Large (*Over 22,000 sf. using exclusively artificial lighting*) Type 5B = Cultivation; Mixed-light; Large (*Over 22,000 sf. using a combination of artificial and natural lighting*) Type 6 = Manufacturer 1 (*Same as MCRSA*) Type 7 = Manufacturer 2 (*Same as MCRSA*) Type 8 = Testing (*Same as MCRSA*) Type 10 = Retailer (*Includes retail sale and delivery*) Type 11 = Distributor (*Same as MCRSA but not mandatory*) Type 12 =Microbusiness (*Can cultivate up to 10,000 sf. and also act as a licensed distributor, Level I manufacturer and retailer*) ****All licenses issued for adult use would be distinct from those issued for medical use, and would be designated as such. E.g., an outdoor cultivator for *medical* cannabis would receive a "Type 1" license, whereas a *non-medical* outdoor cultivator would receive a "Type 1 – Nonmedical" or "Type 1NM" license.**

As you can see, the MCRSA and AUMA are very similar, at least with respect to license types. The key differences are:

(1) The AUMA's addition of Type 5 licenses for large-scale growers, which will not be issued for five (5) years and will not allow for vertical integration;
(2) Unlike the MCRSA, the AUMA does not prohibit vertical integration for other licensees, except for Type 8 testers and Type 5 large growers; and
(3) The AUMA provides for a versatile "microbusiness" license which allows for vertically integrated small farm operations – much like the collective model we've already been using here in California.

a. MCRSA vs. AUMA Licensing

Though the AUMA provides for 19 different types of licenses – most of which mirror the 17 licenses already created by the MCRSA – there are several key differences with respect to licensing:

- **Vertical Integration:** Unlike the MCRSA, the AUMA doesn't prohibit vertical integration of licenses. Instead of being limited to only having up two different license types under the MCRSA, the AUMA instead allows a licensee to hold any number or combination of licenses: cultivator, manufacturer, retailer, distributor and tester. There is one exception, however, for Type 5 cultivators (see below), who cannot hold certain other licenses.

- **(Type 5) New Category of "Large" Cultivation Licenses:** AUMA creates an additional category of Type 5 cultivation licenses, which are the largest cultivation licenses available. This license is created for farms that exceed the MCRSA's current limit of 22,000 sq. ft. indoors or 1-acre outdoors. No Type 5 licenses will be issued before January 1, 2023.[276] Unlike other licensees, the vertical integration for Type 5 cultivators will be limited: they will not be allowed to hold Type 8 (laboratory tester), Type 11 (distributor) or Type 12 (microbusiness) licenses.

- **(Type 12) New Category of "Microbusiness" Licenses:** Not to be confused with the type 12 transporter license und MCRSA, the AUMA replaces Type 12 licenses with a new category of "microbusiness" licenses. This license will allow for vertically integrated small farm operations not exceeding 10,000 sq. ft. –

much like the collective model we've already been using here in California.

- **Diminishes Business Potential for (Type 11) Distributors:** Unlike the MCRSA, the AUMA doesn't *require* that cultivators send their products to Type 11 distributors. It appears that only the new, Type 5 large-scale cultivators will be required to use Type 11 distributors. The remaining licensees will be eligibly to distribute for themselves.

- **Cannabis Cafés:** The AUMA will allow local governments to permit on-site consumption for Type 10 dispensaries and Type 12 microbusinesses in their jurisdiction provided that the sale or consumption of alcohol or tobacco is not allowed on the premises.

3. WHO QUALIFIES FOR AUMA LICENSING?

The AUMA requires licensing authorities to issue state licenses *only* to "qualified applicants,"[277] which naturally begs the question: Who is a "qualified applicant"?

Applicants must comply with local law – First and foremost, only applicants who are in compliance with local law will be considered "qualified" for licensure under the AUMA. This is due to a provision in the AUMA that states that licenses cannot be issued where the activity would violate a local ordinance. In addition, the AUMA states that licensing authorities may deny an application if "[t]he applicant, or any of its officers, directors, or owners, has been sanctioned by a licensing authority or a city, county, or city and county for unauthorized commercial cannabis activities or commercial medical cannabis activities …"[278] This means that if you've been punished for violating local cannabis laws in the past (i.e., you've been convicted of violating Prop D in Los Angeles), your application for state licensing *could* be denied under the AUMA.

Applicants must have resided in California since January 1, 2015 – A California residency provision provides that "no licensing authority shall issue or renew a license to any person or entity that can't demonstrate continuous California residency from or before January 1, 2015."[279] Unless legislators reenact this provision, it will expire in 2020.

Applicants cannot hold liquor or tobacco licenses – The AUMA provides that "[a] licensee shall not also be licensed as a retailer of alcoholic beverages … or of tobacco products."[280]

Applicants cannot be located within 600 feet from a school – In an effort to better protect children from cannabis, the AUMA provides that "[n]o licensee under this division shall be located within a 600-foot radius of a school providing instruction in kindergarten or any grades 1 through 12, day care center, or youth center that is in existence at the time the license is issued, unless a licensing authority or a local jurisdiction specifies a different radius."[281]

Prior criminal convictions – One of the more controversial aspects of the AUMA is the potential disqualification of applicants who have been convicted of certain crimes. Under the AUMA, licenses *may* be denied if the applicant has a prior conviction for an offense that is considered to be "substantially related to the qualifications, function, or duties" of the business for which the application is made. This includes, but is not limited to, serious and violent felonies, felonies involving fraud or deceit, and felonies involving minors in drug-related offenses.[282]

If an applicant has suffered a prior "substantially related" conviction, the "suitability" of the applicant will be judged on a case-by-case basis. In making its suitability determination, the licensing authority will take into consideration several things such as the nature and circumstances of the crime, as well as any evidence of rehabilitation. Based on its review, the licensing authority may use its discretion to deny the applicant if it believes the applicant is not suitable for licensure or if it believes that granting the license would compromise public safety.[283]

If an applicant has *completed* his/her sentence for *certain drug-related offenses* (including possession, possession for sale, manufacture, transportation or cultivation), then the prior conviction will <u>not</u> be considered "substantially related" and cannot be the sole ground for denial of a license. This is a departure from the MCRSA, which makes past drug-related offenses valid grounds for license denial. However, a conviction for any drug-related felony *subsequent* to licensure will be grounds for denial or revocation.

To be safe, if you have been convicted of *any* crime, you should take steps to ensure your best chances at licensure.

4. CRIMINAL PENALTIES UNDER AUMA

One of the most notable provision of the AUMA eliminates and reduces a number of common cannabis crimes, allowing many people with criminal felony records to have their convictions reduced to misdemeanors. The AUMA also allows some people currently serving jail or prison sentences for cannabis crimes to petition for early release.

The following is a summary of the changes that the AUMA would make with respect to criminal penalties in California:

Possession (Health & Safety Code § 11357)[284]

21+ Possession of less than 1 oz. of cannabis or less than 4 grams of concentrated cannabis is legal. Under current law, possession of less than 1 oz. of cannabis is considered an infraction for anyone 18-20yrs and possession of *any* amount of concentrate (without a prescription) is considered a misdemeanor. Quasi-adults (between the ages of 18 and 21) and minors (under 18) can be charged with an infraction and be subject to drug counseling and community service requirements. If a person over the age of 18 is caught possessing on school grounds, however, that person is guilty of a misdemeanor.

Possession of more than 1 oz. of cannabis or more than 4 grams of concentrated cannabis. Under the AUMA, this continues to be a misdemeanor for adults (age 21+). However, quasi-adults (between the ages of 18 and 21) and minors (under 18) would only be guilty of an infraction and would be subject to drug counseling and community service requirements.

Cultivation (Health & Safety Code § 11358)[285]

Less than six plants: Currently, under AUMA, adults (age 21+) can lawfully grow up to six plants for personal use. However, minors (under 18) and quasi-adults (between the ages of 18 and 21) would be guilty of an infraction and would be subject to drug counseling and community service requirements.

More than six plants: All persons age 18+ would be guilty of a misdemeanor.

Felony offenses: Felonies can be charged in the case of repeat offenders, persons with violent or serious priors, and various environmental offenses.

Possession for Sale (Health & Safety Code § 11359)[286]

After the AUMA passed, the mandatory felony for possession for sale was eliminated. All persons age 18+ would now be charged with misdemeanors only. Felony enhancements, however, could be charged in the case of repeat offenders, persons with violent or serious priors, and sale to minors (under 18). Minors (under 18) would be guilty of an infraction and would be subject to drug counseling and community service requirements.

Transportation, Importation, Sale or Gift (Health & Safety Code § 11360)[287]

After the AUMA passed, the mandatory felony for unlawful transportation, importation, sale or gift was eliminated. Any person who transports or gives away less than 1 oz. of cannabis is guilty of an infraction. All persons age 18+ who transport or give away more than 1 oz. of cannabis or *any* amount of concentrate would be guilty of misdemeanors only. Felony enhancements, however, could be charged in the case of repeat offenders, persons with violent or serious priors, sale to minors (under 18) or if the amount exceeds 1 oz. of cannabis or 4 grams of concentrate.

Relief for Current and Prior Offenders[288]

One of the most attractive provisions of the AUMA is a fresh start for those convicted of cannabis related offenses. People with prior cannabis convictions are now able to petition a court for retroactive reduction of their sentence, dismissal of their prior conviction, and/or sealing of their record if the crime would have been a misdemeanor (or would have been legal) under the AUMA. For example, if you were previously convicted of cultivating more than 6 plants, the AUMA would allow you to have your felony reduced to a misdemeanor and then the record of your felony conviction would be ordered sealed.

The AUMA also allows people currently incarcerated for a cannabis-related offense to petition the court for early or immediate release if the crime would have been a misdemeanor (or would have been legal) under the AUMA.

All Other Felonies

Any cannabis-related felony offenses not mentioned above, such as manufacturing cannabis with a volatile substance (Health & Safety Code § 11379.6) or selling cannabis to minors (under 18) (Health & Safety Code § 11361), will continue to remain serious felonies under the AUMA.

5. DRIVING UNDER THE INFLUENCE OF CANNABIS

With the passage of the AUMA – we may run into a new problem – Cannabis DUIs. It's Saturday night and you just got pulled over. You are not drunk, but you did use cannabis — can you get a DUI? Oh yes, but... In California, prosecutors must prove that a driver not only consumed cannabis, but also that he or she was impaired at the time of driving to establish a DUI. This is no easy task.

Although alcohol is easily detected through the use of breathalyzers, detecting cannabis or THC (the active component of cannabis) in your system is a bit more difficult. Without an "objective" scientific test available roadside, law enforcement officers look for "circumstantial evidence of impairment" when they suspect that a driver is driving under the influence of any substance, including cannabis.

"Circumstantial evidence" of cannabis impairment can include statements made to officers, odor of cannabis, and performance on a Field Sobriety Test (FST). Dilated pupils, slurred speech, redness of the eyes, or even a driver's behavior can further determine impairment. The bad news – this determination is pretty subjective and discretionary.

However, these types of observations are not determinative. Drivers who are simply nervous, anxious or scared while being pulled over might portray similar symptoms and be classified as an impaired driver. Because of such a high risk of error, these cases are very hard for prosecutors to prove, but also create a large probability of false arrests. Thus, we need a more concrete way to determine if a driver is under the influence of cannabis.

If you have ever used cannabis – there are probably traces of THC in your system, but determining whether these amounts are dormant or are actually effecting your body currently is the hard part. Why? Cannabis can stay in your system for days and even weeks after it's initially consumed. Further, studies show that THC remains in your mouth and on your breath for up to a few hours. Because it can stay on your breath, a breathalyzer can detect its presence. But, and it's a big BUT, there is no way to determine whether a driver is actually impaired based on some measure of THC in the mouth or lungs. THC does not transport itself along the blood-brain barrier like alcohol does, so the breathalyzer that we use for alcohol- does not work for cannabis!

Blood, urine, and saliva all carry traces of THC. Blood is the most common and accurate test, but saliva tests, while not reliable or accurate, are advantageous, because they can be done roadside. This eight-minute test can detect cocaine, Xanax, methamphetamine, narcotic analgesics and THC, showing cannabis usage within the past few hours.

So what are we doing with this technology? The MCRSA passed by governor Jerry Brown in October 2015, authorized UC San Diego to research new cannabis-specific field sobriety tests. So far, UCSD is exploring the use of oral swab devices to detect THC, however, some states are launching a saliva-based drug-testing program this year.

Saliva tests may be the quick fix, but blood is a lot more accurate. Lets talk numbers! States like Oregon, Colorado, and Washington have established a THC threshold for the bloodstream. On average, these states classify "marijuana impairment" at above five (5) nanograms of active THC per milliliter of blood.

Currently, California does not have an established content limit for drivers suspected of driving under the influence of cannabis. However, California's new Assembly Bill 2740 would establish such limit, making the impairment threshold 5ng/ml or more of THC.

The problem with this threshold is that chronic medical cannabis patients with serious illnesses such as A.I.D.S. and cancer can show 5 ng/ml in the blood for days after using cannabis. Even someone who smoked a lot on the weekend could be convicted of a DUI on Tuesday because of the levels of THC that stayed in their system, making this approach unreliable and overbroad, subjecting undeserving cannabis users to criminal prosecutions.

Possible Effects of AUMA on Cannabis DUIs - In Colorado, cannabis-related traffic deaths have increased 32%, and in Washington, fatal crashes involving drivers under the influence of cannabis doubled. Although scientific evidence is unclear as to how cannabis impairment affects driving, it seems legalized cannabis increases drivers on the road under the influence. In California, we foresee a potential for the same influx of legal issues relating to DUI arrests, especially since California will be gearing up with drug recognition experts. These officers will use all of their expertise and experience to catch this new category of impaired drivers. So, before you leave your house, think twice and maybe call an uber!

6. THE IMPORTANCE OF LOCAL ORDINANCES

Local law compliance is still key under the AUMA. On this issue, the AUMA states:

> **"Nothing in this division shall be interpreted to supersede or limit the authority of a local jurisdiction to adopt and enforce local ordinances to regulate businesses licenses under this division, including, but not limited to, local zoning and land use requirements, business license**

requirements, and requirements related to reducing exposure to second hand smoke, or to completely prohibit the establishment or operation of one or more types of businesses licensed under this division within the local jurisdiction."[289]

What this essentially means is that the AUMA (like the MCRSA) allows cities or counties, like Los Angeles, to continue to ban cannabis businesses if they don't want them and add on regulations that don't conflict with the state's regulations. However, if a city or county chooses to ban all cannabis businesses, it will require a local majority vote and the city or county will not be able to receive any of the tax revenue from the AUMA.

The state now needs until January 2018, to set up the necessary structures to begin issuing licenses for both medical and nonmedical cannabis businesses. In the interim, however, local governments are choosing whether to adopt ordinances to permit or ban such businesses in preparation for state licensing. If a city or county has no ordinance regulating or banning cannabis activity, then the state can unilaterally issue a state license to a business in that city or county under terms fully compliant with the AUMA. This means that a city or county wishing to adopt cannabis regulations will probably do so prior to the date the state begins issuing licenses, which will likely begin in late 2017.

7. SEPTEMBER 1, 2016 DEADLINE

As previously discussed, the MCRSA gives licensing priority to cannabis businesses "that can demonstrate to the authority's satisfaction" that they were "in operation" and "in good standing" with their local governments by January 1, 2016.[290] Very similar to the MCRSA, the AUMA contains a priority licensing standard for applicants "that can demonstrate to the authority's satisfaction that the applicant operated *in compliance with the Compassionate Use Act* and its implementing laws before **September 1, 2016**, or currently operates *in compliance with the MCRSA*."[291]

With respect to local law compliance, the AUMA further provides:

"The bureau shall request that local jurisdictions identify for the bureau potential applicants for licensure based on the applicants' prior operation in the local jurisdiction in compliance with state law, including the Compassionate Use Act and its implementing laws, and any applicable laws."[292]

So, what does this mean? What is this new September 1st deadline and what is its significance? It means that the AUMA has moved up the priority licensing date from January 1st to September 1st. Thus, if you can prove you operated a state and local law- compliant medical CB as of September 1st, you can stand at the front of the line for both medical and nonmedical cannabis licenses under the AUMA. For those who missed the MCRSA's January 1st deadline, the passage of the AUMA might be great news – as it basically gave some of these operators more time to scramble to get their corporate affairs in order, pay their taxes, etc. in order to show compliance with their local jurisdiction by the September 1st deadline. However, if you missed the AUMA deadline – i.e., you cannot show that your business was "in compliance" with state and local law as of September 1st – your business will not be eligible for "priority" status and will need to take a spot at the back of the line.

Why is "priority" status important? Because when you launch a business, timing is everything. Although neither the AUMA nor the MCRSA define the word "priority," a look at the ways in which various other states have handled licensing applications tells us that those with "priority" status in California will almost certainly be the first to obtain state licenses.[293] It is widely anticipated that the number of cannabis businesses will be limited by either the state or local jurisdictions, so the advantage to being among the first state-compliant businesses to market in California cannot be understated. It could have *huge* long-term benefits for *any* licensee in this booming industry. For instance, the state has already indicated that there would be a cap placed on the number of licenses issued for Type 3 cultivators and Type 7 manufacturers, though it is still unclear right now what that limit will be.[294] So, depending on what that number is, there is a very, very real possibility that getting a Type 3 or Type 7 license early could be the only way to getting a license at all![295] In short, for some operators such as the large-scale cultivators or the manufacturers who use butane, priority status could potentially be the make-or-break point for their business.

How can you tell if your business was "in compliance" with state and local law by September 1st? As of right now, there is some ambiguity surrounding what the term "in compliance" actually means because the state hasn't technically defined it yet in the AUMA (or the MCRSA). The Bureau is in the process of defining "in compliance". But based on other states' experience with state licensing, it's probably safe to assume the following:

For starters, your entity should already be registered with the California Secretary of State as an appropriate corporate entity, preferably as a non-profit mutual benefit corporation. Keep in mind that corporate bylaws, articles of incorporation and rules regarding "membership" should be drafted carefully to allow for a smooth transition into for-profit operation when that becomes a "thing" later down the line as licensing becomes available. Your entity should also already be registered with the California BOE, and all federal, state and local taxes should be squared away. You should have also obtained, prior to September 1st, some type of approval or permit from your local authorities to operate your CB. If you haven't yet finished or begun the process with your local authorities, you've already missed the boat for priority licensing. But if you hope to eventually get licensed (i.e., after the first wave of operators), you should still finish your local process ASAP.

8. VERTICAL INTEGRATION

a. *MCRSA – Largely Prohibited*

Under the MCRSA, California now treats cannabis much like it treats alcohol. Noticeable similar to the state's alcohol regulations (also called "tied house" laws), the MCRSA largely prohibits vertical integration – e.g., it prevents cultivators, manufacturers, distributors and retailers from being "tied" to one another. As opposed to the existing closed-loop, vertical integration model in which collectives cultivate their own crop for distribution to its members, the MCRSA implements a three-tiered structure of producers, distributors, and retailers. Subject to only a few exceptions, the MCRSA keeps production (cultivation and manufacturing) separate from retail (dispensaries) by adding the third-party distributor.

The restrictions preventing vertical integration under the MCRSA are complicated.[296] In general, licensees can only hold licenses in up to two separate categories, and the state restricts which combination of licenses may be held. The biggest exception to the MCRSA's prohibition of vertical integration states that if your business was given a local license, prior to July 1, 2015, allowing vertical integration, your business will be grandfathered under the MCRSA. Specifically, the MCRSA states that "[i]n a jurisdiction that adopted a local ordinance, prior to July 1, 2015, allowing or requiring qualified businesses to cultivate, manufacture, and dispense medical cannabis or medical cannabis products, with all commercial cannabis activity being conducted by a single qualified business, upon licensure that business shall not be subject to [the MCRSA provisions preventing vertical integration]" so long as the following conditions are met:

1. The business was cultivating, manufacturing, and dispensing medical cannabis or medical cannabis products on July 1,

2015, and has continuously done so since that date.

2. The business has been in full compliance with all applicable local ordinances at all times prior to licensure.

3. The business is registered with the State Board of Equalization.[297]

The MCRSA further provides that such businesses "are not required to conduct all cultivation or manufacturing within the bounds of a local jurisdiction, but all cultivation and manufacturing shall have commenced prior to July 1, 2015, and have been in full compliance with applicable local ordinances."[298] Such businesses may continue to vertically integrate until January 1, 2026 when that privilege will be repealed.[299]

b. AUMA – MORE PERMISSIVE

The big difference between the MCRSA and the AUMA is that the AUMA *doesn't* prohibit vertical integration of licenses. Rather than being limited to only having up two different license types, the AUMA instead allows a licensee to hold any number or combination of licenses: cultivator, manufacturer, retailer, distributor and tester. There is one exception, however, for Type 5 large-scale growers whose vertical integration will be limited: they will not be allowed to hold Type 8 (laboratory tester), Type 11 (distributor) or Type 12 (microbusiness) licenses. Also, the AUMA provides for a Type 12 "microbusiness" license, which will allow for vertically integrated small farm operations not exceeding 10,000 sq. ft. – much like the collective model we've already been using here in California.

Long story short: The MCRSA largely disfavors vertical integration, whereas the AUMA only prohibits vertical integration for large growers. In any event, being aware of and knowing how to navigate these types of licensing restrictions will be key to maximizing business potential for investors in the California cannabis industry.

9. AUMA: INDUSTRIAL HEMP

There's more to the AUMA than just legalizing recreational pot. A lesser-known provision of the AUMA actually legalizes hemp farming as well. Effective January 1, 2018, the cultivation, production and manufacturing of industrial hemp will be legal without the need of a federal license. All commercial activities related to industrial hemp will now be regulated by the Department of Food and Agriculture.

Pursuant to the federal Farm Bill, the AUMA will allow individuals, agricultural research institutions and institutions of higher learning to cultivate hemp for research purposes.[300] (*See,* detailed discussion of federal laws in "Hemp and CBD," above.)

The AUMA will also allow the cultivation of hemp for commercial purposes, but subject to stricter conditions. For instance, under the AUMA, commercial hemp farmers will be required to obtain a lab report from a DEA-registered testing facility. A random sampling of the dried flowering tops will be tested for THC. To pass as California industrial hemp, the sampling's THC levels must be less than or equal to 0.3%. If the THC levels are higher than 0.3% but less than or equal to 1.0%, additional samples must be submitted and re-tested. If further tests indicate a 0.3% to 1.0% THC level, the hemp must be destroyed within 45 days. If further tests indicate THC levels greater than 1.0%, the hemp must be destroyed within 48 hours.[301]

a. The Interplay with Federal Hemp Laws and CBD

For reasons that none of us can comprehend, industrial hemp – with THC levels below 0.3% – is still classified as a Schedule I drug. In 2014, however, President Obama signed the Agricultural Act of 2014 (or the "Farm Bill") into law. The Farm Bill featured Section 7606, allowing for universities and state department of agriculture to begin cultivating hemp for limited purposes. The law also requires that hemp grow sites be certified by – and registered with – their state. In August 2016, the U.S. Department of Agriculture (USDA), the U.S. Drug Enforcement Administration (DEA) and the U.S. Food and Drug Administration (FDA) released a "Statement of Principles on Industrial Hemp" to clarify the Farm Bill, which legalized the cultivation of industrial hemp for research purposes.

The Statement reiterates that hemp growing "may only take place in accordance with an agricultural pilot program to study the growth, cultivation, or marketing of industrial hemp established by a State department of agriculture or State agency responsible for agriculture in a State where the production of industrial hemp is otherwise legal under State law."[302]

In other words, institutions of higher learning, State departments of agriculture, or persons licensed by State departments of agriculture are free to cultivate hemp under federal law. However, hemp products may *not* be sold for commercial purposes. Moreover, industrial hemp plants and seeds may not be transported across State lines. While the Farm Bill benefits hemp research, it does little to help individual commercial farmers in California. This stems from the fact that although many states (such as

California) have legalized industrial hemp, its production remains illegal under federal law for non-research purposes. [Some, however, have taken the view that that a state can comply with the Farm Bill by enacting laws that allow the private commercial sector to grow and cultivate hemp for *economic* research purposes.

Indeed, if a state is conducting research on the *economic* impact of a hemp industry within its borders, it only makes sense to involve the commercial private sector in order to obtain actual financial data, rather than base research on speculative economic models.] But still, if growing hemp is federally illegal in the U.S., then why do we see hemp everywhere? We use hemp lotion, eat hemp cereal, wear clothing made out of hemp, use reusable hemp shopping bags … the list goes on and on. In fact, the U.S. is the world's largest consumer of hemp products. Yet, we are the only major industrialized country that outlaws hemp. Confused yet?

The reason for this conundrum is that despite the illegality of hemp farming for commercial purposes, hemp and hemp products are legal to import and sell in the U.S. This is due to a 2003 federal court case called *Hemp Industries Association ("HIA"), et al. v. Drug Enforcement Administration*.[303] The *HIA* case involved a dispute between manufacturers of hemp products and the DEA over three DEA rules regarding hemp and THC. The primary rule at-issue (at least for our purposes) was the first one, which purported to interpret both the CSA and the DEA regulations to ban *all* naturally-occurring THC, including the THC found in hemp seed and oil. This rule would have made it illegal for hemp manufacturers to produce and sell their products, even ones that contained only trace amounts of THC.

In striking this rule down, the Ninth Circuit Court of Appeals found that the DEA had exceeded its authority in enacting the rule.[304] In short, the practical effect of the *HIA* case was to strike down the DEA's ban on hemp products that contain only trace amounts of naturally-occurring THC. This essentially opened the door for companies to import hemp from countries that allow it and to sell them throughout the U.S.

This, in turn, also allowed individuals and businesses to legally obtain and sell CBD derived from imported industrial hemp, rather than cannabis. (CBD can be sourced from both cannabis and hemp). The law essentially states that the legality of CBD and CBD products depends on the legality of its source. If the CBD is sourced from cannabis, then the CBD is 100% illegal. Whereas, if the CBD is sourced from imported industrial hemp, then the CBD is legal to use, sell, manufacture and even to ship across state lines. We know – it's a weird state of affairs. But that's simply how the federal hemp laws have evolved to date.

Fast forward to November 2016 – the passage of the AUMA. The practical impact of the AUMA on CBD could not be overstated. Now that hemp production is legal in California, this meant that individuals and businesses could now legally obtain CBD from California-grown hemp. This would allow for better quality CBD than what can be obtained overseas.

This was great news for CBD but, unfortunately, the good news was short-lived. One month after the AUMA passed, in December 2016, the DEA issued regulations that effectively put a stop to attempts to dance around the CSA's definition of "marijuana" when it comes to hemp-derived CBD. The new rule creates a new "Controlled Substances Code Number" for "Marihuana Extract" and extends that classification to all forms of CBD. In response to public comment on its initially proposed rule, the DEA stated that "[f]or practical purposes, all extracts that contain CBD will also contain at least small amounts of other cannabinoids. However, if it were possible to produce from the cannabis plant an extract that contained only CBD … such an abstract would fall within the new drug code," and would thus be federally illegal.[305] The DEA explained the new drug code would enable the agency to separately track quantities of marijuana extract, assisting in compliance with relevant treaty provisions.

So what does this mean for CBD sellers in weed-friendly states like California? It means that the DEA is explicitly saying that it considers your product to be federally illegal under the CSA, despite it being *technically* legal under state law. Importantly, it also means that CBD cannot be shipped or transported across state lines, even if it's to another state where it's legal. If you live in a state which has *not* enacted a hemp law pursuant to the Farm Bill, then you may not legally possess American-made CBD, period.

The hemp industry has since filed a legal challenge against the DEA's new "marihuana extract" rule, citing its seeming inconsistency with the Farm Bill. In a December 2016 press release, the Hemp Industries Association said: "The DEA final rule is concerning to the industry, as it creates confusion in the marketplace among consumers and legitimate businesses alike, and may potentially result in federal agencies improperly treating legal products such as CBD oils, body balms and supplements as controlled substances."[306]

Intelligent attorneys across the country disagree as to whether the new DEA rules pass legal muster when it comes to hemp-derived CBD. But as unhappy as we are with the DEA's statement, we must advise everyone to heed this warning: the DEA has taken the position that using, producing and selling CBD is illegal under federal law. Whether the new DEA rule is ultimately enforced, however, is a whole other story.

On that issue, there are temporary safeguards in place that protect individuals in many states (including California) from prosecution for violations of federal hemp and CBD laws. The Rohrabacher-Farr Amendment (the "Amendment") is the most important of those protections. Originally passed in 2014, the Amendment prohibits the DOJ from spending federal funds to interfere with the implementation of state medical cannabis laws. (Note: The Amendment is silent on recreational use laws and therefore does not apply to recreational cannabis.) This spending ban does not legalize cannabis – it merely states that the DOJ cannot prosecute individuals for cannabis crimes when they are in compliance with state laws.

The Amendment must be renewed every year in order for the safeguards to stay in place. The Amendment was mostly renewed in December 2016, as part of the continuing House resolution known as H.R. 2028, which funds the federal government through April 28, 2017. But unless the Amendment is renewed again, the protections afforded by the Amendment will expire on April 28th.

Many, however, are confident that the Amendment will be renewed again. During a January 11th speech on the floor of the House of Representatives praising the appointment of Jeff Session as Attorney General, Rep. Rohrabacher said: "The [Amendment] currently remains in effect through April 28, though I expect it to be renewed moving forward. With the House and Senate both on record, and Mr. Trump's stated position that the issue should be left to the states, I am confident that the [Amendment] will be renewed."[307]

With regard to hemp, Congress has similarly banned the feds from using federal funds to interfere with industrial hemp. Specifically, the Massie Amendment states that: "None of the funds made available by this act or any other act may be used… to prohibit the transportation, processing, sale or use of industrial hemp that is grown or cultivated in accordance with section 7606 of the Agricultural Act of 2014, *within or outside the State in which the industrial hemp is grown or cultivated.*"[308] Long story short, it is currently debatable whether industrial hemp and hemp-derived CBD is legal under federal law. At a bare minimum, however, the DEA simply has no funds to enforce its rule. For now.

D. LOOKING AHEAD: PENDING CALIFORNIA CANNABIS BILLS (2017-2018)

Ever since the AUMA passed in November 2016, the Legislature has been very busy making important policy decisions regarding the degree to which it will align the MCRSA with the AUMA. Most agree that it makes sense to align the state's regulations to the maximum extent possible.

1. PROPOSED LEGISLATION

To further its efforts to align the AUMA and MCRSA, the Legislature has introduced a combined total of 47 (!!) items of legislation, joint resolutions, budget bills and/or budget proposals for consideration in 2017-2018.

Here is a breakdown of California's pending cannabis legislation:

[Note: When a bill is referenced below as a "spot bill," this means that the bill does not have substantive language in it yet because it is basically a placeholder bill.]

a. CULTIVATION

AB 313 (Gray) Revises the qualifications for the membership to the State Water Resources Control Board by eliminating specified requirements for qualifications in the field of water rights. Transfers authority over water rights matters from the board to the Department of Water Resources.

AB 1254 (Wood) This bill would make diverting or using water for growing cannabis a misdemeanor. The first violation will result in a fine of up to $1,000 or jail time for up to 6 months. The second violation, or a violation during a drought, will result in a fine of up to $5,000 or jail time for up to 1 year.

AB 1420 (Aguiar-Curry) Requires State Water Resources Control Board to give priority to adopting general conditions that permit a registrant to store water for small irrigation use during times of high stream flow in exchange for the registrant reducing diversions during periods of low stream flow. Exempts an entity from the requirement to enter into a lake or streambed alteration agreement with the department under specified circumstances.

AB 362 (Wood) Provides that assessments deposited into the existing Timber Regulation and Forest Restoration Fund, less amounts deducted for refunds and reimbursements, may be, upon appropriation by the Legislature, used for forest resources improvement grants, loans, and projects. Limits the amount of money that can be loaned to the Department of Fish and Wildlife for activities to address environmental damage occurring on forestlands resulting from cannabis cultivation to $500,000, until July 1, 2017.

b. Driving Under the Influence

AB 6 (Lackey) Authorizes law enforcement to use a preliminary oral fluid screen test that indicates presence of a drug or controlled substance as a further investigatory tool to establish reasonable cause to believe the person was driving under the influence.

AB 903 (Cunningam) Amends Prop 64 to require the Department of Highway Patrol to use its annual appropriations from the Marijuana Tax Fund to study the viability of standards for cannabis impairment.

SB 65 (Hill) Makes driving or operating a vehicle, boat, vessel, or aircraft while smoking or ingesting cannabis or cannabis products, or drinking an alcoholic beverage, an offense punishable as an infraction or a misdemeanor.

SB 698 (Hill) Makes it a crime for a person who has between 0.04% and 0.07%, by weight, of alcohol in his or her blood and whose blood contains any controlled substance or 5 mg/ml or more of delta-9-tetrahydrocannabinol to drive a vehicle. Provides for penalties.

AB 702 (Lackey) Repeals the presumption that a person consents to submit to chemical testing of his or her blood or breath and would instead require a motor vehicle driver who is lawfully arrested for a specified DUI offense to submit to chemical testing of his or her blood or breath for the purpose of determining the alcoholic or drug content of his or her blood.

c. GOVERNMENT INVOLVEMENT

AB 171 (Lackey) Amends the MCRSA to require a licensing authority to include in an annual report the number of conditional licenses issued.

AB 1527 (Cooley) Prohibits former state licensing authorities and local government employees who had specified regulatory or licensing responsibilities from being employed by a person or entity licensed under Prop 64 or MCRSA for one year following their employment.

AB 1578 (Jones-Sawyer) Prohibits a state or local agency from taking certain actions without a court order signed by a judge, including using agency money, facilities, property, equipment, or personnel to assist a federal agency to investigate, detain, detect, report, or arrest a person for commercial or noncommercial marijuana or medical cannabis activity authorized by law in the state and transferring an individual to federal law enforcement authorities for purposes of marijuana enforcement.

SB 139 (Wilk) Allows a local government to regulate, by ordinance, the sale of a substance used as a recreational drug that poses a threat to human life or health and a particular risk to minors if specified conditions are met.

SJR 5 (Moorlach) Asks the federal government to reschedule marijuana from a Schedule I drug to an alternative schedule.

d. MARKETING AND ADVERTISING

AB 76 (Chau) Spot bill on prohibition of marketing recreational cannabis to children.

AB 420 (Wood) Requires an advertisement for cannabis or cannabis products to identify the MCRSA licensee by at least the license number.

AB 1143 (Gray) Prohibits highway advertising displays from advertising cannabis.

SB 175 (McGuire) Specifies that marketing, labeling, or packaging of cannabis or cannabis products cannot include use of any similar sounding names to the county that the product was grown in, so as not to mislead consumers as to the origin of the product.

e. EDIBLE PACKAGING AND LABELING

AB 175 (Chau) Requires a manufacturer, prior to introducing an edible cannabis product into commerce in the state, to submit the packaging and labeling to the Bureau of Marijuana Control for approval, and requires the bureau to determine whether the packaging and labeling are in compliance with certain requirements. This bill would specify that those prohibition of the use of any similar sounding name that is likely to mislead consumers as to the origin of the product; amendment adds "advertising" incorrect county of origin as unlawful.

AB 350 (Salas) Specifies that a recreational cannabis product is deemed to be appealing to children or easily confused with commercially sold candy if it is in the shape of a person, animal, insect, fruit, or in another shape normally associated with candy.

SB 663 (Nielsen) Provides that a package or label of cannabis or cannabis products is attractive to children if the package or label has specific characteristics, including any candy, snack food, baked good, or beverage commercially sold without cannabis.

AB 823 (Gipson) Requires a universal symbol for edible marijuana products, design to be developed by BMC.

f. PATIENTS AND EDUCATION

AB 389 (Salas) Requires the Bureau of Marijuana Control to establish a consumer guide to educate the public on the regulation of recreational and medical cannabis, and make it available on its website.

AB 845 (Wood) Authorizes, if federal law authorizes the prescription of a controlled substance containing cannabidiol, a physician to prescribe that substance a legitimate medical purpose in accordance with federal law.

g. COURT PROCEEDINGS

AB 1443 (Levine) Among other provisions, this bill would delete a trial court's authority to create, maintain, and preserve records according to standards and guidelines adopted by the American National Standards Institute or the Association for Information and Image Management, including certain cannabis cases.

AB 208 (Eggman) This bill would make the deferred entry of judgment program a pretrial diversion program. The bill would make that a defendant qualified for the pretrial diversion program if there is no evidence of a contemporaneous violation relating to narcotics or restricted dangerous drugs other than the offense that qualifies him or her for diversion, the charged offense did not involve violence, there is no evidence within the past 5 years of a violation relating to narcotics or restricted dangerous drugs other than a violation that qualifies for the program, and the defendant has no prior conviction for a serious or violent felony within 5 years prior to the alleged commission of the charged offense.

h. PENALTIES

AB 596 (Choi) Amends the Victims' Bill of Rights Act of 2008, Marsy's Law, which entitles the victim of a crime to specified rights, including the right to seek and secure restitution. Provides that entry of judgment may be deferred with respect to a defendant who is charged with certain crimes involving possession of controlled substances and who meets certain criteria. Provides that a sentence to the diversion program qualifies as a conviction for purposes of a victim seeking and securing restitution.

SB 180 (Mitchell) Limits the sentence enhancement imposed for specified crimes relating to controlled substances to only be based on each prior conviction of, or on each prior conviction of conspiracy to violate, the crime of using a minor in the commission of offenses involving specified controlled substances.

i. REGULATION

AB 64 (Bonta) Specifies that licensees under the MCRSA may operate for profit or not for profit. Specifies that a dispensary, producing dispensary, or retailer license may be issued for certain storefront locations. Expands a certain prohibition to apply to advertising or marketing on all interstate highways or state highways. Advances $3M to the CHP and requires that money to be repaid from the Marijuana Tax Fund.

AB 238 (Steinorth) Prohibits a Type 11 (distributor) licensee under the MCRSA from denying employment to an individual because he or she is not party to a collective bargaining agreement. Prohibits an applicant from being denied a license based on that same fact.

AB 416 (Mathis) Spot bill relating to CBD-enriched cannabis.

AB 729 (Gray) Amends Prop 64 to require an authority to suspend a license for violations of the prohibition on engaging in recreational commercial cannabis activities with a person under 21 years of age. Provides for license revocation.

AB 948 (Bonta) Spot bill on cannabis.

AB 1096 (Bonta) Spot bill on regulation of cannabis grown on, but transported off, tribal lands.

AB 1244 (Voepel) Spot bill on the production of concentrated cannabis using butane.

AB 1606 (Cooper) Spot bill on quality standards of edible cannabis products.

j. RESEARCH

AB 1002 (Cooley) Renames the University of California Marijuana Research Program the Center for Center for Cannabis Research and expands the purview of the program to include the study of naturally occurring constituents of cannabis and synthetic compounds that have effects similar to naturally occurring cannabinoids.

k. TAXES, GRANTS AND CASH COLLECTION

AB 844 (Burke) Amends Prop 64 to require applicants for grants to support system navigation services to meet specific minimum performance standards as a condition of grant eligibility.

AB 963 (Gipson) Provides for the suspension or revocation of certain permits and authorizes the denial of an application for a permit in certain cases. Requires a distributor to collect prepayments of cannabis excise and sales taxes. Exempts retail sales of medical cannabis, concentrate, and other specified medical cannabis products from sales and use taxes.

AB 1135 (Wood) Requires the state Department of Public Health and the State Department of Education to establish an inclusive public stakeholder process to determine a disbursement formula for the funds provided to the State Department of Health Care Services from the California Marijuana Tax Fund.

AB 1410 (Wood) Requires a person required to be licensed as a distributor under Prop 64 and the MCRSA to collect a cultivation tax from the taxpayer and give to the taxpayer a receipt in the manner prescribed by the Board of Equalization.

SB 148 (Wiener) Enacts the Cannabis State Payment Collection Law and authorizes the State Board of Equalization or a county to collect cash payments from cannabis-related businesses for a state agency that administers any fee, fine, penalty, or other charge payable by a cannabis-related business. This is a re-introduction of a bill that failed last year.

l. TESTING

SB 311 (Pan) Authorizes a cannabis licensee to perform testing on the licensee's premises of cannabis or cannabis products obtained from another licensee for the purpose of quality assurance.

AB 1627 (Cooley) Moves the authority to regulate testing labs for recreational cannabis to under the Bureau of Marijuana Control, so that it is consistent with medical.

m. BUDGET BILLS AND PROPOSALS

AB 976: Assembly Budget Bill

SB 72: State Budget Bill

Gov. Brown's Cannabis Proposals for the 2017-2018 Budget: The Governor's budget proposes a total augmentation of $51.4 million in 2017-18 across four (4) departments (DCA, DPH, CDFA, and BOE) and about 190 positions across these departments to implement MCRSA and Proposition 64. The budget-year funding would mainly support (1) licensing and enforcement programs in DCA and CDFA, (2) development and implementation of licensing and "track and trace" information technology (IT) systems, and (3) tax administration activities in BOE. The budget also proposes a General Fund loan of up to $62.7 million in 2017-18 to help fund these activities. Furthermore, the administration's budget proposal includes funding and positions in future years, with funding decreasing to $32.1 million and staffing increasing to 219 positions in 2020-21 and ongoing.

2. TIMELINE FOR PROPOSED BILLS

Over the coming months, the proposed bills will be heard and discussed in various committees and floor sessions. In order for a bill to be passed in California, it must be passed by the Legislature by no later than September 15th. If the bill is passed on or before the September 15th deadline, the Governor has until October 15th to sign or veto the bill.

E. CURRENT UNKNOWNS UNDER THE MCRSA AND AUMA.

The passage of the MCRSA and the AUMA was only the beginning. Both laws merely laid the foundation for California's future medical and recreational cannabis licensing framework. But the devil is in the details. It's now up to California's Bureau of Marijuana Control ("Bureau") and other state agencies to create all the rules and regulations to actually implement the state licensing systems.

Creating a brand new regulatory system, however, takes time. Because the state hasn't proposed any rules yet, many in the industry are sort of stuck in a legal limbo and, as a result, there are more questions now than ever about what it takes to be a state-compliant business. Here's a breakdown of the some of the most relevant issues that are still "to be determined" under state law:

1. LOCAL LICENSING

For medical cannabis businesses, the MCRSA requires that all applicants submit evidence that they have "local approval" before they can receive a state license. Local approval can be shown with a "local license, permit or other authorization," meaning some type of "official document granted by a local jurisdiction that specifically authorizes a person to conduct commercial cannabis activity in the local jurisdiction."[309] This is known as the dual-licensing requirement.

The AUMA differs from the MCRSA on this issue. For recreational cannabis businesses, the AUMA does *not* require applicants to submit evidence of local approval with their applications. The AUMA simply states that no state license will be given to an applicant if the activity is in violation of a local ordinance.[310] However, because applicants don't need to submit evidence of local approval, there's no easy way for state licensing agencies to determine whether granting a recreational license will violate local law. The AUMA places the responsibility on the *state* – not the applicant – to be aware of and track *all* local regulations. To accomplish this, the state would have to create some sort of database to keep track of each city's and county's regulations before issuing a state license.

But the state doesn't want to bear the responsibility – i.e., time, effort, expense and risk of liability – of having to determine conformity with local law. And, quite, frankly, we don't blame them. With over 58 counties and 483 incorporated municipalities within the state of California, keeping track of all the local ordinances would be a daunting task. As state lawmakers scramble to better align the MCRSA and AUMA, new rules will probably place the responsibility on the *applicant* – not the state – to show local approval under the AUMA, making it consistent with the dual-licensing protocol established in the MCRSA.

2. RESIDENCY REQUIREMENTS

For now, the MCRSA doesn't include a residency requirement. That means an out-of-state resident (or foreigner) could directly apply for a state license to operate a medical cannabis business in California. This likewise means that a California business entity could directly apply for a state license even if its owners or investors are out-of-state residents.

The AUMA, on the other hand, has a residency provision which states: "[N]o licensing authority shall issue or renew a license to any person that cannot demonstrate continuous California residency from or before January 1, 2015."[311] If the applicant is a business entity, the entity can only satisfy AUMA's residency requirement if all persons "controlling the entity" can demonstrate "continuous California residency from or before January 1, 2015."[312] This residency requirement will last for at least the first two years of recreational licensing – unless the legislature renews it, it expires in 2020.

The AUMA's residency provision is a little murky though because demonstrating California residency essentially boils down to what constitutes "control." The residency requirement applies to "controlling persons" but "controlling" is not defined anywhere in the AUMA. Is a person in "control" if they own 100% of the business? 50%? 20%? Or what if someone owns a very small equity stake in the company, but has no role whatsoever in the operation of the business. Is that person in "control"? Obviously, there is a broad spectrum of possibilities of who could be considered a "controlling person." For this reason, the AUMA's definition of "control" will almost certainly be subject to later regulations. Whether an out-of-state resident (or foreigner) can own or invest in a recreational cannabis business here in California will ultimately depend on how the state later defines "controlling."

3. BANKING

Even though California has now legalized weed, it still doesn't solve the industry's banking problem. Because banks are federally-regulated, and cannabis is illegal under federal law, major banks and credit card companies won't do business with anyone in the weed industry out of fear they'll be penalized by the federal government for money laundering. This is why weed is a cash business. Even in other states that have fully-legalized cannabis, pot shops continue to be mostly cash businesses.

According to Ajax, the fact that weed is a cash industry is "a big concern."[313] Without access to banking, business owners will be forced to carry huge sums of cash to pay state taxes, fees, vendors and employees. This is problematic for obvious public safety reasons, and it could also create massive issues in regards to potential money laundering and tax evasion. The banking conflict has become a top priority for State Treasurer John Chiang, who has convened a Cannabis Banking Working Group made up of representatives from law enforcement, banks, local governments, state regulators and taxing authorities to work on crafting a solution to this problem.[314]

4. FOR-PROFIT VS. NON-PROFIT

Technically, it's still unclear as to whether the MCRSA authorizes medical cannabis businesses to operate for profit. This is because the MCRSA only *implicitly* allows cannabis entities to do so. Specifically, the MCRSA defines an "applicant" as an "[o]wner or owners of a proposed facility, including all persons or entities having ownership interest other than a security interest, lien, or encumbrance on property that will be used by the facility," and defines a "person" as "an individual, firm, partnership, joint venture, association, corporation, limited liability company, estate, trust, business trust, receiver, syndicate, or any other group or combination acting as a unit and includes the plural as well as the singular number." Based on these definitions, it sounds like medical cannabis businesses can operate for-profit, but there's nothing expressly stated in the MCRSA to confirm it. Without an express assurance, medical cannabis businesses will have to continue operating under the current non-profit "collective model" set forth in the CUA and MMP. The only exception would be if the business operated in a local jurisdiction that expressly allowed for for-profit entities.

Luckily, however, there is a bill currently pending in the state legislature seeking to dispel any possible confusion. If passed, AB 64 would *explicitly* provide that medical cannabis businesses can operate for profit.[315] As for the AUMA, the for-profit issue is moot. Unlike medical, recreational pot was never subject to the non-profit rules of the "collective model" because it was considered illegal no matter what. When state licenses roll out in 2018, recreational cannabis businesses will be able to operate for profit.

5. DISTRIBUTORS

The distribution models under the MCRSA and the AUMA differ greatly. Under the MCRSA, all medical cannabis must be sent to an independent distributor (Type 11) prior to testing. Under the AUMA, however, there is no mandatory "middle-man" in the recreational cannabis supply chain. Only large-scale growers (Type 5) will be required to use independents distributors (Type 11) under the AUMA. The remaining licensees will be eligible to distribute for themselves.

The fact that there are two different distribution models would make it more confusing (and costly) to implement a statewide "seed-to-sale" tracking system. For this reason, we would not be surprised if the Bureau implemented an "emergency regulation" requiring that the medical and recreational industries adopt the same distribution model.

6. DELIVERY SERVICES

There has been significant debate about whether the new state laws allow for businesses to operate delivery-only services. Both the MCRSA and AUMA are clear that delivery services will be allowed so long as they have a publicly accessible storefront to serve as a home base, and so long as local laws allow it. But it's unclear whether this will apply to delivery-only services with no brick or mortar. Currently, there is a pending bill that seeks to resolve this ambiguity. If passed, AB 64 would expressly allow delivery-only services under both the MCRSA and AUMA.[316]

7. "CANOPY SIZE" AND "ONE PREMISES"

Different types of cultivation licenses will be issued to growers based on a calculation of the operation's "total canopy size on one premises." This has caused confusion amongst growers because neither the MCRSA or AUMA define "total canopy size" or "one premises." For instance, is "canopy size" measured from leaf to leaf? Or is "canopy size" calculated based on the actual building's measurements? And can two subdivided rooms within one larger room be considered "one premises"? How about two adjacent buildings? Amber Morris – the head of the Department of Food and Agriculture – recently stated at a local cannabis event that the definitions of these terms were still in the works.

8. Priority Licensing

Both the MCRSA and AUMA contain deadlines for priority licensing. The MCRSA states that "[i]n issuing licenses, the licensing authority shall prioritize any facility or entity that can demonstrate to the authority's satisfaction that it was in operation and in good standing with the local jurisdiction by January 1, 2016."[317]

The AUMA also contains "priority" language similar to the MCRSA: "A licensing authority shall give priority in issuing licenses under this division to applicants that can demonstrate to the authority's satisfaction that the applicant operated in compliance with the Compassionate Use Act and its implementing laws before September 1, 2016, or currently operates in compliance with [the MCRSA]."

None of this, however, reveals much about what it means to show "good standing" or "compliance" with state or local laws. The Bureau will likely define these terms and set detailed standards for proving priority status later this year.

9. Number of Available Licenses

The MCRSA states that there will be a limit to the number of state licenses given for manufacturers using volatile solvents (Type 7) and large-scale growers (Type 3). But there is no indication yet as to exactly what those numbers will be. Ultimately, it will be up to the Department of Public Health (DPH) and the Department of Food and Agriculture (DFA) to set those limits. Other than prohibiting large-scale cultivation for the first five years of licensing, the AUMA contains no limitations on the number of recreational licenses that will be available. However, that could change as the state continues to work on issuing its initial rules.

10. Licensing Applications and Fees

The Bureau hasn't determined or revealed yet what the application fees will be for state licenses. Both the AUMA and MCRSA only mandate that license fees be on a "scaled basis" and enough to cover the cost of administrating the programs. In other recreational states, the license application fee has been $250 or less. But in medical states, license application fees have ranged anywhere from approx. $60K in Florida down to $5K in Nevada.[318] To avoid potentially pushing out its existing operators, California will likely try keep its fees competitive and somewhat reasonable.

There is also no indication in either the AUMA or the MCRSA as to what exactly California will require in its licensing applications. However, based on how other cannabis states have handled state licensing, we fully expect California's license applications to be incredibly lengthy. The Bureau is going to want to see every single detail of your proposed cannabis business from start to finish and, at a minimum, will require detailed records of the following: financial and criminal background checks, fingerprints, business and operational plans, floor plans, calculated start-up costs and annual budgets, proof of local law approval, proof of a lease agreement or right to use the proposed real property, proof of insurance, proof of security measures, proof of environmental compliance … etc.

11. LICENSING AVAILABILITY

Under the AUMA, the state is required to begin issuing licenses by January 1, 2018. Despite growing concerns about possible delays, Bureau chief Lori Ajax has repeatedly indicated that the Bureau is "on track to meet that deadline."[319] Ajax has also stated that California's state cannabis regulations will be in place by the 2018 deadline through a streamlined, "emergency regulation" process.[320] But that doesn't mean that the state can issue licenses to everyone on Day One. With the state expecting tens of thousands of license applications to be submitted, Ajax admits not everyone will receive their California cannabis license on January 1st. Instead some could receive temporary licenses while the rest of the applications are being processed.

12. COMBINING MEDICAL AND NON-MEDICAL LICENSES

Under the MCRSA, there are complicated restrictions preventing vertical integration.[321] For example, smaller growers (Types 1 or 2) may hold manufacturing licenses (Types 6 or 7) or a producing dispensary license (Type 10A), but larger growers (Types 3 or 4) can't apply for manufacturing licenses at all. Producing dispensaries (Type 10) can also apply for both manufacturing and cultivation licenses, provided their total cultivation area doesn't exceed 4 acres.[322] And as a general rule, licensees under the MCRSA can only hold licenses in up to two separate categories.

The AUMA, on the other hand, is much more lenient. The AUMA only prohibits vertical integration for testers (Type 8) and large-scale growers (Type 5). Moreover, the AUMA provides for a versatile "microbusiness" license (Type 12) which allows for vertically integrated small farm operations.[323]

While there doesn't appear to be anything in the MCRSA or AUMA that prohibits businesses from having certain combinations of medical *and* non-medical licenses, that could change in the future once the state starts issuing more rules.

13. "Greater Enforcement" by the Trump Administration

Due to recent comments made by White House spokesman Sean Spicer, some people in the industry are getting nervous about what "greater enforcement" of federal drug laws could look like for recreational pot in California. Some even suggest that the state should put recreational licensing on hold until federal enforcement policies are made more clear with respect to recreational cannabis.

However, when asked whether state officials were worried about a possible shift in cannabis policy under the new Trump administration, Bureau chief Ajax stated: "We can't predict what's going to happen at the federal level, and obviously we don't control that part of it. So the bureau is focused on what is under our jurisdiction, which is putting together the state regulatory framework for recreational and medicinal cannabis. That's what we're concentrating on."[324] Ajax further added: "Obviously, we're aware of what's being said, but we still have to focus on what we need to get done by the end of this year. We're still going under the federal guidance that we have under the Cole Memo. That's still in place, until such time as we get a different directive from the federal government."

In other words, unless the feds announce a dramatic shift in federal policy, California is moving ahead as planned with state licensing for recreational pot.

F. 6 Key Steps To Prepare Your Business For State Licensing

To recap all of the above, here are the six key steps you must take in order to position your business for state licensing:

1. Picking the appropraite license type for your business

Review the license types that are available under both the medical and recreational models and figure out now which types make sense for your business. Here is a breakdown of the license types being offered for state licensing:

MCRSA LICENSE TYPES	AUMA LICENSE TYPES
Type 1 = Cultivation; Specialty outdoor; Small. (*Up to 5,000 sf. of canopy, or up to 50 non-contiguous plants*)	Type 1 = Cultivation; Specialty outdoor; Small (*Same as MCRSA*)
Type 1A = Cultivation; Specialty indoor; Small (*Up to 5,000 sf.*)	Type 1A = Cultivation; Specialty indoor; Small (*Same as MCRSA*)
Type 1B = Cultivation; Specialty mixed-light; Small (*Up to 5,000 sf. using exclusively artificial lighting*)	Type 1B = Cultivation; Specialty mixed-light; Small (*Same as MCRSA*)
Type 2 = Cultivation; Outdoor; Small (*Up to 5,000 sf. using a combination of artificial and natural lighting*)	Type 2 = Cultivation; Outdoor; Small (*Same as MCRSA*)
Type 2A = Cultivation; Indoor; Small. (*5,001 -10,000 sf.*)	Type 2A = Cultivation; Indoor; Small (*Same as MCRSA*)
Type 2B = Cultivation; Mixed-light; Small (*5,001 -10,000 sf.*)	Type 2B = Cultivation; Mixed-light; Small (*Same as MCRSA*)
Type 3 = Cultivation; Outdoor; Medium (*10,001 sf. - 1 Acre*)	Type 3 = Cultivation; Outdoor; Medium (*Same as MCRSA*)
Type 3A = Cultivation; Indoor; Medium (*10,001 - 22,000 sf.*)	Type 3A = Cultivation; Indoor; Medium (*Same as MCRSA*)
Type 3B = Cultivation; Mixed-light. Medium (*10,001 - 22,000 sf.*)	Type 3B = Cultivation; Mixed-light; Medium (*Same as MCRSA*)
Type 4 = Cultivation; Nursery	Type 4 = Cultivation; Nursery (*Same as MRSA*)
Type 6 = Manufacturer 1 (*Using non-volatile solvents*)	
Type 7 = Manufacturer 2 (*Using volatile solvents*)	Type 5 = Cultivation; Outdoor; Large (*No artificial lighting greater than 1 Acre*)
Type 8 = Testing	
Type 10 = Dispensary; General	Type 5A =Cultivation; Indoor; Large (*Over 22,000 sf. using exclusively artificial lighting*)
Type 10A = Producing Dispensary; No more than three retail sites	
Type 11 = Distribution	
Type 12 = Transporter	

	Type 5B = Cultivation; Mixed-light; Large (*Over 22,000 sf. using a combination of artificial and natural lighting*)
	Type 6 = Manufacturer 1 (*Same as MCRSA*)
	Type 7 = Manufacturer 2 (*Same as MCRSA*)
	Type 8 = Testing (*Same as MCRSA*)
	Type 10 = Retailer (*Includes retail sale and delivery*)
	Type 11 = Distributor (*Same as MCRSA but not mandatory*)
	Type 12 = Microbusiness (*Can cultivate up to 10,000 sf. and also act as a licensed distributor, Level I manufacturer and retailer*)

In choosing which license type works best for your business, there a couple things you should also take into consideration:

➤ Taxes: CA sales tax, which ranges from 7.5-10%, will apply to the retail sale of adult use cannabis. However, the retail sale of medical cannabis to qualified patients with a state ID card will be exempt from this sales tax.

➤ Vertical integration: The MCRSA largely disfavors vertical integration, whereas the AUMA only prohibits vertical integration for large-scale growers and testers. Being aware of and knowing how to navigate these types of licensing restrictions will be key to maximizing business potential for investors in the California cannabis industry. These licensing restrictions will impact the number and possible combinations of license types that your business will be allowed to have.

2. OBTAINING A SUITABLE STATE AND LOCAL LAW COMPLIANT LOCATION

Choosing a location for a new business is one of the most important decisions an entrepreneur will make. This holds especially true for cannabis business owners. Your location not only has to suit the needs of your specific business – it must also comply with applicable state and local laws. Under state law, all cannabis businesses must be located at least 600 feet away from a school. The AUMA describes a school as any "school providing instruction in kindergarten or any grades 1 through 12, day care center, or youth center that is in existence at the time the license is issued, unless a licensing authority or a local jurisdiction specifies a different radius."

Locals also have the authority to mandate stricter location restrictions than those required by the state. For example, Prop D in Los Angeles required shops to stay at least 1,000 feet away from a school and 600 feet from certain areas such as public parks, libraries, churches and childcare facilities. Though Proposition M will soon replace Prop D in L.A., most expect that the location restrictions under Prop M will remain similar to Prop D's, if not exactly the same. Location restrictions and local zoning laws vary from local government to local government, but as a general rule of thumb usually recommend that business owners choose a location with a buffer of least 1,000 feet from a school or any other location that minors are known to congregate – i.e., a park, a youth center or a dance studio for kids, etc.

Another thing to watch out for is "excessive concentration." The AUMA says that the state may deny a retail license if there is an "excessive concentration" of those licenses already in a given area. What constitutes an "excessive concentration" under the AUMA will turn on two things: (1) local population ratios and (2) whether local law places a cap on the number of licenses available in that area. So when scouting a location, you need to be mindful of whether the area is already saturated with other existing cannabis businesses.

Essentially what all this means is that you can't just locate anywhere. Before throwing money down on a location, be aware of the property's limitations and ensure that the location complies with state and local law.

3. ORGANIZE YOUR FINANCES

The cannabis industry is capital intensive so financial planning is key. Figure out your start-up costs and make sure to keep your start-up budget on track. If you need to secure outside financing, just be aware that that state law is still a little hazy as to who exactly can invest in cannabis businesses and how. For example, the MCRSA doesn't have a residency requirement, but the AUMA, on the other hand, requires that all "controlling persons" of the business be able to demonstrate California residency from or before January 1, 2015. Of course, however, the AUMA doesn't define what a "controlling person" is. And it's unclear whether the MCRSA is going to be later amended to include a residency requirement, similar to the AUMA. The state will be creating more rules on these issues later this year.

For now, make sure your budget accounts for various uncertainties and then add a bit more funding as a cushion. Also take into account the possibility of delays. Though the Bureau has indicated that state licenses will be available by January 1, 2018, not everyone is going to get their state license on Day One. What's more likely to happen on January 1st is that the state will give out a few temporary state license while it processes the rest of the applications.

4. CLEAN UP YOUR CRIMINAL RECORD

Having a criminal record can affect your chances of getting a state license. If you have a prior conviction that is considered "substantially related to the qualifications, functions or duties of the business" that you want to operate, you could be potentially disqualified from getting a state license. "Substantially related" convictions can include felony convictions involving drugs, fraud and/or violence. Depending on your prior conviction(s), there may be possible legal ways to have the conviction reduced, expunged or eliminated altogether. Contact a criminal lawyer ASAP to see if it's possible to get your criminal record cleaned up in time for applications.

5. UNDERSTAND PRIORITY LICENSING

When you launch a business, timing is everything. Especially in a new industry like this, there could be huge benefits to being among the first state-compliant businesses to market in California.

As previously discussed, the MCRSA gives licensing priority to cannabis businesses "that can demonstrate to the authority's satisfaction" that they were "in operation" and "in good standing" with their local governments by **January 1, 2016.**[325] If your business was not "in operation" or in "good standing" with the local government prior to January 1, 2016, your business will not qualify for "priority" status. In this situation, it's important to plan in advance for potential delays in licensing.

Very similar to the MCRSA, the AUMA contains a priority licensing standard for applicants "that can demonstrate to the authority's satisfaction that the applicant operated *in compliance with the Compassionate Use Act* and its implementing laws before **September 1, 2016**, or currently operates *in compliance with the MCRSA.*"[326] Currently, there is some ambiguity surrounding what the term "in compliance" means because the AUMA doesn't define it anywhere. The state will likely define "in compliance" when the Bureau – which is tasked with overseeing the state licensing of cannabis businesses – becomes operational and starts setting all the rules regarding licensing, likely in late 2017. At a minimum, however, the AUMA removes from "priority" status consideration any business that was not in operation prior to September 1, 2016. So if your business was not in operation prior to September 1, 2016, don't expect to get first dibs on state licenses and plan in advance for potential delays in getting one.

6. GET IN COMPLIANCE WITH LOCAL LAW

We cannot stress enough the importance of this. Both the MCRSA and AUMA require compliance with local law so it's critical that you study and understand your local laws *before* you seek a license. If your local jurisdiction requires a local license to operate a cannabis business, then you must obtain that local license first before getting a state license. On the other hand, if your local jurisdiction has a ban or moratorium on cannabis businesses, then no state licenses will be given to any businesses within that jurisdiction. Therefore, it's clear, local law compliance is key – if you cannot comply with laws on the local level, then you will have no chance at compliance on the state level either.

G. CALIFORNIA'S CRIMINAL JUSTICE SYSTEM AND CANNABIS

1. CRIMINAL LAWS & PENALTIES FOR CANNABIS

Unless and until cannabis is legalized, a person arrested for the unlawful possession, cultivation or distribution of cannabis (that does not comply with the provisions of the MCRSA *and* does not meet the criteria for protection under the CUA and MMP, i.e. is not a qualified patient or operating under the guidelines) can be arrested and convicted in California and will be subject to the penalties as outlined in the following chart:

Offense	Type of Penalty	Punishment

Simple Possession (Health & Safety Code § 11357)	Infraction or Misdemeanor	Infraction: max $500 fine Misdemeanor: up to one year (county jail)
Cultivation (Health & Safety Code § 11358)	Felony	16 months to 3 years (county jail)
Sale, Gift or Transport (Health & Safety Code § 11360)	Misdemeanor or Felony	Misdemeanor: max $100 fine Felony: 2 to 4 years (state prison)
Possession for Sale (Health & Safety Code § 11359)	Felony	16 months to 3 years (county jail)
Selling to Minor (Health & Safety Code § 11361)	Felony	3 to 7 years (state prison)
Chemical Extraction (Health & Safety Code § 11358)	Felony	Max $50,000 fine *and* 3 to 7 years (state prison)
Driving with Cannabis (Vehicle Code § 23222(b))	Infraction	Max $100 fine

Unlike federal laws, there are no mandatory minimum sentences attached to these offenses.

2. THE COLLECTIVE AND COOPERATIVE MEDICAL DEFENSE

As noted earlier, the MMP, for the first time ever, provided limited immunity for the collective and cooperative cultivation and distribution of cannabis.[327]

Specifically, Health & Safety Code § 11362.775 provides:

"Qualified patients, persons with valid identification cards, and their designated primary caregivers of qualified patients and persons with identification cards, who associate within the State of California in order <u>collectively or cooperatively</u> to cultivate cannabis for medical purposes, shall not solely on the basis of that fact be subject to state criminal sanctions under Section 11357, 11358, 11359, 1166, 11366.5, or 11570."

In order to raise the collective or cooperative defense in court, the following elements must be proven[328]: **(1) the defendant is a qualified patient or caregiver; and (2) the collective or cooperative was being operated within the scope of those acts immunized by the CUA and MMP.**[329]

The first element is usually the "easiest" to prove. A person's status as a qualified patient can be shown with proof of a verbal or written medical cannabis recommendation from a licensed physician[330] while a person's status as a primary caregiver is typically shown with a written designation by a qualified patient[331]. [Note: The courts have decided that dispensary operators generally do not meet the definition of a primary caregiver.][332]

The second element, however, is often more difficult to establish – mainly because there are so many guidelines (which will be discussed in further detail below) that collectives and cooperatives must adhere to in order to comply with state legislation.

a. MCRSA: COLLECTIVE DEFENSE SUNSET CLAUSE

The MCRSA has created an "**SB 420 collective defense sunset**". This means that the MMP provision affording legal protection to patient collectives and cooperatives, Health & Safety Code §11362.775, will no longer be available to prosecuted medical CBs one year after the BCR posts a notice on its website that the issuance of licenses have commenced. After that date, all medical CBs will have to be licensed, except for individual patient and caregiver gardens <u>serving no more than five patients.</u>

3. MCRSA: CRIMINAL ACTIVITY

Under the MCRSA, many cannabis-related crimes are still charged as felonies. For example, while simple possession is an infraction, acts such as cultivation, possession with intent to sell, transportation, and sales are all still felonies, with a capital "F." Unless and until cannabis is legalized, a person arrested for the unlawful possession, cultivation or distribution of cannabis (that does not comply with the provisions of the MCRSA *and* does not meet the criteria for protection under the CUA and MMP, i.e. is not a qualified patient or operating under the guidelines) can be arrested and convicted in California and will be subject to the penalties as outlined in the following chart:

Offense	Type of Penalty	Punishment
Simple Possession (Health & Safety Code § 11357)	Infraction or Misdemeanor	Infraction: max $500 fine Misdemeanor: up to one year (county jail)
Cultivation (Health & Safety Code § 11358)	Felony	16 months to 3 years (county jail)
Sale, Gift or Transport (Health & Safety Code § 11360)	Misdemeanor or Felony	Misdemeanor: max $100 fine Felony: 2 to 4 years (state prison)
Possession for Sale (Health & Safety Code § 11359)	Felony	16 months to 3 years (county jail)
Selling to Minor (Health & Safety Code § 11361)	Felony	3 to 7 years (state prison)
Chemical Extraction (Health & Safety Code § 11358)	Felony	Max $50,000 fine *and* 3 to 7 years (state prison)
Driving with Cannabis (Vehicle Code § 23222(b))	Infraction	Max $100 fine

Unlike federal laws, there are no mandatory minimum sentences attached to these offenses.

Who can be held criminally liable under the MCRSA?

The answer is easy: businesses operating without a license. However, an exemption from licensing requirements does apply to individual patients who cultivate, possess, or transport exclusively for personal medical use and caregivers who provide for individual patients. Rule of thumb – a license is needed for "commercial activity," which is defined by the MCRSA as providing to no more than five patients.[333] But six patients or more, you've got yourself "commercial activity" and need to get a license.

For those businesses that need a license, the MCRSA creates harsh penalties for failing to comply with the MCRSA. For example:

Criminal penalties – Unlicensed medical CBs will face the same criminal penalties as those in operation unlawfully today, which means – surprise, surprise! – it will still be a misdemeanor to produce medical cannabis commercially without a license. But this time when you waltz into court, you won't be armed with the defense of being a "collective" because the MCRSA will be eliminating SB 420's "collective" defense one year after the state begins issuing licenses. So after that date, businesses either have a license or they don't – talk about the gray smoke clearing.

Heavy fines and strict scrutiny – Regulations mean more rules. More rules mean more rules to break. Under the MCRSA, any person caught engaging in cannabis activity without a license and tracking information can be fined up to twice the cost of a license for *each* separate violation, and yes, a separate fine for each day. Failure to follow the rules also creates grounds for disciplinary action, suspension and revocation of your license, and even shutting down your business and/or destroying all your cannabis plants.

New crime for doctors – Hey, pot doc mills watch out! The MCRSA has created a new misdemeanor crime for doctors found violating good practices in issuing recommendations. It is now unlawful for physicians to accept or offer any sort of remuneration to or from a license-holder in which the doctor or a family member has a financial interest. Moreover, the Medical Board will now assign special priority to investigating physicians who show "[r]epeated acts of clearly excessive recommending of cannabis for medical purposes, or repeated acts of recommending without a good faith prior exam."[334] Don't worry though, patients. This will not substantially affect or impair patients' access to medical recommendations.

4. RETURN OF PROPERTY AFTER CRIMINAL CASE

The Fifth Amendment states that no citizen shall be deprived of life, liberty or property without due process of law, nor shall private property be taken for public use without just compensation. Despite this right, the government regularly seizes property unlawfully, especially if one is found in possession of cannabis. Asset forfeiture is one of the most powerful — and potentially unfair — weapons the government can use against people, regardless of whether they are guilty of a crime. Thus, state and federal officials can seize any cannabis they find despite a person's patient-status.

Under SB 1193, which was approved unanimously by the Senate Public Safety Committee, law enforcement agencies in California that file charges against medical cannabis users have to return any seized cannabis or reimburse the user for it if the charges are dropped or result in acquittal.[335] This bill serves the dual purposes of assisting law enforcement at a practical level with cannabis storage and securing the rights of individuals who are following the law.[336] Further, if there is a legal entitlement to the property that is sought to be returned, the court may not refuse to return it, even if the property was used in the commission of an offense for which the possessor was convicted.[337]

5. IMMIGRATION CONSEQUENCES OF CANNABIS-RELATED CONVICTIONS

Anyone involved in the medical cannabis industry and not a citizen of the U.S. should be very careful. Federal immigration law prescribes serious consequences for cannabis-related offenses. The immigration consequences of a cannabis-related conviction are the same as those for a conviction related to any other controlled substance, such as heroin or cocaine. This is because a cannabis-related conviction is considered an "aggravated felony" under the Immigration and Nationality Act. Thus, anyone convicted of a cannabis related offense as an immigrant can be deported and permanently banned from the United States.[338] This is true regardless of whether the immigrant was convicted under California or federal law.[339]

6. DOES HAVING A CRIMINAL RECORD AFFECT CHANCES OF GETTING A STATE LICENSE?

Yes. Having a criminal record can affect your future chances of getting a state license to operate a cannabis business in California. Under the Medical Cannabis Regulation and Safety Act ("MCRSA") and the Adult Use of Marijuana Act ("AUMA"), all applicants for state licensure must submit their fingerprints for a criminal background check. And the law states that the "licensing authority *may* deny [your] application for licensure or renewal of a state license" if you have been convicted of an offense that is considered "*substantially related*" to the qualifications, functions or duties of the business" that you want to operate.

"Substantially related" convictions that can potentially disqualify you from getting a state license include the following:

- A felony conviction for the illegal possession for sale, sale, manufacture, transportation and/or cultivation of any illegal substance (including cannabis);
- A felony conviction for a "violent" or "serious" crime;
- A felony conviction involving fraud, deceit or embezzlement;

- A felony conviction for a drug-related offense involving a minor; and
- A felony conviction for drug trafficking with certain enhancements.

You may also be disqualified if you have a record of violating local ordinances, such as medical cannabis ordinances, or if you previously had a local license to operate a medical cannabis business that was revoked within 3 years prior to your application for a state license.

The AUMA states that if an applicant in the recreational use industry has completed his/her sentence for certain drug-related offenses (including possession, possession for sale, manufacture, transportation or cultivation), then the prior conviction will not be considered "substantially related" and cannot be the sole ground for denial of a state license. However, this is a departure from the stricter MCRSA, which states that past drug-related offenses are valid grounds for denying licenses to those in the medical cannabis industry. In both industries, a conviction for any drug-related felony *subsequent* to licensure will be grounds for denial or revocation.

Without even taking into consideration the state's requirements, felons could also be disqualified from obtaining licenses on the local level as well. For instance, some cities in Northern California, such as Sacramento, Oakland and San Jose, have already enacted local ordinances stating that persons with certain prior felony convictions will be disqualified from obtaining local licenses to operate CBs within their jurisdictions. And, as we already know, obtaining a local license is key to obtaining a state license.

So, what will happen to your state application if you have a prior "substantially related" conviction? Your application will essentially be "red flagged" for review and will be considered on a case-by-case basis, thus prolonging the application process. The state may determine that you are "otherwise suitable" to receive a license if doing so "would not compromise public safety." At that point, the state will conduct a review of the nature of the crime and any "evidence of rehabilitation" before deciding whether you are suitable for a license. At the end of the day, however, the state is afforded *a lot* of discretion to make these types of case-by-case decisions and many fear that this will effectively result in most felons being denied state licenses.

To be safe, if you have been convicted of *any* crime and want to ensure your best chances at both state and local licensure, here are some recommendations:

1. **Get your felony or misdemeanor conviction reduced and/or eliminated.** Many of the "substantially related" convictions listed under the MCRSA and AUMA can only trigger a failure to obtain a state license if they are *felony* convictions. Luckily, the AUMA allows for many cannabis-related felony convictions to be retroactively reduced or eliminated altogether. Other convictions could also be potentially eligible for reduction under Penal Code § 17(b) or Proposition 47. You should speak with a criminal attorney to see if you qualify.

2. **Get your criminal conviction expunged, if possible.** The AUMA states that an applicant cannot be denied based *solely* on a conviction that has been expunged pursuant to Penal Code § 1203.4. Misdemeanors and certain types of felonies are eligible for expungement under Penal Code § 1203.4. Again, you should speak with a criminal attorney to see if you qualify.

2. **Obtain a certificate of rehabilitation, if possible.** If you do not qualify for expungement, you may be eligible for what is called a "certificate of rehabilitation." A certificate of rehabilitation is a court order which declares that a person who has been convicted of a felony has been rehabilitated after serving state prison time. The AUMA states that an applicant cannot be denied based solely on a "substantially related" conviction for which the applicant has obtained a certificate of rehabilitation. Again, you should speak with a criminal attorney to see if you qualify.

3. **Be a model citizen in the future.** For obvious reasons, the state won't give out licenses to people who show no respect for the law. If you want to obtain a license and keep it in the future, stay out of trouble and play by all the rules.

H. PROP 64 FELONY REDUCTIONS

1. WHY YOU SHOULD REDUCE YOUR FELONY CONVICTIONS UNDER PROP 64

Perhaps you have an old weed-related conviction somewhere in your past. Maybe you even think it was a relatively minor crime – even if it was a felony – and you've since "done your time" and moved on with your life. Maybe you also think that nobody will even care about your conviction anymore because weed is now legal in California.

Unfortunately, even in a legalized state like California, the reality is that a drug-related conviction follows you everywhere, even if it's just a misdemeanor.

Though you may think it's not worth the time, money or effort to get reduction under Proposition 64, here are several reasons why you should definitely reconsider:

- **Employment:** Having a felony on your criminal record will almost always hinder your job prospects. If you reduce your conviction under Proposition 64, you can truthfully say "no" when asked if you've been convicted of a felony on job applications.

- **Getting a Loan:** Some bank institutions and loan agencies believe that a prior felony conviction is an indication that someone is irresponsible and thus less likely to meet their financial obligations. Reducing or eliminating your drug conviction could get you better interest rates when applying for a loan to a buy a car, a home, or even an education.

- **Immigration Benefits:** Because a drug-related conviction can be a basis for deportation, eliminating or reducing a cannabis conviction can significantly impact a noncitizen's ability to remain in the U.S.[340]

- **Gun Rights:** Any felony conviction that is reduced under Proposition 64 is considered a misdemeanor for all purposes. This means that persons who have had their cannabis-related felonies reduced to misdemeanors will have their gun rights restored.

- **Getting a State License:** A felony conviction – even for a cannabis-related offense – can disqualify you from obtaining a state license to operate a medical or recreational cannabis business here in California. Reducing your conviction can greatly increase your chances of getting a state license when applications become available in 2018.

I. CITY COMPLIANCE

2016 was obviously a big year for California cannabis reform given the passage of the MCRSA and AUMA. After nearly 20 years of little to no regulatory guidance from the State, cities and counties have finally been given a clear indication of what is legal under state law and are empowered by the MCRSA and AUMA to license and regulate commercial cannabis activity. Moving forward, it is now up to the cities/counties to take a position and establish their own local ordinances regarding licensing for cannabis growers and dispensaries. Compliance with the MCRSA literally hinges upon compliance with local law. However, with the passage of the AUMA, local government power will be slightly less broad, but cities and counties will still have the final word at the end of the day on allowing cannabis commerce and what types. The major difference being that the AUMA would require a local majority vote to completely ban medical CBs.

With that said, the hot topic for 2017 (and beyond) will undoubtedly be local compliance. The implementation of the MCRSA and AUMA will obviously take some time, but cities and counties will likely use the January 1, 2018 date[341] as a deadline to get their local regulations in order, which means that CBs (especially in Los Angeles) will have a lot of work to do in the next two years in terms of: (1) convincing their local governments to give them a fair chance at state licensing if their local ordinances currently ban dispensaries and/or cultivation; and (2) getting their business ready for a more tightly regulated business landscape. For current and new CBs alike, preparation will be the key theme from now until 2018. Thereafter, it will be the exciting game of state licensing and, ultimately, federal acceptance. Until then, it cannot be emphasized enough how imperative it is that CBs take immediate steps to come into compliance with local law in order to ensure uninterrupted operation during this transitional stage for weed in California.

CHAPTER III.
LOCAL ORDINANCES

A. IMPORTANCE OF LOCAL ORDINANCES UNDER BOTH MCRSA AND AUMA (PROP 64)

We have written extensively about California's passage of the MCRSA and AUMA and what it means to cannabis operators in the State. Now, let's delve into the issue of "local law compliance."

With the implementation of the MCRSA, the issue of what exactly to do about medical cannabis is being brought before city councils and county boards like never before. This is because the MCRSA's **dual-licensing structure** calls for both local *and* state permits – e.g., no person can conduct commercial cannabis activity without BOTH a state license and a local license or permit. Even though the Bureau of Medical Cannabis Regulation ("BMCR" or "the Bureau") issues state licenses under the MCRSA, being in **compliance with local government** rules and regulations is a condition precedent of getting state approval.[342] The AUMA similarly states that no state license will be given to an applicant if the activity is in violation of a local ordinance.[343]

Both the MCRSA and the AUMA also make clear that local governments retain their current right to ban and/or regulate medical cannabis dispensaries and cultivation – meaning, if a local jurisdiction has banned dispensaries and/or cultivation, no medical cannabis business ("medical CBs") within its borders may obtain a state license under the MCRSA.

Compliance with local ordinances also matters if a CB intends on seeking "priority status" pursuant to either the MCRSA or AUMA. Under the MCRSA, medical CBs in compliance with local and state regulations as of January 1, 2018, will be allowed to operate until a state license is issued. However, the State will prioritize the issuance of state licenses to those medical CB's "that can demonstrate to the authority's satisfaction that it was in operation and in good standing with the local jurisdiction by January 1, 2016."[344] This incentivizes current medical CBs to comply with local ordinances because doing so will mean that they will be the first in line for state licensure.

The AUMA also contains "priority" language similar to the MCRSA. Specifically, the AUMA provides that "[a] licensing authority shall give priority in issuing licenses under this division to applicants that can demonstrate to the authority's satisfaction that the applicant operated in compliance with the Compassionate Use Act and its implementing laws before September 1, 2016, or currently operates in compliance with [the MCRSA]."

The key takeaway here is this: State licensing requires compliance with local laws *first* so it's critical that you study and understand your local laws *before* you seek a state license. If your local jurisdiction requires a local license to operate a cannabis business, then you must obtain that local license first before getting a state license. On the other hand, if your local jurisdiction has a ban or moratorium on CBs, then no state licenses will be given to any CBs within that jurisdiction.

Local law compliance is king – if you cannot comply with laws on the local level, then you will have no chance at compliance on the state level either.

B. Local Enforcement Power Under the Constitution

So...how and why are local cities legally able to make up its own rules contrary to the State's rules? Just as the federal CSA empowers states with the discretion to use its police power, the MCRSA and AUMA similarly empower local cities and counties to use their local "police power" to regulate cannabis businesses within their own borders.

As previously discussed, state law merely *exempts* certain conduct from certain state criminal statutes. The MCRSA, AUMA, CUA and MMP do not, as a general rule, prevent counties from regulating or prohibiting medical cannabis businesses or activities via a local ordinance.[345] Indeed, both the MCRSA and AUMA state that nothing in their regulatory schemes "shall be interpreted to supersede or limit existing local authority for law enforcement activity, enforcement of local zoning requirements or local ordinances, or enforcement of local permit or licensing requirements."

The argument here is similar to the prevailing theory surrounding local government's right to limit the number of bars, liquor shops, and other businesses within their jurisdiction. Therefore, they can do the same with dispensaries and grows and any other CB.

Generally, this is true. The California Constitution recognizes the authority of cities and counties to make and enforce, within their borders, "all local, police, sanitary, and other ordinances and regulations not in conflict with general laws." (Cal. Const., art. XI, § 7.) This inherent police power includes broad authority to determine the appropriate use of land within a local jurisdiction's borders. Based on these police powers, the Supreme Court recently held that California's medical cannabis laws do not preempt or override local ordinances that ban medical cannabis facilities.[346]

C. CALIFORNIA CITIES THAT REGULATE CBs

Ever since the MCRSA passed in October 2015, local governments throughout California have been scrambling to put local cannabis laws in place prior to state licensing in January 2018. A major driving force behind this is money. If a city or county chooses to ban all CB's, the city or county will not be able to receive any state or local tax revenue from the sale of recreational or medical weed.

Many cities and counties, including Los Angeles County, have imposed temporary bans or moratoriums on all CB's, aiming to give state legislators time to craft regulations for the state. Many of these local governments have stated that they are utilizing these bans only as "placeholders" to retain local control over regulation, but that they would be open to local regulation in the future. By adopting these placeholder bills, it appears that these local governments are cautiously adopting a "wait-and-see" approach in order to see how the implementation of the MCRSA and AUMA pans out in other cities first. The idea being that – once cities that do pass comprehensive regulation can demonstrate the success of the state and local program – i.e., via tax revenue increases and/or decreases in crime – other cities will undoubtedly follow suit.

As attorneys practicing in this field, one of the most common questions we get is - **What city in California is the best to start a medical or recreational CB?** Although a seemingly simple question, there is no black and white response. It has become clear that each prospective business, operation, and/or individual, requires a case-specific analysis to determine where it should or should not conduct business.

Until state licenses are issued in 2018, all CB's should follow the A.G. Guidelines, which refer to local laws and recommend compliance. According to the A.G. Guidelines, a CB not in compliance with local laws may be running an unlawful operation.[347] Therefore, it is important to pay close attention to local laws to operate legally as a CB.

Absent a local ordinance, the MCRSA will allow 100 square feet of medical cannabis for a patient, and allow caregivers to grow 500 square feet for up to five patients. State licensing for commercial-sized medical cannabis farms is also allowable under the MCRSA, provided locals approve.

Under the AUMA, Californians will be able to lawfully grow up to six indoor or outdoor cannabis plants. Local governments, however, are left free to enact local ordinances *"reasonably regulating"* personal grows. However, *while local governments can completely prohibit outdoor grows, they cannot completely prohibit personal indoor grows.*

Notably, several cities and counties in California have either very strict regulations for CB's, or have banned them altogether. So the question becomes - how does one operate within these cities? The choice is simple - either comply or don't comply. If you don't comply though, you will be operating illegally under local law and you will ruin your chances at state licensing.

With over 58 counties and 483 incorporated municipalities within the state of California, and with local laws constantly changing and evolving on a daily basis, there's simply no easy way to determine whether a particular CB is operating in compliance with local law at any given time. To find out what the current local laws are in your jurisdiction, start by checking your city or county government website for more information. We also suggest contacting the city clerk or looking at recent city agendas to find out what's been going in your city. You may also contact us directly if you would like additional help with navigating your local laws.

1. PROPOSITION M IN LOS ANGELES

In case you missed it, L.A.'s cannabis industry has been stunted for nearly a decade due to the city's fatally flawed regulations. The longstanding ordinance, **Proposition D ("Prop D")**, was a regulatory MESS. Passed in 2013, Prop D didn't give actual licenses to pot shops – it just said that the city would "look the other way" by granting "limited immunity" from city prosecution to a certain 135 dispensaries. This semi-regulation often led to erratic and unpredictable raids and prosecutions of local dispensaries. Hundreds of shops were being shut down by the city, only to have new ones pop up around the corner. Prop D was basically a nightmare for both the industry and the city alike.

With the passage of the Medical Cannabis Regulation and Safety Act (MCRSA) and the Adult Use of Marijuana Act (AUMA), city voters finally decided that the broken-ness of Los Angeles's pot laws could not be tolerated any longer. Because of the new state rules regarding local power and local licensing, the city had to get rid of Prop D if it wanted to partake in the imminent green rush. Both the MCRSA and AUMA require that businesses have "local approval" or be in compliance with local law before they can obtain state license. Therefore, if a local ordinance (like Prop D) didn't provide for actual local permits or licenses to operate a cannabis business, then no businesses in that local jurisdiction could get a state license. And if no businesses in the city could get a state license, then that meant the city would be unable to receive state or local tax revenue from the sale of medical or recreational weed.

Apparently, this proved to be too much green for the city of L.A. to miss out on. On March 7, 2017, in a resounding vote of approval for cannabis regulation, Los Angeles voters approved Prop M with 79.4% of the vote! Now, with the passage of Prop M, it's no longer a question of "if," but "when" and "how" the city of L.A. will regulate the weed industry.

The purpose of Prop M was to amend Prop D in order to make it compatible with the MCRSA and AUMA so that businesses in the city could get state licenses. The initiative was actually the brainchild of City Council President Herb Wesson, Jr., who had stated before that "[t]he city of Los Angeles should explore financial opportunities associated with the recreational use, cultivation, distribution, manufacturing, processing and testing of marijuana." In other words, city officials finally recognized what we've been trying to say all along – that the cannabis industry in L.A. is simply _too_ lucrative for the city to _not_ change.

So what exactly does Prop M say? Honestly, not much. Prop M intentionally gives very few details about how exactly the industry will be governed. It simply states that all the power will be given back to City Council "to amend existing and adopt new regulations regarding cannabis activity in the City," but it doesn't really give specific industry rules for voters to even consider.[348] The only specific rule actually set forth in Prop M is the one thing voters must approve – the establishment of new tax rates for cannabis businesses.

For now, Prop M only hints at a regulatory scheme that would potentially license not only dispensaries in the city, but also cultivators, manufacturers, transporters, testing labs and researchers for both medical and recreational cannabis. The measure further indicates that it would give licensing priority to existing dispensaries in compliance with Prop D.

According to city officials, the broad language of Prop M was by design. A spokeswoman for Wesson wrote in an email to _Marijuana Business Daily_: "The City Council-supported initiative returns industry regulation back to local government, which is why the language is intentionally broad – for now. ... This is the beginning of the City Council's process and everything is on the table and open to discussion."[349] Essentially, the city wants to start from scratch and work with the industry to come up with smarter regulations that are mutually palatable.

City Council hopes to have a complete structure for regulation in place prior to September 30, 2017 – which is when local licenses are expected to be first available. L.A. is poised to become the biggest weed market in the U.S., so the entire country is anxious to see how L.A. puts together its regulatory blueprint. "L.A. alone is larger than two Colorado [markets]; the whole state, twice," says Jared Kiloh, president of the cannabis industry group UCBA Trade Association.[350]

Now with all eyes on L.A., here are some important things to know about Prop M:

1. **There's still a lot for the city to figure out.** Prop M intentionally gives very few details about how exactly the city's industry will be governed. It simply states that all the power will be given back to City Council "to amend existing and adopt new regulations regarding cannabis activity in the City." Public hearings and stakeholder input will play big roles in how City Council decides to craft the rules. For now, Prop M only hints that affirmative licensing will be available for dispensaries, cultivators, manufacturers, transporters, testing labs and researchers for both medical and recreational cannabis.

2. **Local licenses are expected to be available as early as September 30, 2017.** City Council intends to have a complete structure for regulation in place prior to September 30, 2017, which is when local licenses are expected to be first available.

3. **Prop D remains in effect until Prop M formally repeals it.** Prop M states that City Council must adopt an ordinance repealing Prop D effective January 1, 2018. Until then, Prop D still remains the law in L.A.

4. **Prop D dispensaries will get first dibs on local licenses.** When the city starts issuing licenses on September 30th, the 135 dispensaries currently operating in compliance with Prop D will get priority. These Prop D dispensaries will have 60 days to apply for a local permit once they're made available.

5. **There will be local taxes.** Prop M implements new gross receipt taxes on every aspect of the L.A. cannabis industry. Transportation, testing and research start with 1% taxes. Tax rates then increase to 2% for manufacturing, cultivating and any other form of commercial cannabis business. Finally, medical cannabis sales will be subject to a 5% business tax while recreational cannabis sales will be subject to gross receipt taxes of 10%.

6. **Rule-breakers will be harshly punished.** Prop M clarifies that anyone who operates without a city-issued license is in violation of the law and will be subject to potential misdemeanor charges. In addition, violators will be considered a public nuisance and could be hit with huge civil penalties, inc. a max fine of $20K for each day the business is illegally operating. Violators could also have their utilities shut off.

CHAPTER IV.
REAL ESTATE

A. LAND USE, REAL ESTATE & LANDLORD/TENANT ISSUES

1. LOCATION

In 2010, former Governor Arnold Schwarzenegger signed bill AB 2650, which prohibits medical cannabis establishments – including cooperatives, collectives, dispensaries, owners and providers — from operating within a 600-foot radius of a school. This bill took effect January 1, 2011. The bill was intended "to shield children from drugs."[351] AB 2650 is now in effect as Health & Safety Code § 11362.778. It is important to note that, although this regulation only sets a 600 foot restriction, it does not prevent a city, county, or city and county from adopting an ordinance or policy that *further restricts* the location or establishment of a CB by imposing other requirements that need to be met beyond the 600 foot requirement.[352] This means that local governments may choose to require CBs to be located even further than 600 feet away from a school.

Although there are no current state rules outlining a distance between CBs and churches, parks or youth centers, most local ordinances do and thus it is advisable to keep that in mind when choosing a location.

2. RENTING TO A MEDICAL CANNABIS BUSINESS

One of the biggest issues surrounding CBs today is landlord liability. Most landlords and property owners are hesitant to rent to CBs for fear that they may be held liable for the operations of their tenant. Hence, the ever-looming question -- **Can I lose my property if I rent to a CB?** The simple answer to this question is both yes and no.

The federal government can attempt to seize the property of landlords who lease to CBs by initiating a civil forfeiture, based on the fact that a tenant of the property sells medical cannabis. This forfeiture action is based on a showing that it was more probable than not that a crime was being committed on the property.[353] However, in light of the RF Amendment and the *MAMM* case, it seems the likelihood of this occurring is even less now.

a. UNDER FEDERAL LAW

While there are federal enforcement actions in California, the seizure of property under federal law is RARE. Despite the federal government's efforts "to prohibit an owner from providing a place for illegal conduct"[354], there are few, if any, examples of actual asset forfeiture actions by the federal government.[355]

The federal government has attempted to shut down CBs by sending letters to operating dispensaries and to their landlords informing them that their operation is in violation of the CSA and must cease operations within the next 45 days.[356] By sending these blanket warnings, the Federal government works to deprive commercial landlords of the "innocent owner defense" or IOD in forfeiture proceedings. IOD can be used as a defense to federal forfeiture if the property owner did not know that there was a CB operating on his property or upon learning about it, the property owner did all that could be "reasonably expected under the circumstances to terminate such use of the property."[357] Hence, in sending these blanket letters, the Federal government is ensuring that property owners and landlords know there is a CB on their property and thus trying to deprive them of the safety of IOD. After a federal letter is sent, the only way the landlord can rely on the IOD defense to defeat forfeiture is to evict the tenant from the leased premises.[358]

In a widely known case, a landlord in northern California was stopped from trying to evict the biggest dispensary in the country, Harborside Health Centers, even though the federal government was threatening to seize the property.[359] In this case, an argument that Harborside's lease should be terminated due to illegal activity did not succeed because California law allows nonprofit corporations to distribute medical cannabis through a collective model. Although federal law "makes it unlawful to rent, lease, profit from or make available for use... a place for the purpose of unlawfully manufacturing, storing, distributing... cannabis," this has not proven as a justification for going after the landlords.[360]

Adversely, the City of Oakland tried to prevent the forfeiture in a collateral suit in *City of Oakland v. Lynch*,[361] but the Ninth Circuit rejected the action "because the [federal] Government's decision to file the forfeiture action is purely at the agency's discretion by law, and because allowing the [City's] suit to proceed would disrupt the existing [federal] forfeiture framework."[362]

Still, most proceedings are NOT brought against landlords under 21 U.S.C. § 856(a)(2), except where the landlord participated in the cannabis business operation or its proceeds, or the tenant's operation neither complied with federal statutes nor the state's medical cannabis law.[363]

In addition, the city of Oakland sued the federal government in an effort to allow Harborside to continue providing to its 100,000 patients.

Oakland officials warned that a shutdown would lead to a "health crisis."[364] A federal magistrate agreed and Harborside was allowed to continue to operate, at least for now, despite a bid by federal prosecutors to shut it down.[365]

In California, we do not yet have an officially reported case determining whether a landlord has the right to get a court order declaring a lease terminated and evicting the tenant based solely on the tenant's use of medical cannabis. The CUA only addresses criminal liability but, arguably, in conjunction with disability antidiscrimination laws, it might protect tenants from eviction based on their possession, cultivation and use of medical cannabis.

Later, the States' Medical Cannabis Property Rights Protection Act, was introduced to amend the civil forfeiture provisions of the CSA to provide that **no real property may be subject to civil forfeiture to the United States due to medical cannabis-related activities that are performed in compliance with state law**.[366] Furthermore, in May 2014, the Rohrabacher-Farr Amendment approved and renewed for 2015, has now banned the DOJ and, in turn, the DEA from bullying states that legalized medical cannabis. Technically, this means that, although the federal government is still allowed to prosecute and seize assets of CBs in states where it is legal, they are no longer in the business of bullying these businesses. Rep. Sam Farr, co-author of the Amendment put it simply, by saying, "…look, if you are following state law, you are a legal resident doing your business under state law, the feds just can't come in and bust you…[this] just lists the states that have already legalized it only for medical purposes and says, "Federal government…in those states, in those places, you can't bust people."[367]

b. UNDER CALIFORNIA LAW

California typically targets dispensary operators and not landlords. However, Health and Safety Code 11366.5 makes the charge of maintaining a location a crime a landlord could technically be charged with. As a practical matter, District Attorneys do not do this however. This is a "wobbler" offense, which means it can be brought as a felony or misdemeanor depending on the circumstances of the case.

c. UNDER CITY LAW

Even if a CB complies with California law, this does not guaranty that it may continue to operate under a city ordinance. The Inland Empire case held that California's medical cannabis law does not overrule or preempt total local bans. As such, operators and growers are bound by city ordinances that ban, or legalize CBs.[368] A city is fully authorized to take direct action against CBs by banning them altogether as is the case in cities like Ventura County or San Bernardino.[369]

Although public policy discourages actions against landlords, under Los Angeles local ordinance, medical cannabis dispensaries and the landlords who lease space to them can still be prosecuted. A few years ago, the city of Los Angeles filed suit against more than 80 *operators and owners* of facilities alleged to be selling and distributing cannabis for medicinal purposes in violation of the Los Angeles Municipal Code.[370] Los Angeles did so to dissuade potential entrepreneurs who might be contemplating opening similar businesses, as well as to deter property owners from considering renting to cannabis businesses.

3. HOW TO VERIFY IF A DISPENSARY IS LEGAL

In Los Angeles, the only dispensaries currently allowed are those that are Proposition D compliant (under Prop M, more will soon be allowed) for the dispensary to be legal. A quick way to know if the dispensary is indeed compliant, check the 134 list for the dispensary name. The list is a great guide, though the inquiry should begin and not end there. For example, many dispensaries have filed DBAs, are operating under a different name or some illegal shops fraudulently use the name of a Prop D dispensary to avoid detection.[371]

On the other hand, even though a dispensary may not be on the list as one of the coveted 134, it could be compliant with California law and in turn limit exposure/risk to felony charges. The list of Pre-ICO dispensaries in Los Angeles is listed in the Appendix of this book.

CHAPTER V.
BANKING & TAXATION

A. BANKING & CANNABIS

1. THE PROBLEM

"Despite its astounding growth in recent years, the marijuana industry remains hampered by its own banking crisis. [Cannabis] businesses' difficulty in accessing financial services has created problems for businesses and government alike."[372] Banks do not want to do business with CBs for of fear of federal prosecution. Why? Cannabis is federally illegal and banks are bound by federal laws and regulations. Accordingly, revenue from cannabis is considered "drug money" and banks do not want to be complicit in money laundering allegations.[373] As such, banks are terrified of dealing with cannabis sale proceeds.[374] Unfortunately, this means that many legal CBs have no access to the country's most basic banking services – e.g., they cannot apply for a business loan or open a simple checking account – which has forced CBs to deal exclusively in cash.

In addition to the Controlled Substances Act (CSA), there's also the Bank Secrecy Act requiring banks to be vigilant about any AML (Anti-Money Laundering) law violations, for which banks can file a SAR (Suspicious Activity Report). Cash transactions of $10,000 or more require the filing of a CTR (Currency Transaction Report). As if that weren't enough, the Know Your Customer (KYC) doctrine requires banks to monitor their customers' business activities.

Believe it or not, this gauntlet of acronyms causes headaches for the banks, as well as a lot of effort and expenses required to fully comply with these regulations. Furthermore, the risk of error is high, and the punishment for penalties is severe. This banking quagmire not only hurts cannabis businesses but also the banks themselves. So what can be done?

2. THE "SOLUTIONS"

a. *SOME BANKS WILL TAKE THE RISK*

In February 2014, the Obama administration told the banks and CBs that they could be friends. This green light came with the announcement that the federal government would not target banks working with legal and regulated CBs and then issued a set of guidelines. Of course, with thick strings attached.

Under these guidelines, banks now opening accounts for CBs must file suspicious or criminal activities reports, aka (SAR). SAR creates 3 types of reporting - a "limited" reporting, which means the bank is working with a CB believed to be in compliance with federal guidance or state laws, and "priority"/"terminated" reports filed if and when the bank believes the business is in violation of state or federal laws and plans to terminate.

With those rules, some banks started opening their doors to cannabis businesses, but not without hesitation. There is major due diligence, ongoing monitoring, and detailed reporting needed when taking on a CB account. Even so, most banks have still decided not to bother with the cannabis industry. The American Bankers Association says that, "guidance or regulation doesn't alter the underlying challenge for banks. As it stands, possession or distribution of cannabis violates federal law, and banks that support those activities risk of prosecution and sanctions."[375]

Not everyone's running and hiding though. Despite the potential risk, financial institutions in 25 states filed more than 1,700 "limited" reports for cannabis-related businesses receiving banking services.

b. OPERATING IN CASH

Eighty percent of cannabis businesses operate in an all cash environment. There are several obstacles that canna-businesses face because they operate in an all cash environment, including the following items:

1. Protecting cash from theft and misappropriation
2. Operating a successful business
3. Not achieving a good return on investment on your cash

Cash is liquid and one of the easiest assets to pocket. Depending on the size and type of your company, the risk of employee theft of cash is different. However, it's a good practice to have at least two safes to store cash. You'll want additional safes to store your inventory.

| Safe 1 | One safe can have daily cash amounts, and selected employees have access. |

Safe 2	Another safe can have weekly amounts of cash to pay employees, vendors, and other expenses. Access to this safe should be different from the first safe.
Safe 3	A master safe should be located at an off-site location and only the owner(s) should have access to it.

Cash logs also mitigate the risk of theft and misappropriation. A cash log is a log for sums of money entering and leaving. Every purchase and replenishment to the cash log should be supported by a receipt or description of the funds. Include the date of the transaction, the vendor or employee, and the amount. The cash log can be done manually each day or can be entered into the accounting system if your business has the manpower and capacity to do so.

Reconciling your cash funds each day against sales and inventory is the best way to determine if the amount of your cash is correct. If you have multiple safes and locations where cash is stored, then it is recommended to reconcile those on a weekly basis.

At least once a week, perform a full cash count and update your accounting records accordingly. It's good to have two people at different levels perform this.

It is crucial that you can forecast how much money you are going to be spending in the next week (cash outflow) and how much money you plan on making (cash inflow). This will help your business stay successful and ensure you're able to order your product and pay your bills and employees without worry.

c. FORM 8300

California's legalization has opened the floodgates of cannabis cash with nowhere for it to go. In the cannabis industry, where federal law makes banking almost impossible for cannabis businesses its interesting to note that in states where recreational markets thrive, i.e. Colorado, there is greater access to banking. Hello California banking, Prop 64 says it's ok to come out now!

As we have seen in states like Colorado, to comply with federal standards, recreational markets require vigorous compliance and enforcement measures to avoid being targeted. As a result, banks (usually credit unions or community banks) can feel confident that their clients are operating legally. Translation - compliant banking is more prevalent in recreational markets than in those limited to medical cannabis.

Anytime a deposit of $10,000.00 or more is made, federal law requires banks to report the transaction to the IRS or National Security Agencies. Local banks and credit unions will offer their services, but the give and take of it means a new level of reporting and transparency for cannabis businesses. Banks are fully visible to federal government and thus demand transparency from their banking clients. Banks file hundreds of thousands of reports for deposits over 10k. Ultimately, these reports end up in a pile with millions of other reports that may or may not get reviewed and investigated. Not only do banks report this, but the individuals receiving more than 10k are also required to do reporting of their own. Enter Form 8300, stage right.

Transactions that, accumulatively, are more than 10k within a period of a year require that a Form 8300 is filed to report the cash transactions. Generally, a business should file a form 8300 within 15 days of the payment. BUT, be careful, this isn't a one time filing. For any moneys that you get from the same person that continue to build on that $10K, an amended Form 8300 should be filed. Forget being a CB for a second, ANYONE receiving more than $10k – landlords, suppliers, attorneys, vendors - within a year from the same individual needs to file an 8300 or face penalties of up to $1,500,000. OOPS!

Beware. Trying to avoid reporting by making multiple smaller deposits just under the $10,000 reporting threshold is a crime referred to as structuring. Structuring multiple deposits under $10k has little chance to avoid detection and can land you in hot water. Here is why…The Bank Secretary Act (BSA) requires banks to report this activity and banks have detection and compliance systems in place to catch it. This reporting system is very similar to that of the reporting system for deposits made over $10k EXCEPT, every single one of these reports is read and potentially investigated by the IRS.

As banks take on the risk to serve the cannabis industry, they trust that cannabis businesses will operate in line with banking requirements and regulations. As of mid 2016, only 3% of the 7,600 banks in the U.S. were offering some form of financial services to businesses in the marijuana industry. Little by little, as legalization sweeps the nation, state and local banks will slowly trickle behind.

d. ALTERNATIVE BANKING

To enterprising thinkers, there is a silver lining—innovative solutions.

Establish your own private bank. Don't laugh . . . It's not as impossible as you think. Sure, there's a minimum initial startup fee of $500,000, and your ownership group must comprise experienced bankers who can pass an FBI background check. Furthermore, you must show that you have access to at least $10 million in start-up capital. Indeed, the process is arduous, long and expensive. But it can be done, as several flourishing private banking enterprises in Oregon, Washington and Colorado have proven.

> *"As more and more states legalize, constituents will up the pressure on Congress members to take action. This will also force bigger banks to become players. For now, the risks outweigh the potential rewards."*

Another option is to use an online payment system such as PayQwick, the "PayPal for Pot" headquartered in Los Angeles that claims total compliance with banking regulations. Cannabis business owners can use a preloaded PayQwick card to pay vendors, landlords and employees; customers can use it to make cannabis purchases.

A quieter option is opening an account at one of the handful of local banks and credit unions friendly to cannabis-related businesses (CRBs) since the big banks won't deal with them. Due diligence is required to uncover these banks since they still maintain a low profile and avoid undue attention.

e. STATE BALLOT EFFORTS MAY HELP MOTIVATE CONGRESS TO ACT

Although cannabis advocates can claim some victories in Congress, federal legislation to solve the cannabis banking issue has not gained any significant traction. In 2016, many populous and politically-important states voted on legalizing and expanding the legalization of cannabis. California, Nevada, and Massachusetts are among states who passed recreational cannabis in November 16, while Florida voters legalized medical cannabis. Legalization advocates have high hopes for 2017. One weapon in the arsenal for supporters is the fact that the "parade of horribles" — the consequences of legalization cited by anti-cannabis activists — has largely not materialized as more states allow cannabis use.

If legalization at the state level expands, then the constituencies demanding congressional action will also grow. These constituencies include not only cannabis businesses themselves but also the financial institutions that will profit from serving the industry as well as other groups concerned about so much business being conducted in cash. With such widespread interest in a banking solution, Congress may finally provide much-needed relief.

The banking challenges differ from state to state. Washington was proactive in dealing with their challenges. The state's banking regulatory arm worked tirelessly with federal regulators to find a way to have legalized banking services for CRBs. Consequently, Washington banks are upfront about their business relations with CRBs, although even the most basic merchant accounts are expensive to maintain and the flood of paperwork is oppressive.

On the other hand, Colorado took a different path by encouraging the formation of cannabis banking co-ops. However, there are plenty of CRBs doing business with banks and credit unions, though there's much less openness. Just as in Washington, maintaining even a basic merchant account is expensive and cumbersome.

The hope is that the AUMA (Prop 64) and other state marijuana measures will be the impetus for Congress to act. As more and more states legalize, constituents will up the pressure on Congress members to take action. This will also force bigger banks to become players. For now, the risks outweigh the potential rewards. However, if there is outright legalization for recreational cannabis use, the bigger banks will be unable to disregard the industry any longer.

f. SMALL BANKS FACE CHALLENGES SERVING CANNABIS BUSINESSES

Some cannabis businesses *do* have bank accounts — for now. For the most part, banks serving them are smaller community banks. But those banks often lack the resources necessary to ensure that businesses are in compliance with state cannabis laws and federal enforcement guidance. As a result, such banks often close cannabis businesses' accounts once they realize the true costs and burdens of a thorough compliance program. As case studies, look no further than the 2015 decisions of MBank in Oregon and First Security Bank of Nevada to cease serving cannabis businesses. Both banks essentially declared that the compliance resources required to bank such businesses in accordance with federal guidance were too great to justify the potential revenue from servicing such customers.

The small banks that continue serving cannabis businesses are likely to follow one of two paths. They may charge extraordinary fees. Indeed, reports are common of banks charging cannabis businesses as much as $2,000 a month for the privilege of maintaining an account. Second, small banks simply may not perform sufficient due diligence to ensure their clients' compliance. Neither of these paths is conducive to industry growth, but they will remain options for many small banks and desperate businesses, absent legislation.

g. BIGGER BANKS WILL BECOME MORE INTERESTED

For banks, the question of whether to serve cannabis businesses is one of risk versus reward. For larger banks with more sophisticated compliance operations, the risk of serving the cannabis industry has been too high and the potential rewards too low. But recently, the cannabis industry's growing size has increased the profit potential, while more effective cost-efficient risk mitigation methods have become more available.

There are many new tools that banks can leverage to reduce the risk that cannabis industry clients are violating state laws or federal enforcement priorities. For example, many firms with expertise in cannabis regulation now conduct efficient and thorough compliance audits that are tailored to the cannabis laws of a given jurisdiction. These audits, which are often conducted at cannabis business' expense, can reduce the amount of in-house resources needed for the bank to perform compliance due diligence and monitoring. Additionally, data about the licensure and beneficial ownership structures of cannabis businesses is becoming more accessible, giving banks comfort that they know their customers' true identities, as is required by federal law. Better compliance tools at a lower cost, along with higher potential profits, are likely to change the risk-reward calculus of some larger banks.

h. FEDERAL REGULATORS WILL REMAIN RELUCTANT TO PUSH MAJOR POLICY CHANGES

2016 opened with a big blow to the most credible effort to date to form a new financial institution designed to serve cannabis businesses. On Jan. 5, a federal court ruled that the Federal Reserve is not required to open a master account for The Fourth Corner Credit Union, thus denying Fourth Corner the ability to participate in the banking system. The district court explained that because cannabis remains federally illegal, the court would be forcing the Fed to commit a crime if it ordered the master account be granted. Moreover, the court noted the lack of utility of FinCEN's guidance, saying that only congressional action legalizing cannabis would allow banks to serve cannabis businesses. Because the court punted the issue to

Congress, already risk-averse regulators are unlikely to offer further guidance or regulations that would encourage or facilitate cannabis banking on a national level.

B. Taxation & Cannabis

Another hurdle that can cripple the success of CBs is the payment of overinflated federal taxes. Right now CBs are being forced to pay up to 60% to 90% of their revenues in federal taxes due to an obscure, old tax code provision called "Section 280E."376 This is *in addition to* the local and state taxes that CBs also have to pay.

Enacted by Congress in 1982, Section 280E was passed by the Reagan administration in response to a mid-level drug dealer in Minneapolis by the name of Jeffrey Edmondson, who was caught trafficking several pounds of cannabis, cocaine and amphetamines. After the government made him pay taxes on his illicit business earnings, Edmondson was successfully able to declare a hefty list of deductions on his federal income tax return for the various expenses he incurred in dealing drugs. Edmondson, for example, wrote off mileage, food, entertainment, airfare, telephone expenses, rent on his place of business – his apartment – and even $50 for a scale.[377]

Needless to say, this did not go over well with the government. Soon thereafter, Congress passed Section 280E in order to close the Edmondson loophole for good for all future drug dealers. The IRS tax code 280E "Expenditures in connection with the illegal sales of drugs" prevents any company that is directly involved in selling cannabis from receiving the standard tax deductions that other businesses are allowed to take. Under Section 280E, businesses involved in the "trafficking" of controlled substances are now specifically denied tax credits or exemptions, meaning that any logistical expense associated with the sale of a controlled substance, as defined under federal law, will no longer be deductible.378 The IRS tax code 280E allows cannabis producers, processors, manufacturers, and retailers to only deduct their cost of goods sold.

Fast forward three decades, this draconian law is now being applied to state-sanctioned cannabis businesses on the basis that cannabis is still considered illegal under federal law. The end result is that cannabis business owners cannot claim deductions on their federal tax returns for normal and ordinary business expenses such as rent, utilities, and employee salaries, which forces them to pay significantly higher taxes than other businesses. Thus far, the IRS has not expressed much interest in weighing in on the matter, except to point out that only Congress has the authority to stop enforcing the tax code.

In 2011, the agency issued a letter in response to several lawmakers in Colorado, Massachusetts, Arizona and California who had asked the IRS to stop enforcing Section 280E in states where sale of cannabis is legalized.[379] The IRS letter stated: "The result you seek would require Congress to amend either the Internal Revenue Code or the Controlled Substances Act.[380] In short – Denied. Unfortunately, the IRS is right. Congress must either reclassify cannabis as a controlled substance or amend Section 280E in order to "fix" the unequal tax treatment of cannabis businesses. This is yet another example of how cannabis businesses are being held down by federal laws.

1. REDUCING 280E EXPOSURE

a. COSTS OF GOODS SOLD

There are several tools to reducing 280E exposure. Understanding what the Cost of Goods Sold is essential in mitigating 280E exposure.

The IRS defines Cost of Goods Sold (COGS) as "**any expenditure necessary to acquire, construct or extract a physical product** which is to be sold. The seller can have no gain until he recovers the economic investment that he has made directly in the actual item sold."

COGS is anything that directly or indirectly involved in making your product and must be directly or indirectly related to the sale of your product. Cost of Good Examples in the cannabis industry:

1. If you are a grower and have a monthly lease payment for your greenhouse, the lease expense is an indirect cost to your product.
2. If you have machines to process trim into oil, the depreciation on those machines can be allocated to COGS.
3. If you hire trimmers or grow labor, that labor can be allocated to COGS.

Administrative and Selling Costs are not deductible and are not considered cost of goods sold.

1. **Administrative costs** such as cell phone, payroll for staff, gas, meals, entertainment, travel expenses, etc. cannot be allocated to COGS as these costs are not directly involved in making your product.

2. **Selling costs** such as marketing on Weedmaps, trade shows, and paying commissions to sales staff cannot be allocated to COGS. These costs are directly related to *selling* your product or service and aren't considered COGS.

b. ADDITIONAL REVENUE STREAMS

280E doesn't allow expenditures in connection with the illegal sales of drugs to be deducted, but what about sales of products that aren't illegal? Can expenses not related to sales of cannabis be expensed? Yes, but carefully.

If your business has revenue streams that are not related to cannabis, then expenses associated with those revenue streams can be deducted. Ensure you've got adequate supporting documentation to support your 280E strategy. Consult with a CPA or expert if you are unsure.

CHAPTER VI.
INTELLECTUAL PROPERTY ISSUES

Because of the increasingly friendly legal environment for cannabis use – at least in California – medical cannabis business is thriving across the country. It is already a billion-dollar a year business and it is projected to grow 25% (or more) annually by 2018. Like any other emerging industry, with growth comes a host of intellectual property issues. As cannabis businesses begin competing with one another for customers, it becomes all the more important for them to differentiate themselves by enhancing and protecting their brand, equating it with that of superior quality and value in the minds of the consumers. Trademarks, for example, can prevent businesses from using another's brand name, especially if that brand name is being used in a way that damages the reputation or steals business away.

Protecting a medical CB brand can be done in a number of ways, depending on the type of intellectual property at issue. To be clear, intellectual property rights are the rights given to persons and entities over intangible properties, usually thought of as creations of the mind. Rights and protections for owners of intellectual property are based on federal trademark, patent and copyright laws and state trade secret laws. In general, **trademarks** protect a name or symbol that identifies the source of goods or services; **patents** protect inventions of tangible things; **copyrights** protect various forms of written and artistic expression; and a **trade secret** consists of any formula, pattern, device or compilation of information which is used in one's business and which gives that business an opportunity to gain a competitive advantage over other businesses who do not know the secret.

A. TRADEMARKS

Trademarks prevent unfair competition and protect consumers by assuring them that they are buying what they think they are. So what is a trademark? A trademark can be a word (Nike), phrase ("Just do it"), symbol (swoosh), design, or a combination of all. Trademarks are used to enable consumers to identify brands and distinguish goods and/or services of one business from that of another. Take M&Ms for example, consumers see the brown packaging, the M&M character on the front and the distinct font of the brand M&M and automatically buyers know exactly what is inside the package. This branding allows consumers to know the exact product that they are buying.

Trademarks give buyers confidence in a purchase because the branding tells them that it is a familiar product. As a business owner, on the other hand - after investing time and money to develop and promote recognition of the unique and distinctive M&M packaging – it is potentially detrimental to a brand to have another company use distinct markings on a product different than the one the buyer identifies with. Customers viewing a trademark immediately know whom they are dealing with, the reputation of that business and are less likely to look for alternatives. A brand could be the critical factor in driving a customer's purchase decision or use of service. But this concept goes beyond picking a candy bar at the store.

Sometimes, a company's intangible properties - positive brand recognition - constitute the most valuable asset, i.e. Facebook, Instagram, and the ever popular but failed MySpace.

1. FEDERAL PROTECTION

To protect a trademark under federal law, the mark must be registered with the United States Patent and Trademark Office ("USPTO"). There are 2 basic requirements for filing an application with the USPTO:

1) The mark has to be **lawfully** used in commerce, and
2) It must be "distinctive".

The USPTO does not evaluate the originality of the marks itself, nor the product on its own, rather, whether there is a likelihood of confusion as to the company behind the goods or services because of the marks used. The most common reasons for the USPTO to refuse trademark registration are:

- Mark is likely to cause confusion with an existing mark or Pending registration application; (A mark cannot look like or feel like an existing mark, especially if it is in the same class of goods/services.)
- Mark is descriptive of the goods/services (e.g. Salad Spinner for a salad spinner). (If the mark is in a language other than English, the examiner will look to the translation of the word in English to determine registration);
- Mark is a geographic term;
- Mark is a surname;
- Mark is ornamental, or decorative, as applied to the goods (e.g. patterns).

Because cannabis is still federally illegal, the USPTO will not grant registration of a mark that is directly associated with the plant (eg. strain name), or cannabis infused goods (edibles, tinctures, etc....). However, with "wit and creativity" a lawyer can help find a solution to file an application acceptable by the USPTO. Even then, as with all other trademarks, registration is not guaranteed.

So how do consumers and other businesses know the brand is trademarked? The symbol ® is used when the marking, brand, etc. is registered with the USPTO. Marks that are not registered with the USPTO may still enjoy protection, but must use the ™ symbol.

2. STATE PROTECTION

State trademark registration provides similar protection to that of the federal trademark registry, but at the state level. Registering a trademark with a particular state provides protection to that brand in that state and that state alone. State registration does not provide a brand with nationwide protection. For example, another business with a different product in New York may potentially use the same distinct features and symbols as a business that has a registered trademark on those symbols in California. To be protected in the entire country, a mark needs to be registered in each state separately, or as applied to the Cannabis industry, in each state where cannabis is decriminalized.

Unfortunately, California does not currently register trademarks associated with cannabis products. This is a problem considering that cannabis businesses in California are eyeing what could become a $6.4 billion industry. "Not being able to trademark your brand is a huge setback if you're trying to get capital investment," said Nate Bradley, who lobbies for marijuana sellers as the executive director of California Cannabis Industry Association. "If you're not able to protect what you're asking people to invest in, you're not likely to get investments."[381]

A bill recently introduced in the state legislature would help solve this problem. If passed, AB 64 would create a state-level trademark for California cannabis and cannabis products. This would provide cannabis businesses new legal protections and greater access to cash from investors. Right now, the California Secretary of State has the power to register state-level trademarks, but only for items recognized by federal trademark law. AB 64 would change that by allowing the California Secretary of State to register trademarks for cannabis goods and services despite the fact that federal law does not allow such protection.

3. COMMON LAW PROTECTION

A mark that is **not** registered with the state or USPTO, can still be protected under common law. In theory, at least, the owner of an *un*registered mark has the same rights as the owner of a registered mark, except that the common law rights are limited and confined to the territory where the goods or services are found and/or performed (city, county or even state).

Although the cannabis industry does not enjoy the same treatment as other industries when it comes to registration, CBs are still liable for any trademark infringement they may engage in.

In 2014, this exact issue was the hot topic in the case of *Hershey v. TinctureBelle*, in which a Colorado based producer of cannabis edibles was sued by Hershey's Chocolate for trademark infringement when TinctureBelle made cannabis infused candies that too closely resembled iconic products of the chocolate maker.[382] In a settlement in 2014, TinctureBelle agreed to recall and destroy all edibles that looked like the popular Hershey products, or with names that played on their brands.[383]

B. TRADEMARK LICENSING

Another attractive option for CBs is cannabis trademark licensing. Trademark licensing allows owners of a trademark, trade secret (discussed below), or other proprietary know-how to expand their business by licensing its brand to another company.

The cannabis world of 2015 has expanded beyond flower to lotions, serums, vapes, drinks - you name it. We are now seeing more and more product development, branding and celebrity association that needs protection. Hence the idea of trademark licensing is becoming ever so popular. Medical CBs are expanding to license their trade secret, technology etc., via license agreement or consulting agreement to 3rd party companies and even to out-of-state CBs. Licensing ultimately allows the licensor to monetize its brand. However, we caution that these licensing and consulting agreements have the potential to be complex and very complicated given the state-by-state patchwork of cannabis laws.

C. PATENTS

A patent is a property right for an invention granted by the federal government to the inventor. A federal patent gives the inventor the right to exclude others from making, using, offering for sale, or selling their invention throughout the United States. For example, the inventor of a particular grow light or a vape pen could potentially apply for a patent to protect the invention from being made or sold by others. In sharp contrast to the Trademark Office, the Patent Office has been far more liberal in permitting patents for cannabis-related inventions.

One area of patent law that is gaining interest in the industry is a plant patent. As of right now, growers have been unable to secure patents for their cannabis strains, despite the fact that the Patent Office can issue (and has issued in the past) plant patents to those who have "invent[ed] or discover[ed] and asexually reproduce[d] any distinct and new variety of plant."[384] If a grower succeeds in obtaining a patent for his or her cannabis strain, it would be a great achievement since patents are good for 20 years.

D. COPYRIGHTS

Copyright (and patent) is a Constitutional right. Article I, Section 8 of the US Constitution provides that Congress has the power: *"To promote the Progress of Science and useful Arts, by securing for limited Times to Authors and Inventors the exclusive Right to their respective Writings and Discoveries"*.[385]

Copyright protects "an original work that is created and fixed in a tangible medium of expression." Examples of "tangible medium" would be books, pictures, graphics, text, sound recordings and music videos. Ideas, however, are not protected by copyright law. A copyright is composed of a "bundle of rights," namely, the rights to <u>publicly perform, reproduce</u> and <u>display</u> the copyrighted work and to <u>make derivative work</u>.

Copyright exists from the moment an *original* work is created and "fixed in a tangible medium." Which means, an artist need NOT register their work with the copyright office to enjoy copyright protection. Nevertheless, copyright registration provides benefits not available to unregistered work, most notably, the right to file a lawsuit. Accordingly, it is advisable to register for a copyright especially since registering is relatively simple and inexpensive, and the benefits are great.

Here, the good news is that cannabis' status as illegal under Federal law does not effect a CB's protection thereunder. In other words, any cannabis related original creation can be registered with the Copyright Office because copyright registration is not based on the content of a work, but on the work being in a tangible form.

The duration of a Copyright for works created after 1978, whether registered or not, is the life of the author plus 70 years; for works made for hire it's 95 years. After which time, the work enters the public domain, free for anyone and everyone to use.

E. Trade Secrets

A trade secret, like trademark, copyright or patent is an intangible property. A trade secret is defined as secret business information that gives its owner(s) financial or competitive advantage over other businesses because of its secrecy, and for which the owner of the info has to do what it takes to keep it secret. A good example would be an invention not yet registered with the USPTO. A bad example would be secret juicy information about your boss; that would be gossip.

Since a trade secret has value so long as it is unknown to others, to protect the secrecy, make sure that every single person that comes into contact with the information is made aware that it is secret and confidential, usually by signing a non-disclosure agreement or NDA. If a trade secret is leaked (or "misappropriated"), the injured party must file for injunctive relief in state court. Because there are no federal trade secret laws, relief is only available in state court.

Most States' trade secret laws derive from the Uniform Trade Secret Act ("UTSA"). The UTSA is a model law drafted by legal scholars as an attempt to provide uniformity in the law's application. Many states, including California, have adopted UTSA as a model for their own regulation.

CHAPTER VII.
ANCILLARY BUSINESSES & ADVERTISING

A. DEFINITION OF PARAPHERNALIA

Bags, bongs, pipes – what is paraphernalia and is it illegal? The answer to that question is anything but simple. The idea of paraphernalia is not definite. There is no list of items that are, per se, paraphernalia. Anything used to store or consume a drug is not, on its own, considered paraphernalia, and therefore not inherently illegal either. The idea of what constitutes paraphernalia for purposes of criminal prosecution is a term of art, especially under federal law.

1. FEDERAL LAW: PARAPHERNALIA

Although many states have legalized medical cannabis, the cultivation, distribution or possession of cannabis remains a federal crime under the CSA and subject to federal prison and/or fines depending on the quantity of cannabis distributed, cultivated and/or possessed.

Furthermore, federally, *any item primarily used as a conduit for the intake of illegal drugs* constitutes illegal paraphernalia. It follows that it is illegal to sell drug paraphernalia, use any shipping method to move drug paraphernalia, or to import/export drug paraphernalia. Offenders can face a sentence of up to three years and have all drug paraphernalia confiscated.

The challenge comes in classifying exactly what specific items are "paraphernalia" under the federal definition since no actual material items are expressly stated. Therefore, this area of law is broad, complex and open to interpretation. Case law suggests that the federal definition of paraphernalia encompasses a spectrum of products depending on their intended use. Herein lies the beginning of the gray space of interpretation. Thus, determinations of paraphernalia must be made on a case-by-case basis.

Case in point, Tommy Chong's "Chong Bong". In 2003, the federal government was involved in "Operation Pipe Dreams," a national investigation of drug paraphernalia distributors. Amongst those arrested for distribution was Tommy Chong, famous in the 1970s for playing perpetually stoned stooges in movies and later branding and selling "Chong Bongs" through his company, Nice Dreams. This is where the art of interpretation is clearly depicted under the law. It was argued that the bongs were works of art and not for drug use because many of the pipes were too expensive for casual use, and some had been showcased at an art exhibit.

The opposing argument made by the Assistant U.S. Attorney was that despite these pieces used as "art" Chong's appearance in drug-related movies, and iconic status as a glamorizing the illegal use of cannabis was relevant to his "paraphernalia" business because buyers associate his name with illegal drugs. In this case, it was Chong's status as a cannabis icon that insinuated that "Chong Bongs" were intended to be used for the illegal use of cannabis. It is important to note that this legal issue was never actually litigated on its merits in trial, because Chong plead to the charges without the court making a legal determination that "Chong Bongs" were in fact paraphernalia as defined under the law.

The bottom line is that cannabis products and accessories function on a sliding spectrum in which the same product can be determined to be paraphernalia or not based on how the product is promoted, who promotes it, its name, etc... The more the product is surrounded by cannabis, pushed towards cannabis, and the more it is promoted as a cannabis product, the more it fits the definition of paraphernalia as in the Chong case. Again, though, the Chong case only operates as a cautionary tale, since there was no ultimate ruling as to whether the items were indeed "paraphernalia".

2. CALIFORNIA LAW: PARAPHERNALIA

California courts have ruled that, although businesses can still be subject to Federal law while in operating in California, this state has its own laws on paraphernalia that businesses must comply with. While federal law defines paraphernalia under the CSA, California law defines paraphernalia under Health and Safety Code §11364.5. "Paraphernalia" refers to a variety of items that are used for *illegally smoking, or consuming controlled substances or narcotic drugs*. California law, unlike federal law, provides a list of products that can be considered to be "drug paraphernalia" -- water pipes, smoking masks, roach clips, chamber pipes, electronic pipes, bongs, ice pipes etc...[386]

Similar to federal law, drug paraphernalia is not just defined by the product itself. Things like product advertising, product instructions and promotion of the function of the product (all discussed below) are used to determine its status as paraphernalia.

3. ADVERTISING AND PRIMARY INTENT OF THE PRODUCT

An important aspect of advertising is the promotion of the intent of use of the product. Keep in mind that, regardless if a product is promoted as "primarily intended . . . for use" with a controlled substance, evidence must also show the distributor *knew* that the item was likely to be used with illegal drugs.[387] Additionally, a distributor cannot be found criminally liable based on the intentions of the customer.[388] Distributors must intend the product for use with drugs in order for it to be drug paraphernalia.[389]

a. CALIFORNIA VS. FEDERAL LAW

It is important to note the big distinction here, and that is – medical cannabis is legal in California. Even though California's paraphernalia law, on its face, is more definite, a product determined to be paraphernalia may not be subject to prosecution under California drug laws due to the fact that the use of cannabis, medically, is legal. This should not be taken as an invite to freely and unboundedly associate products with cannabis. There is an indistinct boundary between medical and recreational use. However, the extent to which advertising crosses the line from medical to recreational promotion is yet to be concretely determined. It must be kept in mind that, even though recreational language will be voted on in November 2016, recreational cannabis use is still illegal. Therefore, in California, accessories and cannabis associated products also are subject to interpretation as to how much the envelope can really be pushed without a definite point of illegality.

4. ITEMS WITH NO LAWFUL USE = PARAPHERNALIA

It is important to keep in mind that some items have *no other use than with controlled substances*. In this case these items constitute drug paraphernalia regardless of the knowledge or intent of the seller that the product be used with an illegal drug or any negating surrounding circumstances. In California, possession of drug paraphernalia is a misdemeanor, punishable by up to six months in a county jail and a maximum $1,000 fine.[390]

5. LAWFUL SALES OF SMOKING PRODUCTS

Anything defined as drug paraphernalia cannot be legally sold using a mail service or any interstate commerce.[391] However, items that can be shown as intended for tobacco use do not violate the CSA and are thus not subject to punishment under §863. In line with that thought, online retailers and head shops are not actually selling drug paraphernalia. They are selling water pipes, glass tobacco novelty pipes and little, plastic jewelry bags with strict rules banning references to illegal drugs by employees, marketing material, advertisements and customers.

These businesses may legally sell these items for the same reason that it was perfectly legal to buy and sell wine glasses and beer mugs during America's Alcohol Prohibition. You could use wine glasses for grape juice, you could use beer mugs for root beer floats, and you can use a smoking device for tobacco. Unfortunately, there is a larger risk associated with shipping outside California state lines. This exposes business operations to federal jurisdiction and liability under §863 if it is determined that the merchandise being shipped fits the federal definition of paraphernalia.

B. INTERSTATE ADVERTISING & DISCLAIMERS

Businesses producing consumption and storage products (bongs, pipes, etc…) are an ancillary business model because they do not touch the flower or any derivative thereof. Thus, these products can be sold in any state in the United States, regardless of that state's particular position on cannabis law. These businesses, however, must take particular care in their interstate advertising because an advertisement in California demonstrating an "intended use with controlled substances" could also potentially be used in Kansas (where cannabis is not legal), and thus expose the company and its officers to criminal liability.

Therefore, advertisers should err on the side of caution across the board for all states in which you intend to have substantial contacts of business. For example, even if cannabis is legal in California (and in various states across the U.S.), the same advertising message is disseminated to all states in which you do business. Thus, the same message must be appropriate for a state like Kansas (where cannabis is not legal) and for Oregon (where cannabis is both medically and recreationally legal). Things like 18+ disclaimers and adult content (as opposed to appealing to children) are a bit more conducive to national adverting campaigns for these ancillary products.

C. NEW ADVERTISING RULES UNDER THE AUMA

Under the AUMA, there will be new advertising restrictions for cannabis businesses licensed by the state. Effective January 1, 2018, the following restrictions will apply to all licensees:

- All advertising and marketing shall clearly identify the licensee responsible for its content;
- Any advertising or marketing placed in broadcast, cable, radio, print and digital communications shall only be displayed where at least 71.6% of the audience is reasonably expected to be age 21+;[392]
- Any advertising or marketing that involves direct communication or dialogue from a licensee to a prospective

customer shall utilized a method to verify that the recipient is age 21+;
- All advertising shall be truthful and "appropriately substantiated";
- No licensee shall advertise or market in a manner that is false, untrue or tends to create a misleading impression;
- No licensee shall publish or disseminate advertising or marketing material that contains any statement about a brand or a product that is inconsistent with the product's labeling;
- No licensee shall publish or disseminate advertising or marketing material which tends to create the impression that the cannabis originated in a particular place or region, unless the product label states that it is the product's appellation of origin;
- No licensee shall advertise or market on a billboard located on an Interstate Highway or State Highway which crosses the border of any other state;
- No licensee shall advertise in a manner intended to encourage persons under the age of 21 to consume cannabis;
- No licensee shall advertise in a manner known to appeal primarily to persons under the age of 21 (i.e., symbols, language, music gestures, cartoon characters, etc.);
- No licensee shall advertise cannabis on an advertising sign within 1,000 feet of a day care center, school, playground or youth center;
- No licensee shall give away any cannabis or cannabis products as part of a business promotion or other commercial activity;
- No licensee shall publish or disseminate advertising or marketing material that contains any health-related statement that is untrue or tends to create a misleading impression as the effects on health of cannabis consumption.

Currently, the above restrictions under the AUMA will only apply to *licensees*. However, there is a pending state bill – AB 64 – that, if passed, would make these restrictions applicable to all cannabis-related entities regardless of whether they have or need a state license. AB 64 would also extend the AUMA's prohibition on billboards by banning cannabis-related billboards on all highways in California – not just the highways that cross state borders.

D. ADVERTISING ONLINE & POTENTIAL CONFLICTS

Social media companies generally avoid selling ad space to businesses in the cannabis industry. Even (seemingly progressive) tech companies take a hard stance on cannabis marketing. Google and Facebook, for example, forbid the advertising of cannabis (and related products) on their platforms. And they make no exceptions for states that have legalized recreational cannabis. Below is a detailed account of search engines' and social media outlets' policies on cannabis advertisement and promotion.

1. FACEBOOK

According to the Facebook Advertising Guidelines, "Ads may not promote or facilitate the sale or consumption of illegal or recreational drugs, tobacco products, or drug or tobacco paraphernalia." A spokesman for Facebook made the statement that Facebook does allow ads to promote advocacy and the legalization of cannabis, however the ads cannot promote or facilitate the sale or consumption of illegal or recreational drugs. Facebook strictly prohibits the promotion of the sale and use of the drug itself. Promoting advocacy or the legalization of the drug is the type of content Facebook does not want to censor through ads, and is widely considered different than something promoting the actual drug itself. Facebook often revisits their policies, but currently does not have a plan to change this policy.

2. TWITTER

Twitter has a similar drug policy prohibiting the promotion of "drugs and drug paraphernalia globally." The Twitter policy applies to illegal drugs that they define as a "substance sold to induce unnatural euphoria, unnatural highs or lows, psychoactive effects, or altered reality," and all accessories related to drug use like bongs or pipes and even products or services that feature access to drugs like a dispensary directory.

3. INSTAGRAM

Instagram, which is owned by Facebook, also has strict regulations around cannabis marketing, and recently came under fire for suspending accounts belonging to businesses in the cannabis industry. Instagram says they only review inappropriate behavior on accounts reported by other users, so it is impossible for the company to stop everyone who uploads photos of cannabis. Instagram, at least in theory, is OK with people who enjoy recreational cannabis, as long as they don't try to use the platform to sell it. However, content moderators are paid to troll photos posted to

Instagram each day and continue to remove cannabis-related accounts that cross that line.

4. APP STORE

Apple, on the other hand, individually reviews each app (and subsequent update) before it makes it to the App Store, and so has communicated to developers a slightly firmer policy on what flies and what doesn't. Apple claims the most important factor when determining which apps can stay in its App Store is whether the features in the app promote only medical, not recreational, use.

5. GOOGLE

Google's official AdWords policy doesn't allow the "promotion of illegal drugs, legal or synthetic highs, herbal drugs, chemicals and compounds with psychoactive effects, drug paraphernalia, or aids to pass drug tests." Google specifically cites cannabis as one of the several drugs for which it does not allow ads and confirms that the company hasn't made any changes to the current policy, but that updates and reviews of their AdWords policies are frequent.

Currently, Google does not allow:

1. Products or services marketed as facilitating recreational drug use;
2. Promotion of instructional content about producing, purchasing, or using recreational drugs;
3. Tobacco or any products containing tobacco;
4. Products that form a component part of a tobacco product, as well as products and services that directly facilitate or promote tobacco consumption. Examples: Rolling papers, pipes, tobacco filters, hookah lounges, cigar bars.

These ad policies aren't exclusive to Google, Facebook and Twitter -- other major search engines, like Bing and Yahoo, also have strict bans for drug-related advertisements on their websites and specifically site "recreational" drugs as part of the ban. Posting photos of cannabis or promoting its use/ possessing cannabis for recreational use on the internet, can end up feeling like driving over the speed limit: Nearly everyone does it, but only a select few get pulled over and fined.

CHAPTER VIII.
KNOW YOUR RIGHTS & ENCOUNTERS WITH LAW ENFORCEMENT

Even qualified patients or valid operators of legal collectives, can be subject to a criminal investigation and a law enforcement interrogation. Accordingly, anybody who uses medical cannabis and/or is involved with a CB should be prepared in advance to protect his or her rights during a law enforcement encounter. Although arrest in some situations may be unavoidable, by asserting your rights, you ensure the best defense possible.

1. ASSERT YOUR RIGHT TO REMAIN SILENT

During an investigation or interrogation, police officers are trained to gather incriminating evidence. Although it may not look like the bright room interrogation shown on television, anything said during a "casual encounter" or a "friendly conversation," is admissible in a court of law. Therefore, in most situations, it is not advisable to volunteer any information, rather it's better to assert your right to remain silent. During a law enforcement encounter that involves a cop asking you questions or trying to engage you in conversation, ask: *"Am I being detained or arrested?"* If you are not being detained or arrested, walk away. If you are being detained or arrested, the only things you should say to them are these magic words: *"I do not consent to a search. I wish to remain silent and want a lawyer."* [Note: In order to invoke your right to remain silent, you must actually say the words "I wish to remain silent." Ironically, silence does not count.]

2. WHAT TO DO IF YOU ARE BEING DETAINED

Police can only **detain** a suspect if they have **reasonable suspicion** to believe that he or she has committed, are committing, or about to commit a crime. Reasonable suspicion must be more than a mere hunch. The police must be able to put their reasonable suspicion into words. For example, if an officer stops an individual, it's not enough for the officer to say, "He looked like he was up to something." The officer has to be more specific, giving details such as, "He was sitting in the driver's seat of the car and there was smoke emitting from the car windows that smelled like the strong odor of cannabis."

A detention is supposed to only last a short time and should not involve changing location, such as going to the local precinct. Though not as serious as an arrest, **a detention still means that a person is not free to leave.**

During a detention, an officer may pat a suspect down and go into his or her bag to make sure that you don't have any weapons. This is called a *Terry* stop. Officers are not supposed to go into a suspect's pockets unless they feel a weapon while patting them down. An officer might order a suspect to empty their pockets and the natural inclination might be to obey the command. However, know, you are within your rights to refuse. If you do empty your pockets, it could be considered consent and anything they find in your pockets may be used against you.

If an officer is asking you questions you are not comfortable answering, you may ask: **"Am I being detained or arrested?"** If you are not being detained or arrested, walk away. If you are being detained or arrested, the only things you should say to them are these magic words: ***"I do not consent to a search. I wish to remain silent and want a lawyer."*** You can provide them with a copy of your medical cannabis recommendation, but say nothing else. Remain silent.

3. WHAT TO DO IF YOU ARE BEING ARRESTED

A detention can very easily turn into an arrest. Officers can make an arrest only if they have probable cause to believe that the suspect was involved in a crime. Probable cause is more than reasonable suspicion, but less than the actual level of proof required to convict a person at trial.

Once a suspect is arrested, officers can strip-search him or her and go through their car and any belongings. By law, an officer strip-searching a suspect must be the same gender as the suspect.

After arrest and before interrogation the law requires the police to advise a suspect of his or her *Miranda* rights. That means that, if the police are asking a suspect questions but have not initiated an arrest or the person is not "in custody", then the law does not require a *Miranda* advisement. More importantly, if the police arrest a suspect and do not initiate questions, they don't have to give a Miranda advisement, but if *the suspect* goes ahead and makes "spontaneous incriminating statements", those can be used as evidence in a court of law. For example, Johnny Walker is arrested for a DUI, but not interrogated nor read his rights. While in the back of the police car, he starts screaming at the police, "give me a break, it's Friday and the whiskey was flowing, I had to take advantage!" Because Johnny spontaneously uttered those statements and he was not prompted by police questioning, those statements are admissible against him in court. If you realize that you accidentally started answering questions, re-invoke your rights by saying the magic words: ***"I wish to remain silent and want a lawyer."*** Then stop talking.

4. WHAT TO DO IF YOU ARE BEING QUESTIONED

Police Officers are trained to interrogate effectively during an investigation and gather information out of a suspect. That is their job. They are legally allowed to lie when they're investigating, and they are trained to manipulate the subject. To ensure you do not say the wrong thing, it is advisable that you assert your rights and utter the magic words, **"I am going to remain silent. I want to see a lawyer."**

Here are some examples of lies that an officer is authorized to tell a suspect to gather incriminating evidence:

"You're not a suspect—just help us understand what happened here and then you can go."

"If you don't answer my questions, I'll have no choice but to arrest you. Do you want to go to jail?"

"If you don't answer my questions, I'm going to charge you with resisting arrest."

"All of your friends have cooperated, and we let them go home. You're the only one left."

Do not fall for these types of sneaky tricks. Again, if you say anything to the cops after invoking your rights, it is considered a waiver of your rights and anything you say can be used against you. If you forget your decision to remain silent and start talking to the officers, you can and should re-invoke your rights by saying the magic words: *"I wish to remain silent and want a lawyer."*

5. WHAT TO DO IF YOU ARE BEING SEARCHED

Any time the police try to conduct a search of your person or property, say: *"I do not consent to this search."* Although this may not stop them, your lawyer may be able to get evidence thrown out in court later. This is important because you might have something on you that is technically illegal like a pocketknife that's too long. Although we encourage you to assert your constitutional rights, NEVER never physically resist when an officer tries to conduct a search because you could get hurt and charged with assault.

Furthermore, any time officers try to search something *connected* to you, say: *"I do not consent to this search."* Keep saying it, loudly enough for witnesses to hear. This is true for your body, your car, your house, your garage – anything. It's also true if the cops have a search warrant. There might be a technical problem with the warrant that only comes up later.

Saying *"I do not consent to this search"* may seem a little formal and awkward, but it helps keep the police from claiming you gave them permission to search. Many defendants have been at a disadvantage in court because they are too polite or too intimidated to clearly refuse the search, or they were not aware that they do not have to consent. For example, if you said, "I'd rather you didn't search," it could be argued that you were reluctantly allowing the police to proceed.

6. What to Do if You Are Stopped in Your Car

Stop the car in a safe place as quickly as possible. Turn off the car, turn on the internal light, open the window part way and place your hands on the wheel. Do not make sudden movements.

Upon request, show the officer your driver's license, registration and proof of insurance. If a cop asks to step out of the car, you must do so.

If an officer asks to look inside your car, say the magic words: *"I do not consent to this search."* If the officer has probable cause to believe that your car contains evidence of a crime, your car can be searched without your consent. Nevertheless, you do not have to (nor should you) make things easier for him/her. By giving the cop consent to search your car, it eliminates the need for him or her to show later in court that he/she had probable cause to search your car. By refusing to give your consent, your lawyer will be better equipped to challenge the evidence obtained during the warrantless search of your car.

Both drivers and passengers have the right to remain silent. Anything you say to the police can be used against you and your friends. Whenever the cops ask you anything besides your name and address, it's safest to say: *"I am going to remain silent. I want to see a lawyer."* The cops are then legally required to stop questioning you. They probably won't, so just keep repeating it. Say it loud enough for witnesses to hear.

7. What to Do if an Officer Shows Up at Your Door

If the police show up at your home or business, you do not have to open the door or let them in unless they have a warrant. If they try to invite themselves in, stand in the doorway and refuse to give them permission by saying: *"I do not consent to your entering."* You do not need to speak to them or answer their questions. If you do choose to speak to the officer, step outside and close the door.

You should never consent to a search. If the cops try to search your home or business, say the magic words: ***"I do not consent to a search. I wish to remain silent and want a lawyer."*** This may not stop them from forcing their way in and searching anyway, but if they search you illegally, they probably won't be able to use the evidence against you in court. You have nothing to lose from refusing to consent to a search and lots to gain. Do not physically resist officers when they are trying to search, because you could get hurt and/or charged with resisting arrest or assault and battery. Just keep repeating the magic words: ***"I do not consent to a search. I wish to remain silent and want a lawyer."***

8. WHAT TO DO IF AN OFFICER HAS A SEARCH WARRANT

If the police show up at your home or business with a search warrant, ask to see it. Make sure it is signed and has your correct address and a reasonably recent date (not more than a couple of weeks old). If you point out a flaw in a warrant, the police may ask you to let them in anyway. Just say no. (The police may threaten to tear your home or business apart if they have to go back and get another warrant, but the search will be destructive anyway, even if you let the police in immediately.) Whether or not the police have a warrant which looks perfectly okay to you, still say the magic words: ***"I do not consent to a search. I wish to remain silent and want a lawyer."*** It's possible that there's a hidden flaw in the warrant which your lawyer may be able to find later on.

Do not physically resist the police when they are executing their search warrant because you're likely to get hurt and charged with resisting or assaulting an officer. Stand aside and let the police through the door and remain silent throughout the search.

APPENDIX

APPENDIX I

FEDERAL LAW

Ogden Memo - Memorandum For Selected United States Attorneys: Investigations And Prosecutions In States. Authorizing The Use Of Medical Marijuana

October 19, 2009

MEMORANDUM FOR SELECTED UNITED STATES ATTORNEYS

FROM: David W. Ogden, Deputy Attorney General

SUBJECT: Investigations and Prosecutions in States <u>Authorizing the Medical Use of Marijuana</u>

This memorandum provides clarification and guidance to federal prosecutors in States that have enacted laws authorizing the medical use of marijuana. These laws vary in their substantive provisions and in the extent of state regulatory oversight, both among the enacting States and among local jurisdictions within those States. Rather than developing different guidelines for every possible variant of state and local law, this memorandum provides uniform guidance to focus federal investigations and prosecutions in these States on core federal enforcement priorities.

The Department of Justice is committed to the enforcement of the Controlled Substances Act in all States. Congress has determined that marijuana is a dangerous drug, and the illegal distribution and sale of marijuana is a serious crime and provides a significant source of revenue to large-scale criminal enterprises, gangs, and cartels. One timely example underscores the importance of our efforts to prosecute significant marijuana traffickers: marijuana distribution in the United States remains the single largest source of revenue for the Mexican cartels.

The Department is also committed to making efficient and rational use of its limited investigative and prosecutorial resources. In general, United States Attorneys are vested with "plenary authority with regard to federal criminal matters" within their districts. USAM 9-2.001. In exercising this authority, United States Attorneys are "invested by statute and delegation from the Attorney General with the broadest discretion in the exercise of such authority." *Id.* This authority should, of course, be exercised consistent with Department priorities and guidance.

The prosecution of significant traffickers of illegal drugs, including marijuana, and the disruption of illegal drug manufacturing and trafficking networks continues to be a core priority in the Department's efforts against narcotics and dangerous drugs, and the Department's investigative and prosecutorial resources should be directed towards these objectives. As a general matter, pursuit of these priorities should not focus federal resources in your States on individuals whose actions are in clear and unambiguous compliance with existing state laws providing for the medical use of marijuana. For example, prosecution of individuals with cancer or other serious illnesses who use marijuana as part of a recommended treatment regimen consistent with applicable state law, or those caregivers in clear and unambiguous compliance with existing state law who provide such individuals with marijuana, is unlikely to be an efficient use of limited federal resources.

On the other hand, prosecution of commercial enterprises that unlawfully market and sell marijuana for profit continues to be an enforcement priority of the Department. To be sure, claims of compliance with state or local law may mask operations inconsistent with the terms, conditions, or purposes of those laws, and federal law enforcement should not be deterred by such assertions when otherwise pursuing the Department's core enforcement priorities.

Typically, when any of the following characteristics is present, the conduct will not be in clear and unambiguous compliance with applicable state law and may indicate illegal drug trafficking activity of potential federal interest:

- unlawful possession or unlawful use of firearms;
- violence;
- sales to minors;
- financial and marketing activities inconsistent with the terms, conditions, or purposes of state law, including evidence of money laundering activity and/or financial gains or excessive amounts of cash inconsistent with purported compliance with state or local law;
- amounts of marijuana inconsistent with purported compliance with state or local law;
- illegal possession or sale of other controlled substances; or
- ties to other criminal enterprises.

Of course, no State can authorize violations of federal law, and the list of factors above is not intended to describe exhaustively when a federal prosecution may be warranted. Accordingly, in prosecutions under the Controlled Substances Act, federal prosecutors are not expected to charge, prove, or otherwise establish any state law violations. Indeed, this memorandum does not alter in any way the Department's authority to enforce federal law, including laws prohibiting the manufacture, production, distribution, possession, or use of marijuana on federal property. This guidance regarding resource allocation does not "legalize" marijuana or provide a legal defense to a violation of federal law, nor is it intended to create any privileges, benefits, or rights, substantive or procedural, enforceable by any individual, party or witness in any administrative, civil, or criminal matter. Nor does clear and unambiguous compliance with state law or the absence of one or all of the above factors create a legal defense to a violation of the Controlled Substances Act. Rather, this memorandum is intended solely as a guide to the exercise of investigative and prosecutorial discretion.

Finally, nothing herein precludes investigation or prosecution where there is a reasonable basis to believe that compliance with state law is being invoked as a pretext for the production or distribution of marijuana for purposes not authorized by state law. Nor does this guidance preclude investigation or prosecution, even when there is clear and unambiguous compliance with existing state law, in particular circumstances where investigation or prosecution otherwise serves important federal interests.

Your offices should continue to review marijuana cases for prosecution on a case-by-case basis, consistent with the guidance on resource allocation and federal priorities set forth herein, the consideration of requests for federal assistance from state and local law enforcement authorities, and the Principles of Federal Prosecution.

cc: All United States Attorneys

Lanny A. Breuer
Assistant Attorney General Criminal Division

B. Todd Jones
United States Attorney
District of Minnesota
Chair, Attorney General's Advisory Committee

Michele M. Leonhart
Acting Administrator
Drug Enforcement Administration

H. Marshall Jarrett
Director
Executive Office for United States Attorneys

Kevin L. Perkins
Assistant Director
Criminal Investigative Division
Federal Bureau of Investigation

Cole Memo - Memorandum For Selected United States Attorneys: Guidance Involving Marijuana Enforcement

MEMORANDUM FOR ALL UNITED STATES ATTORNEYS

FROM: James M. Cole,
Deputy Attorney General

SUBJECT: Guidance Regarding Marijuana Enforcement

In October 2009 and June 2011, the Department issued guidance to federal prosecutors concerning marijuana enforcement under the Controlled Substances Act (CSA). This memorandum updates that guidance in light of state ballot initiatives that legalize under state law the possession of small amounts of marijuana and provide for the regulation of marijuana production, processing, and sale. The guidance set forth herein applies to all federal enforcement activity, including civil enforcement and criminal investigations and prosecutions, concerning marijuana in all states.

As the Department noted in its previous guidance, Congress has determined that marijuana is a dangerous drug and that the illegal distribution and sale of marijuana is a serious crime that provides a significant source of revenue to large-scale criminal enterprises, gangs, and cartels. The Department of Justice is committed to enforcement of the CSA consistent with those determinations. The Department is also committed to using its limited investigative and prosecutorial resources to address the most significant threats in the most effective, consistent, and rational way. In furtherance of those objectives, as several states enacted laws relating to the use of marijuana for medical purposes, the Department in recent years has focused its efforts on certain enforcement priorities that are particularly important to the federal government:

• Preventing the distribution of marijuana to minors;

• Preventing revenue from the sale of marijuana from going to criminal enterprises, gangs, and cartels;

• Preventing the diversion of marijuana from states where it is legal under state law in some form to other states;

• Preventing state-authorized marijuana activity from being used as a cover or pretext for the trafficking of other illegal drugs or other illegal activity;

- Preventing violence and the use of firearms in the cultivation and distribution of marijuana;

- Preventing drugged driving and the exacerbation of other adverse public health consequences associated with marijuana use;

- Preventing the growing of marijuana on public lands and the attendant public safety and environmental dangers posed by marijuana production on public lands; and

- Preventing marijuana possession or use on federal property.

These priorities will continue to guide the Department's enforcement of the CSA against marijuana-related conduct. Thus, this memorandum serves as guidance to Department attorneys and law enforcement to focus their enforcement resources and efforts, including prosecution, on persons or organizations whose conduct interferes with anyone or more of these priorities, regardless of state law.[1]

Outside of these enforcement priorities, the federal government has traditionally relied on states and local law enforcement agencies to address marijuana activity through enforcement of their own narcotics laws. For example, the Department of Justice has not historically devoted resources to prosecuting individuals whose conduct is limited to possession of small amounts of marijuana for personal use on private property. Instead, the Department has left such lower-level or localized activity to state and local authorities and has stepped in to enforce the CSA only when the use, possession, cultivation, or distribution of marijuana has threatened to cause one of the harms identified above.

The enactment of state laws that endeavor to authorize marijuana production, distribution, and possession by establishing a regulatory scheme for these purposes affects this traditional joint federal-state approach to narcotics enforcement. The Department's guidance in this memorandum rests on its expectation that states and local governments that have enacted laws authorizing marijuana-related conduct will implement strong and effective regulatory and enforcement systems that will address the threat those state laws could pose to public safety, public health, and

---

[1] These enforcement priorities are listed in general terms; each encompasses a variety of conduct that

other law enforcement interests. A system adequate to that task must not only contain robust controls and procedures on paper; it must also be effective in practice. Jurisdictions that have implemented systems that provide for regulation of marijuana activity must provide the necessary resources and demonstrate the willingness to enforce their laws and regulations in a manner that ensures they do not undermine federal enforcement priorities.

In jurisdictions that have enacted laws legalizing marijuana in some form and that have also implemented strong and effective regulatory and enforcement systems to control the cultivation, distribution, sale, and possession of marijuana, conduct in compliance with those laws and regulations is less likely to threaten the federal priorities set forth above. Indeed, a robust system may affirmatively address those priorities by, for example, implementing effective measures to prevent diversion of marijuana outside of the regulated system and to other states, prohibiting access to marijuana by minors, and replacing an illicit marijuana trade that funds criminal enterprises with a tightly regulated market in which revenues are tracked and accounted for. In those circumstances, consistent with the traditional allocation of federal-state efforts in this area, enforcement of state law by state and local law enforcement and regulatory bodies should remain the primary means of addressing marijuana-related activity. If state enforcement efforts are not sufficiently robust to protect against the harms set forth above, the federal government may seek to challenge the regulatory structure itself in addition to continuing to bring individual enforcement actions, including criminal prosecutions, focused on those harms.

The Department's previous memoranda specifically addressed the exercise of prosecutorial discretion in states with laws authorizing marijuana cultivation and distribution for medical use. In those contexts, the Department advised that it likely was not an efficient use of federal resources to focus enforcement efforts on seriously ill individuals, or on their individual caregivers. In doing so, the previous guidance drew a distinction between the seriously ill and their caregivers, on the one hand, and large-scale, for-profit commercial enterprises, on the other, and advised that the latter continued to be appropriate targets for federal enforcement and prosecution. In drawing this distinction, the Department relied on the common-sense judgment that the size of a marijuana operation was a reasonable proxy for assessing whether marijuana trafficking implicates the federal enforcement priorities set forth above.

As explained above, however, both the existence of a strong and effective state regulatory system, and an operation's compliance with such a system, may allay the threat that an operation's size poses to federal enforcement interests. Accordingly, in exercising prosecutorial discretion, prosecutors should not consider the size or commercial nature of a marijuana operation alone as a proxy for assessing whether marijuana trafficking implicates the Department's enforcement priorities listed above. Rather, prosecutors should continue to review marijuana cases on a case-by-case basis and weigh all available information and evidence, including, but not limited to, whether the operation is demonstrably in compliance with a strong and effective state regulatory system. A marijuana operation's large scale or for-profit nature may be a relevant consideration for assessing the extent to which it undermines a particular federal enforcement priority. The primary question in all cases - and in all jurisdictions – should be whether the conduct at issue implicates one or more of the enforcement priorities listed above.

As with the Department's previous statements on this subject, this memorandum is intended solely as a guide to the exercise of investigative and prosecutorial discretion. This memorandum does not alter in any way the Department's authority to enforce federal law, including federal laws relating to marijuana, regardless of state law. Neither the guidance herein nor any state or local law provides a legal defense to a violation of federal law, including any civil or criminal violation of the CSA. Even in jurisdictions with strong and effective regulatory systems, evidence that particular conduct threatens federal priorities will subject that person or entity to federal enforcement action, based on the circumstances. This memorandum is not intended to, does not, and may not be relied upon to create any rights, substantive or procedural, enforceable at law by any party in any matter civil or criminal. It applies prospectively to the exercise of prosecutorial discretion in future cases and does not provide defendants or subjects of enforcement action with a basis for reconsideration of any pending civil action or criminal prosecution. Finally, nothing herein precludes investigation or prosecution, even in the absence of anyone of the factors listed above, in particular circumstances where investigation and prosecution otherwise serves an important federal interest.

cc: Mythili Raman
       Acting Assistant Attorney General, Criminal Division

       Loretta E. Lynch
       United States Attorney
       Eastern District of New York
       Chair, Attorney General's Advisory Committee

       Michele M. Leonhart
       Administrator
       Drug Enforcement Administration

H. Marshall Jarrett
Director
Executive Office for United States Attorneys

Ronald T. Rosko
Assistant Director
Criminal Investigative Division
Federal Bureau of Investigation

Guidelines For Federal Prosecution Of Marijuana Related Cases - Department Of Justice Memorandum To DEA, HIDTA, And Federal Task Force Partners In California

Department of Justice Memorandum

To: DEA, HIDTA, Federal task force partners in California for internal law enforcement use only.
Not for public use or circulation

From: California United States Attorneys

This memorandum outlines factors that all four California U.S. Attorneys Offices (the USAOs) agree may render a particular marijuana case suitable for federal prosecution. Identification of these factors is intended to assist federal, state and local law enforcement agencies in determining whether a particular marijuana case has significant potential for federal prosecution and conducting investigations in a manner that develops the best evidence to support federal prosecution (Footnote 1). The USAOS will consider for federal prosecution cases investigated by federal, state or local law enforcement agencies that implicate federal interests as reflected in the factors. Cases investigated by federal agencies will generally be given priority over cases adopted from state or local investigations. The factors listed below are relevant to the USAOs consideration of whether a marijuana case should be prosecuted federally but the presence or absence of one or more of the factors will not guarantee or preclude federal prosecution in any case. In general the federal interest will be greater in prosecuting leaders and organizers of the criminal activity as opposed to lower level workers.

The memorandum is intended as prospective guidance only, is not intended to have the force of law and is not intended to, does not, and may not be relied on to create any right, privilege or benefit, substantive or procedural, enforceable by any person or entity against any type of the USAOs, DOJ or the United States.

1) Domestic distribution cases.

Federal prosecution of a case of domestic distribution of marijuana should generally involve at least 200 or more kilograms of marijuana and also include additional factors that reflect a clear federal interest in prosecution (Footnote 2—This guidance for domestic distribution cases does not apply to cases involving distribution within or smuggling into a federal prison.18 USC 1791). Typically the more marijuana above 200 kilograms the better the potential for federal prosecution. Domestic distribution cases involving quantities of marijuana below 200kilograms should demonstrate an especially strong federal interest or should not be prosecuted with marijuana distribution as the sole federal charge. Set forth below is a non-exhaustive list of factors that USAOs believe indicate a federal interest in a domestic distribution case.

*Distribution by an individual or organization with provable ties to an international drug cartel or a poly-drug trafficking organization.

*Distribution of significant quantities to persons or organizations outside California.

*Distribution by individuals with significant prior criminal histories.

*Distribution by individuals with provable ties to a street gang that engages in drug trafficking involving violent conduct.

*Distribution for the purpose of funding other criminal activities.

*Distribution near protected locations or involving underage or vulnerable people (e.g. in violation of 21 USC 859 persons under 21, 860 near schools, playground and colleges, 861 employment of persons under 18).

*Distribution involving the use or presence of firearms or other dangerous weapons including cases that would support charges under 18 USC 924c.

*Distribution generating significant profits that are used or concealed in ways that would support charges of federal financial crimes such as tax evasion, money laundering or structuring. Note: Generation of significant profits alone generally will not be viewed as a factor weighing in favor of federal prosecution.

*Distribution in conjunction with other federal crimes involving violence or intimidation.

2. Cultivation cases.

Federal prosecution of a marijuana case involving cultivation on non-federal or non-tribal land, indoor or outdoor, should generally involve at least 1,000 marijuana plants so that the quantity necessary to trigger the ten-year mandatory minimum sentence can be clearly proven and also include additional factors that reflect a clear federal interest in prosecution. Typically, the more marijuana above 1,000 plants, the better the potential for federal prosecution. Non-federal or non-tribal land cases involving quantities below 1,000 plants should demonstrate an especially strong federal interest or should not be prosecuted with marijuana cultivation as the sole federal charge. Federal prosecution of a marijuana case involving cultivation on federal or tribal land should generally involve at least 500 marijuana plants and also include additional factors that reflect a clear federal interest in prosecution. Cases on federal or tribal land involving quantities below 500 plants will be considered if they demonstrate a strong federal interest, if the cultivation has caused significant damage to federal or tribal lands or has occurred in an area of exclusive federal jurisdiction (Footnote 3-- The USAOs will consider the totality of circumstances with respect to all marijuana plant quantities in these guidelines. For example, the presence of especially mature, large or robust plants will generally weigh in favor of prosecution while the presence of seedlings or immature plants will generally weigh against prosecution). Set forth below is a non-exhaustive list of factors that the USAOs believe indicate a federal interest that may justify federal prosecution of a marijuana case involving cultivation whether on federal, tribal or other lands.

*Cultivation causing significant environmental damage, risk to human health or interference with particularly sensitive land or significant recreational interests, ie damage to wilderness area or wildlife, danger to innocent families using a recreation area or use of toxic or dangerous chemicals.

*Cultivation by an individual or organization with provable ties to an international drug cartel or poly-drug trafficking organization.

*Cultivation of significant quantities on behalf or persons or organizations outside California.

*Cultivation by individuals with significant prior criminal histories.

*Cultivation by individuals with provable ties to a street gang that engages in drug trafficking involving violent conduct.

*Cultivation for the purpose of funding other criminal activities.

*Cultivation near protected locations or involving under-age or vulnerable people (eg, in violation…

*Cultivation involving the use or presence of fire-arms, booby traps or other dangerous weapons including cases that would support charges under 18 USC 924c.

*Cultivation generating significant profits that are used or concealed in ways that would support charges for federal financial crimes such as tax evasion, money laundering or structuring.. Note—generation of significant profits alone will not be viewed as a factor weighing in favor of federal prosecution.

*Cultivation in conjunction with other federal crimes involving violence or intimidation

3. Dispensary cases.

Given California state law, prosecution of marijuana stores or "dispensaries" purporting to comply with state law face additional challenges. Federal prosecution of a case involving a marijuana store should generally involve a) provable sales through seizures or records of over 200 kilograms or 1000 plants per year. b) sales clearly in violation of state law, eg sales to persons without legitimate doctors' recommendations, side-sales occurring outside of the store or shipping to persons outside of California (Note—selling for profit, though a violation of state law, typically alone will not alone satisfy this requirement), and c) additional factors that reflect a federal interest in prosecution. Set forth below is a non-exhaustive list of such additional factors. Nothing herein should be taken as a limitation on investigation by federal law enforcement to determine the existence of these factors. However, search warrants or other more intrusive investigative techniques directed at marijuana stores should be closely coordinated with the USAOs.

*Marijuana "inventory" obtained from cultivation on federal or tribal land.

*Targets involved in cultivation or distribution outside of the dispensary that merits federal prosecution based on consideration of factors set forth in sections 1 and 2 above.

*Targets using profits from the dispensary to support other criminal activity.

*Store linked to physician providing marijuana recommendations without plausible legitimate justification, eg doctor on site providing recommendation with no on-site examinations or legitimate medical procedures. *Targets have significant prior criminal histories.

*Targets have provable ties to a street gang that engages in drug trafficking involving violent conduct.

*Store operations involve the use or presence or firearms or other dangerous weapons including cases that would support charges under 18 USC 924.
*Store generates significant profits that are used/concealed in ways that would support charges for federal financial crimes such as tax evasion, money laundering or structuring. Note--generation of significant profits alone generally will not be viewed as a factor weighing in favor of federal

prosecution

*Store operations in conjunction with other federal crimes involving violence or intimidation.

*Store employs minors under 18 and/or sells a significant portion of marijuana to minors under the age of 21 especially where evidence that minors aren't using for medical purposes

4. Civil forfeiture.

The USAOs general preference is to pursue forfeiture through criminal forfeiture or civil forfeiture filed in parallel with a criminal case. Nevertheless circumstances may arise in which civil forfeiture alone is the best option. Those cases will generally involve one or more of the following:

*Significant forfeitable assets clearly traceable to marijuana trafficking in violation of federal criminal law that would merit federal prosecution based on consideration of factors set forth in sections 1-3 above.

*Significant forfeitable assets clearly traceable to non-marijuana related violations of federal law such as structuring or money-laundering. Large scale "medical marijuana" cultivation operations that 1) are operating in violation of state law 2) involve real property that has been the subject of a warning letter or similar prior notice or 3) involve real property that has been the subject of a prior forfeiture proceeding arising from marijuana cultivation or a property owner who has been a claimant in such proceedings or individual targets not subject to criminal prosecution eg fugitives or persons whose involvement in marijuana trafficking is too marginal to justify criminal prosecution including off-site land lords and non-resident owners falsely claiming ignorance of tenant's marijuana trafficking.

SIGNIFICANT FEDERAL CASE LAW

SIGNIFICANT CASES REGARDING FEDERAL LAWS.

Preemption – 9th and 10th Amendment

New York v. United States (1992) 505 U.S. 144

Held: **Congress Cannot Force the States to Implement Federal Regulations**

The state of New York filed suit against the federal government, questioning the authority of Congress to regulate state waste management. Congress enacted the Low-Level Radioactive Waste Policy Amendments Act of 1985 (the "Act"). The Act attempted to force states to arrange for the disposal of radioactive waste. New York claimed the Act violated the Tenth Amendment of the United States Constitution, by invading the sovereignty of the state. It was ultimately held that Congress does not have the authority to force a state to adopt a federal regulatory program. Although monetary and access incentives are allowed, the Tenth Amendment is violated when Congress directs states to regulate a particular field and in a particular way – this is called "commandeering." Thus, Congress cannot "commandeer" the state legislative process.

Printz v. United States (1997) 521 U.S. 898

Held: **Federal Government Cannot Force the States to Implement Federal Regulations**

Printz and others filed suit alleging that the federal government does not have the power to enact that Brady Handgun Violence Prevention Act, an act that required state and local law enforcement to do background checks before issuing firearm permits. The federal government may not require state law enforcement agents to administer the background checks required by the Act. The requirements of the Act violate the federal separation of powers because it removes Presidential oversight from a federal program and requires the state to exercise oversight. Because the Act is a federal statute, the Constitution of the United States relegates the authority. By putting the enforcement in the hands of state and local officials, Congress has stripped the federal executive of the constitutional duty to enforce federal legislation.

Gonzales v. Raich (2005) 545 U.S. 1

Held: **State-Compliant Medical Marijuana Still Violates Federal Law**

In *Raich, supra,* 545 U.S. 1, the United States Supreme Court ruled (6-3) that even when individuals or businesses are cultivating, possessing, or distributing medical marijuana in accordance with state law, they are still violating federal marijuana laws. In support of its holding, the *Raich* reasoned that the Commerce Clause of the United States Constitution grants the federal government jurisdiction to prosecute marijuana offenses under the CSA – even if the marijuana is grown for medical purposes and not distributed across state lines – because the intrastate medicinal marijuana market contributes to the interstate illicit marijuana market.

U.S. v. Rosenthal (9th Cir. 2006) 454 F.3d 943

Held: **Under Federal Law It Is Irrelevant If A Defendant Complied With State Medical Marijuana Laws, Thus No Such Evidence May Be Presented To The Jury**

Rosenthal was found guilty of cultivating cannabis, conspiracy to cultivate, and maintaining a place where drugs are manufactured under Federal Marijuana and Controlled substances laws. However, the judge did not allow the jury to hear evidence regarding Prop. 215 or Rosenthal's deputization by the city of Oakland to grow medical cannabis. Jurors publicly recanted their "guilty" verdict after finding out all the facts that were left out of the trial. Rosenthal appealed to the Ninth Circuit. In response to the reversal of Rosenthal's convictions, the federal government re-indicted Rosenthal. Rosenthal was, again, convicted of cultivating marijuana and, again, was given a sentence of one-day, time-served.

Medial necessity and Recommendations for Marijuana Use

United States v. Oakland Buyers' Cooperative (2001) 532 U.S. 483

Held: **No Medical Necessity Exception to CSA**

In *Oakland Buyers Coop, supra,* 532 U.S. 483, a cooperative was organized to distribute marijuana to qualified patients for medical use purposes in compliance with California law. In an 8-0 opinion, the Supreme Court held that there is no medical necessity exception to the CSA's prohibitions on manufacturing and distributing marijuana. "The statute reflects a determination that marijuana has no medical benefits worthy of an exception, wrote Justice Thomas, therefore "medical necessity is not a defense to manufacturing and distributing marijuana."

Conant v. Walters (9th Cir. 2002) 309 F.3d 269

Held: **Doctors Cannot Be Punished for Recommending the Use of Medical Marijuana**

When California passed the CUA in 1996, the United States government threatened physicians with the loss of their license. In response, physicians and patients filed a class action lawsuit seeking to enjoin the federal government from doing so. In *Conant,* the Ninth Circuit found in favor of the physicians and patients and held that the government could not punish, or threaten to punish, physicians for recommending the medical use of marijuana. The court stated that the government's policy struck at the core of First Amendment interests of physicians and patients. "An integral component of the practice of medicine is the communication between a doctor and a patient. Physicians must be able to speak frankly and openly to patients. That need has been recognized by the courts through the application of the common law doctor-patient privilege."[393] It continued: "Being a member of a regulated profession does not, as the government suggests, result in a surrender of First Amendment rights.... To the contrary, professional speech may be entitled to 'the strongest protection our Constitution has to offer.'"[394] (*Id.*)

Medical Defense

U.S. v. Steele Smith (2009)

Held: **Defendants can present a medical marijuana defense based on conspiracy as a specific intent crime**

In November of 2007, the DEA arrested Steele Smith, director of C-3 medical cannabis caregiver service. Steele was indicted along with three others on charges of cultivating 1,289 plants at various addresses. For the first time, a medical marijuana defense was allowed to be raised in a federal case. In April 2010, it was held that if any defendant chooses to testify, they may testify as to the context of why they did what they did, even if it involves medical marijuana issues under state law. However, the jury will still be instructed that any testimony involving medical marijuana will not be a defense. Steele Smith pled guilty and was sentenced to 8 months and 21 days.

Rescheduling Marijuana

United States v. Pickard, et al. 2015 US Dist Lexis 51109

Held: **Congress acted rationally in classifying marijuana as a Schedule I Substance.**

Here, the constitutionality of the classification of marijuana as an illegal Schedule I controlled substance was challenged. In this case, the defendants were charged with growing marijuana in Shasta-Trinity National Forest, a federally designated national forest in northern California. Schweder argued that even if marijuana had been classified as a Schedule I substance, there is no rational basis for that classification.

United States v. Kettle Falls (2015)

In August 2012, the DEA raided the property of a marijuana-growing family in Washington and seized 68 marijuana plants, charging each of the five family members – each of whom are qualified patients – with conspiracy, manufacturing, distribution and firearm charges. Though the medical and recreational use of marijuana is legal in the state of Washington, the government alleged that the family members – known as the "Kettle Falls Five" – were not perfectly following state marijuana laws in operating their grow. The case is extremely controversial and has sparked national outrage mainly due to recent claims by the federal government that it would not be spending federal dollars to go after medical marijuana patients in states where it is legal, but yet the DOJ has spent more than $3 million so far to prosecute the Kettle Falls Five, and could spend up to $13 million to send them to prison if convicted. In March 2015, a federal jury acquitted the Kettle Falls Five of all charges except for one: a single charge of manufacturing between 50 and 100 plants. The defendants await their sentencing in June 2015. Though the manufacturing charge is not subject to a mandatory minimum sentence, the Kettle Falls Five still face a sentencing range of up to 20 years. This case is significant because the federal authorities have clearly used the Kettle Falls Five to set an example to the rest of the country of how dogged they are willing to be in pursuing criminal charges against marijuana growers in states that have decriminalized marijuana.

9th Circuit Interpretation of Rohrbacher-Farr Amendment

United States v. McIntosh (2016)

Held: **Rohrbacher-Farr prevents prosecution of medical cannabis businesses that are in "strict compliance" with state law.**

In *United States v. McIntosh,* the U.S. Court of Appeals for the Ninth Circuit (which includes California) issued an opinion ruling that the Amendment prohibits the DOJ from prosecuting cannabis suppliers who "fully comply" with state laws allowing medical cannabis within their borders. The defendants in *McIntosh* argued that prosecuting them violated the Amendment, which states that "none of the funds made available in this Act to the Department of Justice" to "prevent [states] from implementing their own State laws that authorize the use, distribution, possession or cultivation of medical marijuana." The Ninth Circuit agreed with the defendants, explaining that even though the Amendment is "not a model of clarity," it prohibited the DOJ from spending money on prosecuting people "who engaged in conduct permitted by the State Medical Marijuana Laws and who fully complied with such laws."

The *McIntosh* decision is actually very complicated and has several limitations. For one, the *McIntosh* case applies *only* to medical cannabis (and nothing else) in the specific geographic area covered by the Ninth Circuit: Alaska, Arizona, California, Hawaii, Idaho, Montana, Nevada, Oregon, Washington, Guam and the Northern Marianas Islands. Secondly, it could prove difficult for these 10 defendants to ultimately pass the test under *McIntosh*. The ruling makes clear that there is *no guarantee* that any of the defendants' convictions will actually be thrown out. Finally, and of certainly no small import, the *McIntosh* opinion hints that its ruling could only be temporary if Congress does not renew the Rohrbacher-Farr Amendment.

United States v. Marin Alliance For Medical Marijuana 139 F.Supp.3d 1039 (2015)

Held: **The DOJ is prohibited from spending public money to enforce the CSA against medical cannabis dispensaries in California**

In 1998, the DOJ filed suit against MAMM and several other California dispensaries on the grounds that they were distributing cannabis in violation of the CSA. In 2002, a permanent injunction was entered against MAMM prohibiting it from operation. MAMM ignored the injunction and continued operating for nine (9) more years. Throughout the case, there was never a dispute that MAMM was operating in compliance with state law. MAMM filed a motion arguing that the newly-enacted Amendment warranted taking another look at the injunction entered against it. Judge Breyer agreed and revisited the injunction. Although he did not grant MAMM's request to lift the injunction entirely, he did order that the injunction could only be enforced against MAMM insofar as MAMM violated state law. Based upon a plain reading of the Amendment, the judge held that the DOJ was prohibited from spending public money to enforce the CSA against medical cannabis dispensaries in California. MAMM, if it so chooses, is now free to operate as a dispensary in California without fear of federal prosecution.

APPENDIX II

CALIFORNIA LAW

Attorney General Guidelines For The Security and Non-Diversion Of Marijuana Grown For Medical Use

EDMUND G. BROWN JR.
Attorney General

DEPARTMENT OF JUSTICE
State of California

**GUIDELINES FOR THE SECURITY AND NON-DIVERSION
OF MARIJUANA GROWN FOR MEDICAL USE**
August 2008

In 1996, California voters approved an initiative that exempted certain patients and their primary caregivers from criminal liability under state law for the possession and cultivation of marijuana. In 2003, the Legislature enacted additional legislation relating to medical marijuana. One of those statutes requires the Attorney General to adopt "guidelines to ensure the security and nondiversion of marijuana grown for medical use." (Health & Saf. Code, § 11362.81(d).[2]) To fulfill this mandate, this Office is issuing the following guidelines to (1) ensure that marijuana grown for medical purposes remains secure and does not find its way to non-patients or illicit markets, (2) help law enforcement agencies perform their duties effectively and in accordance with California law, and (3) help patients and primary caregivers understand how they may cultivate, transport, possess, and use medical marijuana under California law.

I. SUMMARY OF APPLICABLE LAW

A. California Penal Provisions Relating to Marijuana.

The possession, sale, cultivation, or transportation of marijuana is ordinarily a crime under California law. (See, e.g., § 11357 [possession of marijuana is a misdemeanor]; § 11358 [cultivation of marijuana is a felony]; Veh. Code, § 23222 [possession of less than 1 oz. of marijuana while driving is a misdemeanor]; § 11359 [possession with intent to sell any amount of marijuana is a felony]; § 11360 [transporting, selling, or giving away marijuana in California is a felony; under 28.5 grams is a misdemeanor]; § 11361 [selling or distributing marijuana to minors, or using a minor to transport, sell, or give away marijuana, is a felony].)

B. Proposition 215 - The Compassionate Use Act of 1996.

On November 5, 1996, California voters passed Proposition 215, which decriminalized the cultivation and use of marijuana by seriously ill

---

[2] Unless otherwise noted, all statutory references are to the Health & Safety Code.

individuals upon a physician's recommendation. (§ 11362.5.) Proposition 215 was enacted to "ensure that seriously ill Californians have the right to obtain and use marijuana for medical purposes where that medical use is deemed appropriate and has been recommended by a physician who has determined that the person's health would benefit from the use of marijuana," and to "ensure that patients and their primary caregivers who obtain and use marijuana for medical purposes upon the recommendation of a physician are not subject to criminal prosecution or sanction." (§ 11362.5(b)(1)(A)-(B).)

The Act further states that "Section 11357, relating to the possession of marijuana, and Section 11358, relating to the cultivation of marijuana, shall not apply to a patient, or to a patient's primary caregiver, who possesses or cultivates marijuana for the personal medical purposes of the patient upon the written or verbal recommendation or approval of a physician." (§ 11362.5(d).) Courts have found an implied defense to the transportation of medical marijuana when the "quantity transported and the method, timing and distance of the transportation are reasonably related to the patient's current medical needs." (*People v. Trippet* (1997) 56 Cal.App.4th 1532, 1551.)

C. Senate Bill 420 - The Medical Marijuana Program Act.

On January 1, 2004, Senate Bill 420, the Medical Marijuana Program Act (MMP), became law. (§§ 11362.7-11362.83.) The MMP, among other things, requires the California Department of Public Health (DPH) to establish and maintain a program for the voluntary registration of qualified medical marijuana patients and their primary caregivers through a statewide identification card system. Medical marijuana identification cards are intended to help law enforcement officers identify and verify that cardholders are able to cultivate, possess, and transport certain amounts of marijuana without being subject to arrest under specific conditions. (§§ 11362.71(e), 11362.78.)

It is mandatory that all counties participate in the identification card program by (a) providing applications upon request to individuals seeking to join the identification card program; (b) processing completed applications; (c) maintaining certain records; (d) following state implementation protocols; and (e) issuing DPH identification cards to approved applicants and designated primary caregivers. (§ 11362.71(b).)

Participation by patients and primary caregivers in the identification card program is voluntary. However, because identification cards offer the holder protection from arrest, are issued only after verification of the cardholder's status as a qualified patient or primary caregiver, and are immediately verifiable online or via telephone, they represent one of the best ways to ensure the security and non-diversion of marijuana grown for medical use.

In addition to establishing the identification card program, the MMP also defines certain terms, sets possession guidelines for cardholders, and recognizes a qualified right to collective and cooperative cultivation of medical marijuana. (§§ 11362.7, 11362.77, 11362.775.)

D. Taxability of Medical Marijuana Transactions.

In February 2007, the California State Board of Equalization (BOE) issued a Special Notice confirming its policy of taxing medical marijuana transactions, as well as its requirement that businesses engaging in such transactions hold a Seller's Permit. (http://www.boe.ca.gov/news/pdf/medseller2007.pdf.) According to the Notice, having a Seller's Permit does not allow individuals to make unlawful sales, but instead merely provides a way to remit any sales and use taxes due. BOE further clarified its policy in a June 2007 Special Notice that addressed several frequently asked questions concerning taxation of medical marijuana transactions. (http://www.boe.ca.gov/news/pdf/173.pdf.)

E. Medical Board of California.

The Medical Board of California licenses, investigates, and disciplines California physicians. (Bus. & Prof. Code, § 2000, et seq.) Although state law prohibits punishing a physician simply for recommending marijuana for treatment of a serious medical condition (§ 11362.5(c)), the Medical Board can and does take disciplinary action against physicians who fail to comply with accepted medical standards when recommending marijuana. In a May 13, 2004 press release, the Medical Board clarified that these accepted standards are the same ones that a reasonable and prudent physician would follow when recommending or approving any medication. They include the following:

> 1. Taking a history and conducting a good faith examination of the patient;
> 2. Developing a treatment plan with objectives;
> 3. Providing informed consent, including discussion of side effects;
> 4. Periodically reviewing the treatment's efficacy;
> 5. Consultations, as necessary; and
> 6. Keeping proper records supporting the decision to recommend the use of

medical marijuana.
(http://www.mbc.ca.gov/board/media/releases_2004_05-13_marijuana.html.)

Complaints about physicians should be addressed to the Medical Board (1-800-633-2322 or www.mbc.ca.gov), which investigates and prosecutes alleged licensing violations in conjunction with the Attorney General's Office.

F. The Federal Controlled Substances Act.

Adopted in 1970, the Controlled Substances Act (CSA) established a federal regulatory system designed to combat recreational drug abuse by making it unlawful to manufacture, distribute, dispense, or possess any controlled substance. (21 U.S.C. § 801, et seq.; *Gonzales v. Oregon* (2006) 546 U.S. 243, 271-273.) The CSA reflects the federal government's view that marijuana is a drug with "no currently accepted medical use." (21 U.S.C. § 812(b)(1).) Accordingly, the manufacture, distribution, or possession of marijuana is a federal criminal offense. (*Id.* at §§ 841(a)(1), 844(a).)

The incongruity between federal and state law has given rise to understandable confusion, but no legal conflict exists merely because state law and federal law treat marijuana differently. Indeed, California's medical marijuana laws have been challenged unsuccessfully in court on the ground that they are preempted by the CSA. (*County of San Diego v. San Diego NORML* (July 31, 2008) --- Cal.Rptr.3d ---, 2008 WL 2930117.) Congress has provided that states are free to regulate in the area of controlled substances, including marijuana, provided that state law does not positively conflict with the CSA. (21 U.S.C. § 903.) Neither Proposition 215, nor the MMP, conflict with the CSA because, in adopting these laws, California did not "legalize" medical marijuana, but instead exercised the state's reserved powers to not punish certain marijuana offenses under state law when a physician has recommended its use to treat a serious medical condition. (See *City of Garden Grove v. Superior Court* (*Kha*) (2007) 157 Cal.App.4th 355, 371-373, 381-382.)

In light of California's decision to remove the use and cultivation of physician recommended marijuana from the scope of the state's drug laws, this Office recommends that state and local law enforcement officers not arrest individuals or seize marijuana under federal law when the officer determines from the facts available that the cultivation, possession, or transportation is permitted under California's medical marijuana laws.

II. DEFINITIONS

A. **Physician's Recommendation:** Physicians may not prescribe marijuana because the federal Food and Drug Administration regulates prescription drugs and, under the CSA, marijuana is a Schedule I drug, meaning that it has no recognized medical use. Physicians may, however, lawfully issue a verbal or written recommendation under California law indicating that marijuana would be a beneficial treatment for a serious medical condition. (§ 11362.5(d); *Conant v. Walters* (9th Cir. 2002) 309 F.3d 629, 632.)

B. **Primary Caregiver:** A primary caregiver is a person who is designated by a qualified patient and "has consistently assumed responsibility for the housing, health, or safety" of the patient. (§ 11362.5(e).) California courts have emphasized the consistency element of the patient-caregiver relationship. Although a "primary caregiver who consistently grows and supplies . . . medicinal marijuana for a section 11362.5 patient is serving a health need of the patient," someone who merely maintains a source of marijuana does not automatically become the party "who has consistently assumed responsibility for the housing, health, or safety" of that purchaser. (*People ex rel. Lungren v. Peron* (1997) 59 Cal.App.4th 1383, 1390, 1400.) A person may serve as primary caregiver to "more than one" patient, provided that the patients and caregiver all reside in the same city or county. (§ 11362.7(d)(2).) Primary caregivers also may receive certain compensation for their services. (§ 11362.765(c) ["A primary caregiver who receives compensation for actual expenses, including reasonable compensation incurred for services provided . . . to enable [a patient] to use marijuana under this article, or for payment for out-of-pocket expenses incurred in providing those services, or both, . . . shall not, on the sole basis of that fact, be subject to prosecution" for possessing or transporting marijuana].)

C. **Qualified Patient:** A qualified patient is a person whose physician has recommended the use of marijuana to treat a serious illness, including cancer, anorexia, AIDS, chronic pain, spasticity, glaucoma, arthritis, migraine, or any other illness for which marijuana provides relief. (§ 11362.5(b)(1)(A).)

D. **Recommending Physician:** A recommending physician is a person who (1) possesses a license in good standing to practice medicine in California; (2) has taken responsibility for some aspect of the medical care, treatment, diagnosis, counseling, or referral of a patient; and (3) has complied with accepted medical standards (as described by the Medical Board of California in its May 13, 2004 press release) that a reasonable and prudent physician would follow when recommending or approving medical marijuana for the treatment of his or her patient.

III. GUIDELINES REGARDING INDIVIDUAL QUALIFIED PATIENTS AND PRIMARY CAREGIVERS

A. State Law Compliance Guidelines.

1. **Physician Recommendation**: Patients must have a written or verbal recommendation for medical marijuana from a licensed physician. (§ 11362.5(d).)

2. **State of California Medical Marijuana Identification Card**: Under the MMP, qualified patients and their primary caregivers may voluntarily apply for a card issued by DPH identifying them as a person who is authorized to use, possess, or transport marijuana grown for medical purposes. To help law enforcement officers verify the cardholder's identity, each card bears a unique identification number, and a verification database is available online (www.calmmp.ca.gov). In addition, the cards contain the name of the county health department that approved the application, a 24-hour verification telephone number, and an expiration date. (§§ 11362.71(a); 11362.735(a)(3)-(4); 11362.745.)

3. **Proof of Qualified Patient Status**: Although verbal recommendations are technically permitted under Proposition 215, patients should obtain and carry written proof of their physician recommendations to help them avoid arrest. A state identification card is the best form of proof, because it is easily verifiable and provides immunity from arrest if certain conditions are met (see section III.B.4, below). The next best forms of proof are a city- or county-issued patient identification card, or a written recommendation from a physician.

4. **Possession Guidelines**:

   a) **MMP**:[3] Qualified patients and primary caregivers

---

[3] On May 22, 2008, California's Second District Court of Appeal severed Health & Safety Code § 11362.77 from the MMP on the ground that the statute's possession guidelines were an unconstitutional amendment of
Proposition 215, which does not quantify the marijuana a patient may possess. (See *People v. Kelly* (2008) 163 Cal.App.4th 124, 77 Cal.Rptr.3d 390.) The Third District Court of Appeal recently reached a similar conclusion in *People v. Phomphakdy* (July 31, 2008) --- Cal.Rptr.3d ---, 2008 WL 2931369. The California Supreme Court has granted review in *Kelly* and the Attorney General intends to seek review in *Phomphakdy*.

who possess a state issued identification card may possess 8 oz. of dried marijuana, and may maintain no more than 6 mature or 12 immature plants per qualified patient. (§ 11362.77(a).) But, if "a qualified patient or primary caregiver has a doctor's recommendation that this quantity does not meet the qualified patient's medical needs, the qualified patient or primary caregiver may possess an amount of marijuana consistent with the patient's needs." (§ 11362.77(b).) Only the dried mature processed flowers or buds of the female cannabis plant should be considered when determining allowable quantities of medical marijuana for purposes of the MMP. (§ 11362.77(d).)

    b)   **Local Possession Guidelines:** Counties and cities may adopt regulations that allow qualified patients or primary caregivers to possess medical marijuana in amounts that exceed the MMP's possession guidelines. (§ 11362.77(c).)

    c)   **Proposition 215**: Qualified patients claiming protection under Proposition 215 may possess an amount of marijuana that is "reasonably related to [their] current medical needs." (*People v. Trippet* (1997) 56 Cal.App.4th 1532, 1549.)

B.   **Enforcement Guidelines**.

1.   **Location of Use**: Medical marijuana may not be smoked (a) where smoking is prohibited by law, (b) at or within 1000 feet of a school, recreation center, or youth center (unless the medical use occurs within a residence), (c) on a school bus, or (d) in a moving motor vehicle or boat. (§ 11362.79.)

2.   **Use of Medical Marijuana in the Workplace or at Correctional Facilities:** The medical use of marijuana need not be accommodated in the workplace, during work hours, or at any jail, correctional facility, or other penal institution. (§ 11362.785(a); *Ross v. RagingWire Telecomms., Inc.* (2008) 42 Cal.4th 920, 933 [under the Fair Employment and Housing Act, an employer may terminate an employee who tests positive for marijuana use].)

3.   **Criminal Defendants, Probationers, and Parolees:**

Criminal defendants and probationers may request court approval to use medical marijuana while they are released on bail or probation. The court's decision and reasoning must be stated on the record and in the minutes of the court. Likewise, parolees who are eligible to use medical marijuana may request that they be allowed to continue such use during the period of parole. The written conditions of parole must reflect whether the request was granted or denied. (§ 11362.795.)

4. **State of California Medical Marijuana Identification Cardholders**: When a person invokes the protections of Proposition 215 or the MMP and he or she possesses a state medical marijuana identification card, officers should:

> a) Review the identification card and verify its validity either by calling the telephone number printed on the card, or by accessing DPH's card verification website (http://www.calmmp.ca.gov); and

> b) If the card is valid and not being used fraudulently, there are no other indicia of illegal activity (weapons, illicit drugs, or excessive amounts of cash), and the person is within the state or local possession guidelines, the individual should be released and the marijuana should not be seized. Under the MMP, "no person or designated primary caregiver in possession of a valid state medical marijuana identification card shall be subject to arrest for possession, transportation, delivery, or cultivation of medical marijuana." (§ 11362.71(e).) Further, a "state or local law enforcement agency or officer shall not refuse to accept an identification card issued by the department unless the state or local law enforcement agency or officer has reasonable cause to believe that the information contained in the card is false or fraudulent, or the card is being used fraudulently." (§ 11362.78.)

5. **Non-Cardholders**: When a person claims protection under Proposition 215 or the MMP and only has a locally-issued (i.e., non-state) patient identification card, or a written (or verbal) recommendation from a licensed physician, officers should use their sound professional judgment to assess the validity of the person's medical-use claim:

> a) Officers need not abandon their search or investigation. The standard search and seizure rules apply to the

enforcement of marijuana-related violations. Reasonable suspicion is required for detention, while probable cause is required for search, seizure, and arrest.

b) Officers should review any written documentation for validity. It may contain the physician's name, telephone number, address, and license number.

c) If the officer reasonably believes that the medical-use claim is valid based upon the totality of the circumstances (including the quantity of marijuana, packaging for sale, the presence of weapons, illicit drugs, or large amounts of cash), and the person is within the state or local possession guidelines or has an amount consistent with their current medical needs, the person should be released and the marijuana should not be seized.

d) Alternatively, if the officer has probable cause to doubt the validity of a person's medical marijuana claim based upon the facts and circumstances, the person may be arrested and the marijuana may be seized. It will then be up to the person to establish his or her medical marijuana defense in court.

e) Officers are not obligated to accept a person's claim of having a verbal physician's recommendation that cannot be readily verified with the physician at the time of detention.

6. **Exceeding Possession Guidelines**: If a person has what appears to be valid medical marijuana documentation, but exceeds the applicable possession guidelines identified above, all marijuana may be seized.

7. **Return of Seized Medical Marijuana:** If a person whose marijuana is seized by law enforcement successfully establishes a medical marijuana defense in court, or the case is not prosecuted, he or she may file a motion for return of the marijuana. If a court grants the motion and orders the return of marijuana seized incident to an arrest, the individual or entity subject to the order must return the property. State law enforcement officers who handle controlled substances in the course of their official duties are immune from liability under the CSA. (21 U.S.C. § 885(d).) Once the marijuana is returned, federal authorities are free to exercise jurisdiction over it. (21 U.S.C. §§ 812(c)(10), 844(a); *City of Garden Grove v. Superior Court (Kha)* (2007) 157 Cal.App.4th 355, 369, 386, 391.)

IV. GUIDELINES REGARDING COLLECTIVES AND COOPERATIVES

Under California law, medical marijuana patients and primary caregivers may "associate within the State of California in order collectively or cooperatively to cultivate marijuana for medical purposes." (§ 11362.775.) The following guidelines are meant to apply to qualified patients and primary caregivers who come together to collectively or cooperatively cultivate physician-recommended marijuana.

A. Business Forms: Any group that is collectively or cooperatively cultivating and distributing marijuana for medical purposes should be organized and operated in a manner that ensures the security of the crop and safeguards against diversion for non-medical purposes. The following are guidelines to help cooperatives and collectives operate within the law, and to help law enforcement determine whether they are doing so.

1. **Statutory Cooperatives:** A cooperative must file articles of incorporation with the state and conduct its business for the mutual benefit of its members. (Corp. Code, § 12201, 12300.) No business may call itself a "cooperative" (or "coop") unless it is properly organized and registered as such a corporation under the Corporations or Food and Agricultural Code. (*Id.* at § 12311(b).) Cooperative corporations are "democratically controlled and are not organized to make a profit for themselves, as such, or for their members, as such, but primarily for their members as patrons." (*Id.* at § 12201.) The earnings and savings of the business must be used for the general welfare of its members or equitably distributed to members in the form of cash, property, credits, or services. (*Ibid.*) Cooperatives must follow strict rules on organization, articles, elections, and distribution of earnings, and must report individual transactions from individual members each year. (See *id.* at § 12200, et seq.) Agricultural cooperatives are likewise nonprofit corporate entities "since they are not organized to make profit for themselves, as such, or for their members, as such, but only for their members as producers." (Food & Agric. Code, § 54033.) Agricultural cooperatives share many characteristics with consumer cooperatives. (See, e.g., *id.* at § 54002, et seq.) Cooperatives should not purchase marijuana from, or sell to, non-members; instead, they

should only provide a means for facilitating or coordinating transactions between members.

2. **Collectives:** California law does not define collectives, but the dictionary defines them as "a business, farm, etc., jointly owned and operated by the members of a group." (*Random House Unabridged Dictionary*; Random House, Inc. © 2006.) Applying this definition, a collective should be an organization that merely facilitates the collaborative efforts of patient and caregiver members – including the allocation of costs and revenues. As such, a collective is not a statutory entity, but as a practical matter it might have to organize as some form of business to carry out its activities. The collective should not purchase marijuana from, or sell to, non-members; instead, it should only provide a means for facilitating or coordinating transactions between members.

B. Guidelines for the Lawful Operation of a Cooperative or Collective: Collectives and cooperatives should be organized with sufficient structure to ensure security, non-diversion of marijuana to illicit markets, and compliance with all state and local laws. The following are some suggested guidelines and practices for operating collective growing operations to help ensure lawful operation.

1. **Non-Profit Operation**: Nothing in Proposition 215 or the MMP authorizes collectives, cooperatives, or individuals to profit from the sale or distribution of marijuana. (See, e.g., § 11362.765(a) ["nothing in this section shall authorize . . . any individual or group to cultivate or distribute marijuana for profit"].

2. **Business Licenses, Sales Tax, and Seller's Permits**: The State Board of Equalization has determined that medical marijuana transactions are subject to sales tax, regardless of whether the individual or group makes a profit, and those engaging in transactions involving medical marijuana must obtain a Seller's Permit. Some cities and counties also require dispensing collectives and cooperatives to obtain business licenses.

3. **Membership Application and Verification**: When a patient or primary caregiver wishes to join a collective or cooperative, the group can help prevent the diversion of marijuana for non-medical use by having potential members

complete a written membership application. The following application guidelines should be followed to help ensure that marijuana grown for medical use is not diverted to illicit markets:

> a) Verify the individual's status as a qualified patient or primary caregiver. Unless he or she has a valid state medical marijuana identification card, this should involve personal contact with the recommending physician (or his or her agent), verification of the physician's identity, as well as his or her state licensing status. Verification of primary caregiver status should include contact with the qualified patient, as well as validation of the patient's recommendation. Copies should be made of the physician's recommendation or identification card, if any;
>
> b) Have the individual agree not to distribute marijuana to non-members;
>
> c) Have the individual agree not to use the marijuana for other than medical purposes;
>
> d) Maintain membership records on-site or have them reasonably available;
>
> e) Track when members' medical marijuana recommendation and/or identification cards expire; and
>
> f) Enforce conditions of membership by excluding members whose identification card or physician recommendation are invalid or have expired, or who are caught diverting marijuana for non-medical use.

4. Collectives Should Acquire, Possess, and Distribute Only Lawfully Cultivated Marijuana: Collectives and cooperatives should acquire marijuana only from their constituent members, because only marijuana grown by a qualified patient or his or her primary caregiver may lawfully be transported by, or distributed to, other members of a collective or cooperative. (§§ 11362.765, 11362.775.) The collective or cooperative may then allocate it to other members of the group. Nothing allows marijuana to be purchased from outside the collective or cooperative for distribution to its members. Instead, the cycle should be a closed circuit of marijuana cultivation and consumption with no purchases or sales to or from non-members. To help prevent diversion of medical marijuana to nonmedical markets, collectives and cooperatives should document each member's contribution of labor, resources, or money to the enterprise. They also should track and record the source of their marijuana.

5. **Distribution and Sales to Non-Members are Prohibited**: State law allows primary caregivers to be reimbursed for certain services (including marijuana cultivation), but nothing allows individuals or groups to sell or distribute marijuana to non-members. Accordingly, a collective or cooperative may not distribute medical marijuana to any person who is not a member in good standing of the organization. A dispensing collective or cooperative may credit its members for marijuana they provide to the collective, which it may then allocate to other members. (§ 11362.765(c).) Members also may reimburse the collective or cooperative for marijuana that has been allocated to them. Any monetary reimbursement that members provide to the collective or cooperative should only be an amount necessary to cover overhead costs and operating expenses.

1. **Permissible Reimbursements and Allocations:** Marijuana grown at a collective or cooperative for medical purposes may be:

    a) Provided free to qualified patients and primary caregivers who are members of the collective or cooperative;

    b) Provided in exchange for services rendered to the entity;

    c) Allocated based on fees that are reasonably calculated to cover overhead costs and operating expenses; or

    d) Any combination of the above.

2. **Possession and Cultivation Guidelines**: If a person is acting as primary caregiver to more than one patient under section 11362.7(d)(2), he or she may aggregate the possession and cultivation limits for each patient. For example, applying the MMP's basic possession guidelines, if a caregiver is responsible for three patients, he or she may possess up to 24 oz. of marijuana (8 oz. per patient) and may grow 18 mature or 36 immature plants. Similarly, collectives and cooperatives may cultivate and transport marijuana in aggregate amounts tied to its membership numbers. Any patient or primary caregiver exceeding individual possession

guidelines should have supporting records readily available when:

    a) Operating a location for cultivation;
    b) Transporting the group's medical marijuana; and
    c) Operating a location for distribution to members of the collective or cooperative.

3. **Security**: Collectives and cooperatives should provide adequate security to ensure that patients are safe and that the surrounding homes or businesses are not negatively impacted by nuisance activity such as loitering or crime. Further, to maintain security, prevent fraud, and deter robberies, collectives and cooperatives should keep accurate records and follow accepted cash handling practices, including regular bank runs and cash drops, and maintain a general ledger of cash transactions.

C. Enforcement Guidelines: Depending upon the facts and circumstances, deviations from the guidelines outlined above, or other indicia that marijuana is not for medical use, may give rise to probable cause for arrest and seizure. The following are additional guidelines to help identify medical marijuana collectives and cooperatives that are operating outside of state law.

1. **Storefront Dispensaries:** Although medical marijuana "dispensaries" have been operating in California for years, dispensaries, as such, are not recognized under the law. As noted above, the only recognized group entities are cooperatives and collectives. (§ 11362.775.) It is the opinion of this Office that a properly organized and operated collective or cooperative that dispenses medical marijuana through a storefront may be lawful under California law, but that dispensaries that do not substantially comply with the guidelines set forth in sections IV(A) and (B), above, are likely operating outside the protections of Proposition 215 and the MMP, and that the individuals operating such entities may be subject to arrest and criminal prosecution under California law. For example, dispensaries that merely require patients to complete a form summarily designating the business owner as their primary caregiver – and then offering marijuana in exchange for cash "donations" – are likely unlawful. (*Peron, supra*, 59 Cal.App.4th at p. 1400 [cannabis club owner was not the primary caregiver to thousands of patients where he did not consistently assume responsibility for their housing, health, or safety].)

2. **Indicia of Unlawful Operation:** When investigating collectives or cooperatives, law enforcement officers should be alert for signs

of mass production or illegal sales, including (a) excessive amounts of marijuana, (b) excessive amounts of cash, (c) failure to follow local and state laws applicable to similar businesses, such as maintenance of any required licenses and payment of any required taxes, including sales taxes, (d) weapons, (e) illicit drugs, (f) purchases from, or sales or distribution to, non-members, or (g) distribution outside of California.

SIGNIFICANT CALIFORNIA CASE LAW

SIGNIFICANT CASES REGARDING CALIFORNIA LAW

Protection of the Compassionate Use Act

People v. Trippett, (1 Dist. 1997) 56 Cal.App.4th 1532

Held: **CUA Also Applies to Transportation of Cannabis**

The CUA applies retroactively to qualified individuals who were in the process of being criminally charged before the statute was put into effect. The transportation of cannabis is implied under the CUA if the quantity transported and the method, timing and distance of the transportation are reasonably related to the patients' current medical needs. Thus, it was held that the amount of cannabis a patient may legally possess is an amount "reasonably related" to current medical need. The court found that the physician's opinion regarding frequency and dosage were sufficient to establish such amounts. The court also found that qualified individuals cannot possess "unlimited quantities" of cannabis.

People v. Mower, (2002) 28 Cal.4th 457

Held: **CUA Provides a Limited Immunity From Prosecution**

In a unanimous ruling, the California Supreme Court in *Mower* granted medical cannabis patients powerful legal protection against state prosecution for cannabis-related crimes. The court ruled that the CUA is more than just an affirmative defense to criminal prosecution for the possession and cultivation of cannabis, it is a "limited immunity" from prosecution.[395] Defendant must be found guilty "beyond a reasonable doubt," rather than merely by "preponderance of evidence," a weaker standard that had been previously used by the courts. In powerful language, the court declared: "[T]he possession and cultivation of cannabis is no more criminal – so long as its conditions are satisfied - than the possession and acquisition of any prescription drug with a physician's prescription."[396] To protect patients from unnecessary prosecution, the *Mower* court established a two-part process for patients who are arrested. First, they are entitled a to a pre-trial hearing, where they can have their cases dismissed if they show a "preponderance of the evidence" that they are entitled to protection under the CUA. Afterwards, if they are brought to trial, they need only raise a "reasonable doubt to prove their innocence."[397]

Rules Governing Patient and Caregiver

People v. Konow, (2004) 32 Cal.4th 995

Held: **Defendant May "Informally Suggest" That a Judge Dismiss Criminal Charges in the" Interests of Justice"**

In *Konow,* the court established that a defendant may "informally suggest" that the court dismiss a criminal complaint "in the interests of justice," upon properly submitting a physician's recommendation. This is also known as a motion to dismiss under Penal Code § 1385. In fact, if a court fails to consider a motion to dismiss under § 1385, the defendant is considered to have been denied a "substantial right affecting the legality of the proceedings."[398] In so holding, the court also expressly approved of a magistrate dismissing the complaint at an early stage in a medical cannabis case.[399]

People v. Mentch, (2008) 45 Cal.4th 274

Held: **Medical Cannabis Providers Do Not Qualify as "Primary Caregivers" Under the CUA if Their Primary Role is Only to Supply Cannabis**

In a blow to medical cannabis providers, the California Supreme Court held in *Mentch* that defendants are not entitled to a CUA defense as "primary caregivers" if their primary role is only to supply cannabis to patients. The court noted: "We hold that a defendant whose caregiving consisted principally of supplying cannabis and instructing on its use, and who otherwise only sporadically took some patients to medical appointments, cannot qualify as a primary caregiver under the [CUA] ..."[400] [Note: Los Angeles District Attorney Steve Cooley argues that the rationale underlying this decision makes the sale of medical cannabis to patients illegal[401], but there is absolutely nothing in *Mentch* that directly addresses this issue. In fact, we find this interpretation to be extremely strained and do not believe a court would agree with Cooley's interpretation of *Mentch*.]

People v. Hochanadel, (Dist.4 2009) 176 Cal.App.4th 997

Held: **Storefront Dispensaries Are Not Legal "Caregivers"**

Defendants were operators of a medical cannabis dispensary where police executed a search warrant and found a growing operation, cannabis for sale and cannabis on drying racks. Under the A.G. Guidelines, cooperatives must file articles of incorporation with the state and follow strict rules on organization. The court primarily focused on what constituted a storefront dispensary. A person who only provides medical cannabis to a patient is not found to be a patients' primary caregiver. A caregiver is one who constantly provides housing, health or safety to a patient in addition to supplying medical cannabis. It was held that dispensaries thus cannot operate as "caregivers." Storefront dispensaries may lawfully operate, and receive financial reimbursement for medical cannabis, if formed as a collective or cooperative.

People v. Wayman, (2010) 189 Cal.App.4th 215

Held: **Transportation of Cannabis Must Be Reasonably Related to Medical Needs**

In this Orange County case, the defendant was entitled to use medical cannabis under the CUA, but kept his entire stash in his car in order to appease his mother, whom he lived with. The defendant was convicted of transporting cannabis. His medical cannabis defense didn't hold up because the quantity transported and the method, timing, and distance of the transportation were not reasonably related to his current medical needs. The court held that if the defendant were leaving town for an extended period of time, then that might justify his possession of four ounces of cannabis in his car. However, the defendant couldn't transport his entire stash at all times simply to appease his mother. It was held that a medical cannabis defense to transporting cannabis must show that the transportation was reasonable related to medical needs.

People v. Kelly, (2010) 47 Cal. 4th 1008

Held: **No More Actual Limits on "Permissible Quantity" of Medical Cannabis Possession**

In this case, a patient had more than 12 ounces of cannabis – an amount that exceeded the allowable limit under the MMP at the time. The Court of Appeal reversed the defendant's conviction for possession on the ground that the MMP's quantity limitations constituted an unconstitutional amendment of the CUA. In a unanimous decision, it was determined that the CUA's only limit on the amount of cannabis someone may possess is that it must be "reasonably related to the patient's current medical needs."

Rules governing Collectives and Cooperatives

People v. Colvin, (2012) 203 Cal.App.4th 1029

Held: **Cooperatives/Collectives May Cultivate and Transport Medical Cannabis in Aggregate Amounts Tied To Membership Numbers and The Law Does Not Require All Or Any Specified Number Of A Cooperative/Collectives Patients To Physically Take Part In The Cultivation Of Cannabis**

Defendant was arrested after being pulled over transporting several pounds from one of his collectives to his second collective in Los Angeles County. The appellate court found that the defendant's transportation of the cannabis was covered under the MMP and therefore should be acquitted. Notably, the evidence showed that the defendant had 14 offsite grows and the Court did not find this to disqualify him for the medical cannabis defense. The court held that collectives and cooperatives may cultivate and specifically transport medical cannabis in aggregate amounts tied to its membership numbers. In addition, the Colvin decision affirmed that possession of extracted or concentrated forms of medical cannabis was legal under state law.

People v. Jackson, (2012) 148 Cal.Rptr.3d 375

Held: **Cooperative/Collective Members Do Not Have to Be Directly Involved in Cultivation and There Are No Limits on Membership Size**

Defendant was involved in a medical cannabis collective of which the collective members were qualified patients, however, the court determined that the members did not collectively cultivate the cannabis and thus the MMP defense was not available. The court held that cannabis cooperative and collectives do not have to be directly involved in the cultivation or administration of the business. There are thus no numerical limits on how many members may be associated, the MMP defense is available to qualified patients who associate with a non-profit collective to purchase their medical cannabis.

People v. Mitchell, (2014) 225 Cal.App.4th 1189

Held: **MMP Defense Does Not Apply to Growers Selling Cannabis to "For-Profit" Collectives**

In *Mitchell,* the defendant was a qualified patient who was growing over 200 cannabis plants for a "for-profit" collective. When police arrested the defendant, he claimed that the plants belonged to him, and not any other qualified patients, and that he was planning on selling the cannabis to a "for-profit" collective. The court held that the MMP collective defense did not apply because the defendant was involved in a "for-profit" operation and he could not prove that the plants were collectively owned by qualified patients.[402]

People v. Orlosky, (Jan. 16, 2015, No. D064468)

Held: **Even Informal Agreements May Constitute Collective**

In ORLOSKY, the defendant and his friend were both users of medical cannabis and grew cannabis on their property for their own medicinal use and, if any were left over, for others who also had medical cannabis recommendations. Two patients growing cannabis for themselves do not need to form a formal business entity, so long as they are not distributing to anyone else and the amount of cannabis is reasonable for their medical conditions. However, the court of appeals decided that even an informal arrangement among patients to cultivate cannabis for their medical use may constitute a collective.

People v. Anderson, (Jan. 9, 2015, No. F066737)

Held: **Growing Members Can Sell to Consumer Members So Long As It Is Done on a Non-Profit Basis**

In *Anderson,* a qualified patient was arrested after law enforcement seized over 187 plants on his property. During trial, the prosecution presented evidence that Anderson had sold cannabis to a dispensary. The defense presented evidence that Anderson was a member of the collective and was in the process of starting a collective of his own with friends and family. During his closing arguments, the prosecutor emphasized to the jury that any sales of cannabis was illegal and that the operation was also illegal because no one was helping Anderson with the plants. The jury convicted Anderson on the cultivation charge and Anderson appealed. On appeal, the court reversed the conviction and ruled that under the MMP, it is legal for growing members of a collective to sell cannabis to the collective, so long as the collective is not for profit, and the cannabis is distributed to only qualified patient-members of the collective.[403] The court further held that Anderson could have been in the initial phases of starting a collective and thus the amount of cannabis could have been lawful.

Garden Grove v. Superior Court (Kha) (Dist.4 2007) 157 Cal.App.4th 355

Held: Police Must Return Medical Cannabis That Was Improperly Seized From Qualified Patient

In *Kha,* a qualified patient was pulled over by police for a traffic stop. During the stop, the police searched his vehicle without his consent and seized approximately 8 grams of cannabis. When the defendant showed police his physician's recommendation, the police insisted that it was still illegal under federal law. After the defendant's case was later dismissed in court, he immediately asked for and obtained a court order for the return of his cannabis. However, when the defendant tried to get his cannabis back from police, they refused. On appeal, the court upheld the duty of the state and local authorities to return a qualified patient's medical cannabis. The court noted that the defendant was: "a qualified patient whose marijuana possession was legally sanctioned under state law. That is why he was not subjected to a criminal trial, and that is why the state cannot destroy his marijuana. It is also why the police cannot continue to retain his marijuana. Because [the defendant] is legally entitled to possess it, due process and fundamental fairness dictate that it be returned to him."[404] The bright line rule stemming from this case is that if cannabis is seized from a qualified medical cannabis patient who is legally entitled to possess it, the police *must* return the cannabis.

People v. Urziceanu (Dist. 3 2005) 132 Cal.App.4th 747

Held: Mistake of Law Defense is Available to Conspiracy Charge

Prior to the opening of his dispensary, the defendant spoke with law enforcement officials, attorneys and members of the DA's office to ensure that his medical cannabis dispensary was compliant with state law. After opening his dispensary to the public, defendant was charged with conspiracy to sell cannabis. In order to commit the crime of conspiracy, the defendant must have a specific intent to violate cannabis laws. Thus, because conspiracy requires specific intent, a true mistake of the law would be a defense to such charge. It is held that a Defendant is entitled to the mistake of law defense for the conspiracy charge to sell cannabis. However, had the Defendant been charged with the sale of cannabis or transportation, the defense would be unavailable to him because specific intent is not required for that particular charge. The *Urziceanu* court also affirmed the legality of collectives and cooperatives under the MMP.

APPENDIX III

LOCAL ORDINANCES, PROPOSITION D & PROPOSITION M

LOS ANGELES PRE- ICO DISPENSARY LIST

PROPOSITION D: EXISTING MEDICAL MARIJUANA BUSINESSES
TIMELY REGISTERED UNDER ICO, TUO AND MEASURE M

This document provides information compiled by the City of names, addresses, and tax registration numbers for all medical marijuana businesses that timely registered under the three threshold requirements for limited immunity in Sections 45.19.6.3 B, C and E(i) of Ordinance 182580, known as Proposition D. This information is not a final determination of whether or not any particular business has met or failed the restrictions of Sections 45.19.6.3 B, C and E(i). To be entitled to limited immunity, businesses must satisfy these three threshold requirements AND all other requirements of Section 45.19.6.3 of Proposition D. Please refer to Proposition D Frequently Asked Questions also posted on the City Attorney website.

#	ICO and TUO Name(s)		BTRC Number(s)	BTRC Address(es)	BTRC Name(s)	BTRC dba Name
1	420 For The People Cooperative Inc	ICO	0002208457-0001-0	15300 Devonshire 91345	420 For The People Cooperative Inc	Same as Legal Name
	Same	TUO	Same	Same	Same	Same
		L050	Same	Same	Same	Same
2	Mary Jane's Collective	ICO	0002181863-0001-2	7805 Sunset 90046	Aaron Whitney	Mary Jane's Medical Cannabis Collective
	Aaron Whitney dba: Mary Jane's Medical Cannabis Collective	TUO	Same	4901 Melrose 90029	Same	Same
		L050	Same	4901 Melrose 90029	Aaron Whitney	Mary Jane's Medical Cannabis Collective
3	Absolute Herbal Pain Solutions	ICO	0002203172-0001-4	901 La Brea 90036	Absolute Herbal Pain Solutions Inc	Same as Legal Name
	Absolute Herbal Pain Solutions, Inc	TUO	Not Resubmitted per TUO			
		L050	0002203172-0001-4	2201 San Pedro 90011-1158	Same	Same
4	Advanced Patients Collective	ICO	0002086145-0001-8	1580 Gower 90028	Advanced Patients' Collective / Hollywood Patient's Collective	Kush Mart
	Advanced Patients' Collective	TUO	Same	Same	Same	Same
		L050	Same	Same	Same	Same
5	After Care	ICO	0002082405-0002-7	18749 Napa 91324	Charles A Harper / After Care	After Care
	After Care Collective, A Cooperative Corporation	TUO	Same	Same	Same	Same
		L050	Same	Same	Same	Same
6	Alternative Medicinal Caregivers	ICO	0002205123-0001-4	13611 Sherman 91405	Alternative Medicinal Caregivers Inc	Rite Meds
	Alternative Medicinal Caregivers Inc	TUO	Not Resubmitted per TUO		Same	Same
		L050	0002205123-0001-4	8537 Reseda 91324-4630	Alternative Medicinal Caregivers Inc	Same
7	Alternative Medicine Group	ICO	0002331857-0001-1	10964 Ventura 91604	Alternative Medicine Group	Same as Legal Name
	Alternative Medicine Group, Inc	TUO	Same	Same	Same	Same
		L050	Same	Same	Same	Same
8	Arts District Patient Collective Inc. dba: Arts District Healing Center transitioning to : Arts District Healing Center Cooperative	ICO	0002243958-0001-4	620 1st 90012-4302	Arts District Patients Collective Inc / Arts District Healing Center / James Shaw	Arts District Healing Center / Metropolitan Caregivers
	Arts District Patients Collective, Inc dba Arts Healing Center ("ADPC")	TUO	0002243958-0001-4	Same	Same	Same
		L050	0002243958-0001-4	Same	Same	Arts District Healing Center / Metropolitan Caregivers
9	Ashmoon Caregivers	ICO	0002195649-0001-1	22053 Sherman 91303 / 21610 Ventura 91364	Ashmoon LLC	Ashmoon Caregivers
	Ashmoon Inc / Ashmoon Caregivers	TUO	Same	21610 Ventura 91364 / 22647 Ventura Blvd 91364	Same	Same
		L050	Same	21610 Ventura 91364-1921	Ashmoon Inc / Ashmoon Caregivers (Marijuana Dispensary)	Same

PROPOSITION D: EXISTING MEDICAL MARIJUANA BUSINESSES
TIMELY REGISTERED UNDER ICO, TUO AND MEASURE M

#	ICO and TUO Name(s)		BTRC Number(s)	BTRC Address(es)	BTRC Name(s)	BTRC dba Name
10	Balboa Care Givers Inc	ICO	0002198520-0001-7	16900 Sherman 91406	Balboa Caregivers Inc	Same as Legal Name
	Same	TUO	Same	Same	Same	Same
		L050	Same	Same	Same	Same
11	Beach Enlightenment and Compassionate Healing Center	ICO	0002224443-0001-1	310 Culver 90293	Beach Enlightenment & Compassionate Healing Center	Same as Legal Name
	Beach Enlightenment and Compassionate Healing Center Inc	TUO	Same	Same	Same	Same
		L050	Same	Same	Beach Enlightenment and Compassionate Healing Center Inc	Same
12	Buds and Roses Collective	ICO	0002212464-0001-2	13235 Ventura 91604	Buds & Roses Collective Inc / Buds & Roses	Buds & Roses
	Buds and Roses Collective Inc	TUO	Not Resubmitted per TUO	Same	Same	Same
		L050	0002212464-0001-2	13235 Ventura 91604	Buds & Roses Collective Inc / Buds & Roses	Same
13	California's Finest Compassionate Co-op	ICO	0002262577-0001-0	8552 Venice 90034	Californias Finest Compassionate Cooperative Inc	Cali's Finest
	California's Finest Compassionate Co-op / C.F.C.C. / Cali's Finest	TUO	Same	Same	Same	Same
		L050	Same	8540 Venice 90034-2549	Same	Same
14	Cahuenga Caregivers Inc	ICO	0002200695-0001-3	5656 Cahuenga 91601	Cahuenga Caregivers Inc	Same as Legal Name
	Cahuenga Caregivers Inc / No Ho Compassionate Caregivers	TUO	Same	Same	Same	Same
		L050	Same	Same	Same	Same
15	California Alternative Care Givers	ICO	0002097999-0001-3	122 Lincoln 90291	California Alternative Care Givers Christian Alliance Inc	Same as Legal Name
	California Alternative Caregivers	TUO	Same	Same	Same	Same
		L050	Same	Same	Same	Same
16	California Caregivers Alliance	ICO	0002115894-0001-2	2815 Sunset 90026	Barr Corporation / California Caregiver's Alliance	California Caregiver's Alliance
	California Caregivers Alliance / Barr Corporation	TUO	Not Resubmitted per TUO	Same	Same	Same
		L050	0002115894-0001-2	2815 Sunset 90026	Barr Corporation / California Caregiver's Alliance	Same
17	California Compassionate Care Network	ICO	0002174731-0001-0	4664 Lankershim 91602	California Compassionate Care Network LLC	Same as Legal Name
	California Compassionate Care Network / CCCN	TUO	Same	Same	Same	Same
		L050	Same	4720 Vineland 91602-1222	Same	Same
18	California Herbal Remedies	ICO	0002095479-0001-1	5470 Valley 90032	Erik Margerum / California Herbal Remedies	California Herbal Remedies
	California Herbal Remedies Inc	TUO	Not Resubmitted per TUO	Same	Same	Same
		L050	0002095479-0001-1	5470 Valley 90032	Erik Margerum / California Herbal Remedies	Same
19	California Organic Treatment Center Inc	ICO	0002205101-0001-8	6757 Santa Monica 90038	California Organic Treatment Center Inc	Same as Legal Name
	California Organic Treatment Center Inc / Eden Therapy	TUO	Same	Same	Same	Same
		L050	Same	Same	Same	Same
20	California Patients Alliance	ICO	0002184860-0010-0	8271 Melrose 90046 / 1220 N. Gardner Unit 106 90046	California Patients Alliance Incorporated	Same
	California Patients Alliance / California Patient's Alliance Inc	TUO	Not Resubmitted per TUO	Same	Same	Same
		L050	0002184860-0010-0	8271 Melrose 90046	California Patients Alliance Incorporated	Same

PROPOSITION D: EXISTING MEDICAL MARIJUANA BUSINESSES
TIMELY REGISTERED UNDER ICO, TUO AND MEASURE M

#	ICO and TUO Name(s)		BTRC Number(s)	BTRC Address(es)	BTRC Name(s)	BTRC dba Name
21	Canna Health	ICO	0002211289-0001-9	5208 Pico 90019	Kit Shum / Cannahealth Caregiver	Cannahealth Caregiver
	Cannahealth Caregivers Inc / Canna Health	TUO	Same	Same	Same	Same
		L050	Same	7101 Sunset 90046-4411	Same	Same
22	Canto Diem Collective Inc	ICO	0002184683-0001-5	5419 Sunset 90027	Cantodiem Dispensing Collective Inc	Same as Legal Name
	Cantodiem Dispensing Collective Inc	TUO	Not Resubmitted per TUO		Same	Same
		L050	0002184683-0001-5	5419 Sunset 90027	Cantodiem Dispensing Collective Inc	Same
23	Care California Consultation Inc	ICO	0002246086-0001-4	2202 Figueroa 90007	Care California Consultation Inc	Same as Legal Name
	Care California Consultation Inc	TUO	Not Resubmitted per TUO	Same	Same	Same
		L050	0002246086-0001-5	643 Olive 90014-3608	Care California Consultation Inc	Same
24	Chinatown Patient Collective	ICO	0002220929-0001-3	987 Broadway 90012	Chinatown Patient Collective Inc	Same as Legal Name
	Chinatown Patient Collective / Chinatown Patient Collective Inc	TUO	Same	Same	Same	Same
		L050	Same	Same	Same	Same
25	Chronicpractor Caregiver	ICO	0002225069-0001-1	5751 Adams 90016	Clarence L Ross / Chronicpractor Caregiver Inc	Same as Legal Name
	Chronicpractor Caregiver Inc / Chronicpractor Caregiver / CPC / Chronic Practor Care Giver	TUO	Same	Same	Chronicpractor Caregiver Inc	Same
		L050	Same	Same	Same	Same
26	Collective Caregivers Pharmacy and/or 2 AM Pharmacy	ICO	0002072981-0001-4	8239 Canoga 91304	Holistic Supplements LLC	Collective Caregivers Pharmacy and 2 AM Pharmacy
	Holistic Supplements LLC dba: 2 AM Dispensary	TUO	Same	Same	Same	Same
		L050	Same	Same	.	Same
27	Collective Pharmaceuticals Inc VNCC	ICO	0002248953-0001-8	7026 Van Nuys 91405	Collective Pharmaceutical Inc / Van Nuys Compassionate Caregivers	Same as Legal Name
	Collective Pharmaceuticals Inc / Van Nuys Compassionate Caregivers	TUO	Not Resubmitted per TUO		Same	Same
		L050	0002248953-0001-8	7026 Van Nuys 91405	Collective Pharmaceutical Inc / Van Nuys Compassionate Caregivers	Same
28	Compassion Union Inc	ICO	0002274712-0001-2	1260 Soto 90023	Compassion Union Inc	Same as Legal Name
	Same	TUO	Same	Same	Same	Same
		L050	Same	Same	Same	Same
29	Compassionate Care of Studio City	ICO	0002060233-0001-7	11314 Ventura 91604	Calvin Frye / CCSC / Compassionate Caregivers	CCSC / Compassionate Caregiver of Studio City
	Same	TUO	Same	Same	Same	Same
		L050	Same	11422 Moorpark 91602-2010	Same	Same
30	Compassionate Patient Resources Inc	ICO	0002202307-0001-0	19237 Ventura 91356	Compassionate Patient Resources Inc	Same
	Same	TUO	Same	Same	Same	Same
		L050	Same	Same	Same	Same

PROPOSITION D: EXISTING MEDICAL MARIJUANA BUSINESSES
TIMELY REGISTERED UNDER ICO, TUO AND MEASURE M

	ICO and TUO Name(s)		BTRC Number(s)	BTRC Address(es)	BTRC Name(s)	BTRC dba Name
31	Cornerstone Collective	ICO	0002212486-0001-9	4623 Eagle Rock 90041	Metaverse Collective Corporation	Cornerstone Collective
	Cornerstone Research Collective / Cornerstone / Cornerstone Collective / CRC	TUO	Same	Same	Same	Same
		L050	Same	Same	Cornerstone Research Collective / Cornerstone Collective	Same
32	Coultrock Enterprises Inc dba: LAX Compassionate Caregivers (LAXCC)	ICO	0002178151-0001-7	6218A Manchester 90045	Coultrock Enterprises, Incorporation	LAX Compassionate Caregivers
	Coultrock Enterprises Inc / LAX Compassionate Caregivers	TUO	Same	Same	Same	Same
		L050	Same	8332 Lincoln 90045	Same	Same
33	Cruz Verde Inc dba: Green Cross	ICO	0002178173-0001-3	1658 Carson 90501	Cruz Verde Inc	Same as Legal Name
	Same	TUO	Not Resubmitted per TUO			
		L050	0002178173-0001-3	1658 Carson 90501	Cruz Verde Inc	Same
34	Cyon Corporation Inc. dba: Canna Med of Northridge	ICO	0000765934-0001-4	9349 Melvin 91324	Cyon Corp	Cigarettes Unlimited
	Cyon Corporation dba: Canna Med of Northridge	TUO	0002053218-0001-8	9345 Melvin 91324	Cyon Corporation / Cannamed of Northridge - Collective	Cannamed of Northridge-Collective
		L050	Same	Same	Same	Same
35	D.E.C. Medical	ICO	0002274920-0001-2	8717 Woodman 91331 / 13664 Ottoman 91331	Jereme Fishel / DEC Medical Inc	Same as Legal Name
	D.E.C. Medical Inc / DEC Medical / D.E.C. Medical	TUO	Same	Same	Same	Same
		L050	Same	6309 Van Nuys 91401-6629	DEC Medical	Same
36	Delta-9 T.H.C.	ICO	0002201665-0001-0	1321 Carson 90501	Delta-9 T.H.C.	Same as Legal Name
	Delta-9 Torrance Herbal Collective / Delta-9 T.H.C.	TUO	Not Resubmitted per TUO			
		L050	0002201665-0001-0	1321 Carson 90501	Delta-9 T.H.C.	Same
37	Discount Caregivers	ICO	0002569972-0001-2	21315 Saticoy 91304	Ruben Diaz	Same as Legal Name
	Same	TUO	Same	Same	Discount Caregivers	Same
		L050	Same	Same	Same	Same
38	Divine Wellness Center Inc	ICO	0002239633-0001-7	5056 Lankershim 91601	Divine Wellness Center Inc	Same as Legal Name
	Same	TUO	Same	Same	Same	Same
		L050	Same	Same	Same	Same
39	Downtown Collective	ICO	0002183298-0001-1	1600 Hill 90015	Danilo P Marquez / Downtown Collective	Downtown Collective
	Downtown Collective Inc / DTC / Downtown Collective	TUO	Same	1616 Hill 90015	Danilo P Marquez	Same
		L050	Same	1600 Hill 90015	Same	Same
40	DTPG	ICO	0002189128-0001-1	1753 Hill 90015	Alfred A Garcia / DTPG	DTPG
	DTPG, Inc. / Downtown Patients Group	TUO	Same	Same	Same	Same
		L050	Same	Same	Same	Same
41	Eight One Eight	ICO	0002257223-0001-9	7232 Sepulveda 91405	Anthony Di Lorenzo / Michael Shadsirat / Eight One Eight	Same as Legal Name
	Eight One Eight / 818 Collective	TUO	Same	Same	Same	Same
		L050	Same	Same	Same	Same

PROPOSITION D: EXISTING MEDICAL MARIJUANA BUSINESSES
TIMELY REGISTERED UNDER ICO, TUO AND MEASURE M

	ICO and TUO Name(s)		BTRC Number(s)	BTRC Address(es)	BTRC Name(s)	BTRC dba Name
42	Fountain of Wellbeing, The	ICO	0002273685-0001-6	3835 Fountain 90029	Charlie M Ferrell / Fountain of Wellbeing	Fountain of Wellbeing
	Fountain of Wellbeing / FWB	TUO	Not Resubmitted per TUO		Same	Same
		L050	0002273685-0001-6	3835 Fountain 90029	Charlie M Ferrell / Fountain of Wellbeing	Same
43	Gourmet Green Room	ICO	0002207858-0001-0	2000 Cotner 90025 / 12021 Wilshire Unit 684 90025	Gourmet Green Room Inc	Same as Legal Name
	Gourmet Green Room / GGR	TUO	Not Resubmitted per TUO		Same	Same as Legal Name
		L050	Same	2000 Cotner 90025	Gourmet Green Room Inc	Same
44	Grateful Meds LLC	ICO	0002245971-0001-4	744 La Brea 90038	MMD Inc / Grateful Medications Compassionate Caregivers	Same as Legal Name
	MMD Inc; Grateful Meds; Grateful Meda Compassionate Caregivers; Grateful Medications Compasionate Caregivers	TUO	Not Resubmitted per TUO			
		L050	0002245971-0001-4	1437 La Brea 90028-7505	MMD Inc	Same
45	Green Dragon Caregiver Inc	ICO	0002240228-0001-4	7423 Van Nuys 91405	Green Dragon Caregiver Inc	Same as Legal Name
	Same	TUO	Same	Same	Same	Same
		L050	Same	Same	Same	Same
46	Green Earth Pharmacy	ICO	0002243160-0001-6	6811 Woodman 91405	Mohamad Anouti / Green Earth Pharmacy	Same as Legal Name
	The Green Earth Farmacie, Inc / Mohamad Anouti dba Green Earth Pharmacy	TUO	Same	Same	Same	Same
		L050	Same	Same	Same	Same
47	Greenlight Discount Pharmacy	ICO	0002179615-0002-7	15507 Cobalt 91342	Natalie Batae Clark / Green Light Discount Pharmacy	Green Light Discount Pharmacy
	Green Light Discount Pharmacy / Zen Medical Garden "Co-op Entities"	TUO	Not Resubmitted per TUO	Same	Same	Same
		L050	0002179615-0002-7	Same	Same	Same
48	Green Plant Therapy, Inc	ICO	0002257519-0001-7	2900 Riverside 90039	Green Plant Therapy Inc / Green Planet Co-op	Green Plant Co-op
	Same	TUO	Not Resubmitted per TUO	Same	Holistic Plant	Holistic Plant
		L050	0002257519-0001-7	Same	Green Plant Therapy Inc / Holistic Plant / Green Plant Co-op	Green Plant Co-op
49	Greenhouseherbs LLC dba: The Greenhouse Greenhouse Organics Inc dba: The Greenhouse Herbs, LLC dba: The Greenhouse	ICO	0002168149-0001-3	5156 Sepulveda 91403 / 5315 Zelzah #3 91316	Jeffrey Mark Berg	The Greenhouse
		TUO	Same	5156 Sepulveda 91403	Joshua/Rasalind Pomerantz Michael Kumar / The Greenhouse	Same
		L050	Same	Same	Same	Same
50	Healthy Herbal Care Plus "HHC+"	ICO	0002211791-0001-7	313 Virgil 90004	Bulkin Mikhail / HHC Plus Inc	HHC Plus Inc
	HHC Plus Inc / Healthy Herbal Care Plus	TUO	Same	Same	Same	Same
		L050	Same	Same	Same	Same
51	Herbal Healing Center	ICO	0002263119-0001-1	5507 Laurel Canyon 91607	Timothy James Cullen / Herbal Healing Center	Herbal Healing Center
	Herbal Healing Center	TUO	Same	Same	Same	Same
		L050	Same	Same	Same	Same

PROPOSITION D: EXISTING MEDICAL MARIJUANA BUSINESSES
TIMELY REGISTERED UNDER ICO, TUO AND MEASURE M

#	ICO and TUO Name(s)		BTRC Number(s)	BTRC Address(es)	BTRC Name(s)	BTRC dba Name
52	H.P.R.C. / Herbal Pain Relief Center	ICO	0002232461-0001-1	21521 Sherman 91303	Herbal Pain Relief Center Cooperative Inc	Same as Legal Name
	Herbal Pain Relief Center Cooperative / Herbal Pain Relief Center	TUO	Same	Same	Same	Same as Legal Name
		L050	Same	Same	Same	Same as Legal Name
53	Herbal Relief Caregivers Inc	ICO	0002231724-0001-8	6850 Van Nuys 91405	Herbal Relief Caregivers Inc	Same as Legal Name
	Same	TUO	Same	Same	Same	Same as Legal Name
		L050	Same	6446 Lankershim 91606-2812	Same	Same as Legal Name
54	Herbal Solutions LLC	ICO	0002182264-0001-5	22728 Ventura 91364	Herbal Solutions LLC / Herbal Solutions	Same as Legal Name
	Herbal Solutions LLC / Herbal Cooperative Solutions	TUO	Same	Same	Herbal Solutions LLC	Same as Legal Name
		L050	Same	19654 Ventura 91356-2970	Same	Same as Legal Name
55	Herbalcure	ICO	0002221186-0001-3	11318 Pico 90064 / 767 Isabel #2 90065	Herbalcure Corporation	Same as Legal Name
	Herbalcure Corporation / Herbalcure	TUO	Same	11318 Pico 90064	Herbalcure Corporation / Herbalcure	Same as Legal Name
		L050	Same	Same	Same	Same as Legal Name
56	Highland Park Patient Collective	ICO	0002190335-0001-9	5716 Figueroa 90042	Highland Park Patient Collective Inc / Highland Park Patient Collective	Same as Legal Name
	Highland Park Patient Collective Inc	TUO	Same	Same	Highland Park Patient Collective Inc	Same as Legal Name
		L050	Same	Same	Same	Same as Legal Name
57	Holistic Alternative Inc	ICO	0002247944-0001-1	21001 Sherman 91303 / 6698 Paso Fino St 92880	Holistic Alternative Inc	Same as Legal Name
	Same	TUO	Same	Same	Same	Same as Legal Name
		L050	Same	Same	Same	Same as Legal Name
58	Holistic Care of Studio City	ICO	0002236381-0001-0	12406 Ventura 91604	Vincent Nicoletti / CCSC	Same as Legal Name
	Holistic Care of Studio City / Holistic Pain Relief	TUO	Not Resubmitted per TUO	264 Rampart 90057-1404	Same	Same as Legal Name
		L050	Same	Same	Same	Same as Legal Name
59	Holistic Healing Alternative Inc	ICO	0002226675-0001-2	1400 Olive 90015	Holistic Healing Alternatives Inc	Same as Legal Name
	Same	TUO	Same	Same	Same	Kenmore Medical
		L050	Same	261 Kenmore 90004-5604	Same	Same
60	Hollywood Holistic	ICO	0002173088-0001-5	1543 Sawtelle 90025	Hollywood Holistic Inc	Same as Legal Name
	Hollywood Holistic Inc / Hollywood Holistic II	TUO	Same	Same	Same	Same as Legal Name
		L050	Same	Same	Same	Same as Legal Name
61	Hyperion Healing Inc	ICO	0002274403-0001-9	1913 Hyperion 90027	Hyperion Healing	Same as Legal Name
	Hyperion Healing / Hyperion Healing Inc	TUO	Same	Same	Same	Same as Legal Name
		L050	Same	Same	Same	Same as Legal Name
62	Infinity Medical Alliance Inc dba RC Alliance	ICO	0002246573-0001-8	1147 Robertson 90035	Infinity Medical Alliance Inc	Same as Legal Name
	Infinity Medical Alliance Inc	TUO	Not Resubmitted per TUO			
		L050	0002456876-0001-3	1151 Robertson 90035-1468	Same	Same

PROPOSITION D: EXISTING MEDICAL MARIJUANA BUSINESSES
TIMELY REGISTERED UNDER ICO, TUO AND MEASURE M

#	ICO and TUO Name(s)		BTRC Number(s)	BTRC Address(es)	BTRC Name(s)	BTRC dba Name
63	Ironworks Collective	ICO	0002112115-0001-9	4100 Lincoln 90292	Ironworks Collective Inc / Ironworks Collective	Ironworks Collective
	Ironworks Collective Inc / Ironworks Collective	TUO	Same	Same	Same	Same
		LO50	Same	Same	Same	Same
64	KB Center for Compassionate Care Inc	ICO	0002190532-0001-1	9960 Canoga 91311	KB Center for Compassionate Care Inc	Same as Legal Name
	Same	TUO	Not Resubmitted per TUO			Same
		LO50	Same	Same	Same	Same
65	Korea Town Collective LLC	ICO	0002132954-0001-7	3567 3rd 90020	Korea Town Collective LLC / Korea Town Collective	Same as Legal Name
	Koreatown Collective, LLC / Koreatown Collective	TUO	Same	Same	Same	Same
		LO50	Same	Same	Same	Same
66	Kushism Inc	ICO	0002244476-0001-9	7555 Woodley 91406	Kushism, Inc	Same as Legal Name
	Same	TUO	Same	Same	Same	Same
		LO50	Same	Same	Same	Same
67	L.A. Area Herbal Delivery dba: Hollywood Home Remedies	ICO	0002275065-0001-2	1607 El Centro 90028	L.A. Area Herbal Delivery	Hollyweed
	L.A. Area Herbal Delivery dba: Hollyweed and Hollywood Home Remedies	TUO	Same	Same	Same	Same
		LO50	Same	Same	Same	Same
68	LA Wonderland Caregivers	ICO	0002256288-0001-6	4406 Pico 90019 / 4410 Pico 90019	LA Wonderland Caregivers LLC	Same as Legal Name
	LA Wonderland Caregivers LLC / LA Wonderland Caregivers	TUO	Same	Same	Same	Same
		LO50	Same	Same	Same	Same
69	Living Earth Wellness Center Inc	ICO	0002211556-0001-9	4207 Pico 90019	Living Earth Wellness Center Inc	Same as Legal Name
	Same	TUO	Not Resubmitted per TUO			Same
		LO50	Same	1803 Western 90006-5813	Same	Same
70	Woodland Hills Treatment Center	ICO	0002286459-0001-5	5338 Alhama 91364	Vladimir Ganelin / Woodland Hills Treatment Center	Same as Legal Name
	Lizbor Inc dba: Woodland Hills Treatment Center	TUO	Not Resubmitted per TUO			Same
		LO50	0002406834-0001-8	5338 Alhama 91364-2101	Lizbor Inc	Woodlandhills Treatment Center WHTC
71	Natural Remedies Inc	ICO	0002206249-0001-4	6231 Santa Monica 90038	Natural Remedies Inc	Same as Legal Name
		TUO	Same	1551 Calle Patricia 90272	Same	Same
	Los Angeles Natural Remedies, Inc / Natural Remedies Caregivers / Natural Remedies Collective / Natural Remedies	LO50	Same	927 Western 90029-3215	Same	Same
72	Los Angeles Valley Caregivers Inc	ICO	0002227446-0001-7	6657 Reseda 91335	Los Angeles Valley Caregivers, Inc.	Same as Legal Name
	Los Angeles Valley Caregivers Inc / L.A.V.C.	TUO	Same	Same	Same	Same
		LO50	Same	Same	Same	Same
73	Los Angeles Wellness Center LLC	ICO	0002289515-0001-2	312 Olympic 90015	Los Angeles Wellness Center LLC / Paul Scott	Same as Legal Name
	Los Angeles Wellness Center LLC / IMCC Wellness Center	TUO	Not Resubmitted per TUO			Same
		LO50	Same	Same	Los Angeles Wellness Center LLC	Same

PROPOSITION D: EXISTING MEDICAL MARIJUANA BUSINESSES
TIMELY REGISTERED UNDER ICO, TUO AND MEASURE M

	ICO and TUO Name(s)		BTRC Number(s)	BTRC Address(es)	BTRC Name(s)	BTRC dba Name
74	Marina Caregivers Cooperative Inc	ICO	0002072463-0001-5	3007 Washington 90292	Marina Caregivers Cooperative Inc / Marina Caregivers	Same as Legal Name
	Marina Caregivers Cooperative Inc / M.C.C. Inc	TUO	Not Resubmitted per TUO		Same	Same
		L050	Same	730 Washington 90292-5543	Marina Caregivers Cooperative Inc	Same
75	McFlower Corporation / Delta 9 Caregivers	ICO	0002165101-0001-1	7648 Van Nuys 91405 / P.O. Box 73 91408	McFlower Corp	Delta 9 Caregivers
	Same	TUO	Same	Same	McFlower Corp / Kind Caregivers Prop-215 SB420	Same
		L050	Same	7648 Van Nuys 91405	McFlower Corp	Same
76	Medical Caregivers Association	ICO	0002117413-0001-1	4344 Eagle Rock 90041	Medical Caregivers Association	Same as Legal Name
	Medical Caregivers Cooperative, Inc / Medical Caregivers Association	TUO	Same	Same	Same	Same
		L050	Same	1804 Broadway 90031-2525	Medical Caregivers Cooperative	Same
77	Medical Marijuana Relief Center	ICO	0002226606-0001-1	14303 Ventura 91423	Glen Tim LeVangie / Medical Marijuana Relief Center	Medical Marijuana Relief Center
	MMRC, inc / Medical Marijuana Relief Center	TUO	Same	Same	Same	Same
		L050	Same	Same	Same	Same
78	Melrose Herbal Collective	ICO	0002259291-0001-7	7257 Melrose 90046	Trevor Davis Angone / Melrose Herbal Collective	Melrose Herbal Collective
	Melrose Herbal Collective / California Herbal Remedies	TUO	Same	Same	Same	Same
		L050	Same	22700 Western 90501-4951	Same	Same
79	Mid City Cannabis Club Inc. dba La Brea Collective	ICO	0002210665-0004-3	812 La Brea 90036	Mid City Cannabis Club Inc. / La Brea Collective	La Brea Collective
	Mid City Cannabis Club Inc. / Benefit Corporation dba La Brea Collective	TUO	Same	Same	Daniel Sosa / La Brea Collective	Same
		L050	Same	5057 Pico 90019-4129	Mid City Cannabis Club Inc. / La Brea Collective	Same
80	Mother Nature's Remedy	ICO	0002086566-0001-2	17302 Saticoy 91406	Mother Nature's Remedy Caregivers Inc / David Slocum	Same as Legal Name
	Mother Nature's Remedy Caregivers Inc / Mother Nature's Remedy	TUO	Same	Same	Same	Same
		L050	Same	Same	Mother Nature's Remedy Caregivers Inc	Same
81	Nature's Cure Inc	ICO	0002260907-0001-2	4577 Valley 90032	Natures Cure Inc / Nature's Cure	Nature's Cure Inc
	Same	TUO	Same	Same	Same	Same
		L050	Same	2107 Manchester 90047-2953	Same	Same
82	Nature's Natural Collective Care	ICO	0002189025-0001-0	6951 Reseda 91335	Nature's Natural Collective Care Inc	Same as Legal Name
	Same	TUO	Same	Same	Same	Same
		L050	Same	Same	Same	Same
83	New Age Compassion Care Center LLC	ICO	0002220478-0001-6	19973 Ventura 91364 / 20929 Ventura #47-154 91364	New Age Compassion Care Center LLC	Same as Legal Name
	New Age Compassion Care Center LLC / New Age Compassion Care Center	TUO	Not Resubmitted per TUO	Same	Same	Same
		L050	0002189250-001-0	19720 Ventura 91364-6308	New Age Compassion Care Center Corp	Same
84	New Apothecary Inc dba Apothecary 420	ICO	0002245640-0001-4	330 Western 90004	New Apothecary Inc / Apothecary 420 / Edward Skopinsky	Apothecary 420
	New Apothecary, Inc / Apothecary 420	TUO	0002187797-0001-7	Same	The Apothecary, Inc / Medical Marijuana Facility in Compliance with State and City Laws	Same
		L050	0002245640-0001-4	Same	Same	Same

PROPOSITION D: EXISTING MEDICAL MARIJUANA BUSINESSES
TIMELY REGISTERED UNDER ICO, TUO AND MEASURE M

#	ICO and TUO Name(s)		BTRC Number(s)	BTRC Address(es)	BTRC Name(s)	BTRC dba Name
85	Nile Collective Corporation	ICO	0002275032-0001-0	1501 Pacific 90291	Nile Cooperative Corporation / Nile Collective	Nile Collective
	Nile Cooperative Corporation / Nile Collective Corporation	TUO	Same	Same	Same	Same
		L050	Same	Same	Same	Same
86	North Hollywood Compassionate Caregivers	ICO	0002269618-0001-1	4854 Lankershim 91601	Hakop Paronyan / North Hollywood Compassionate Caregivers	North Hollywood Compassionate Caregivers
	North Hollywood Compassionate Caregivers, Inc. / North Hollywood Compassionate Caregivers	TUO	Same	Same	North Hollywood Compassionate Care Givers Inc	Same
		L050	Same	Same	Same	Same
87	Northridge Caregivers Co-op Inc (NCI)	ICO	0002207291-0001-3	12517 Oxnard 91606	Northridge Caregivers Co-op Inc	Same as Legal Name
	Northridge Caregivers Co-op, Inc. / Northridge Caregivers, Inc.	TUO	Not Resubmitted per TUO	Same	Same	Same
		L050	0002207291-0001-3	12517 Oxnard 91606-4458	Same	Same
88	Organic Century Farmacy	ICO	0002193580-0001-2	404 7th 90014	Organic Century Farmacy Inc	Same as Legal Name
	Same	TUO	Not Resubmitted per TUO	Same	Same	Same
		L050	0002193580-0001-2	Same	Same	Same
89	Organic Green Treatment Center	ICO	0002239788-0001-6	2626 Figueroa 90007	Arutyun Yegoyan / Organic Green Treatment Center	Organic Green Treatment Center
	Organic Green Treatment Center / Adams/Hill Discount Center	TUO	Same	2606 Hill 90007 / 2626 Figueroa 90007	Same	Same
		L050	Same	1337 Flower 90015-2907	Same	Same
90	Patients Against Pain Inc	ICO	0000382947-0002-9	6240 Laurel Canyon 91606	Patients Against Pain Inc / Patients Against Pain	Same as Legal Name
	Same	TUO	Same	Same	Same	Same
		L050	Same	Same	Same	Same
91	PCLA / Patients and Caregivers Los Angeles Inc	ICO	0002201626-0001-0	5763 Pico 90019	Patients and Caregivers Los Angeles Inc	Same as Legal Name
	Patients and Caregivers Los Angeles Inc	TUO	Not Resubmitted per TUO	Same	Same	Same
		L050	0002201626-0001-0	6141 Vineland 91606-4913	Same	Same
92	Patients Corp dba: Foothill Wellness Center	ICO	0002237919-0001-7	7132 Foothill 91042 / 5495 Cochran #112 93063	Patients Corp / Benefit Care Givers	Foothill Wellness Center
	Same	TUO	Not Resubmitted per TUO	Same	Same	Same
		L050	0002237919-0001-7	7132 Foothill 91042	Patients Corp / Foothill Wellness Center	Same
93	Perennial Holistic Wellness Center	ICO	0002207035-0001-3	14542 Ventura 91403	Sammar Mustafa Humeid	Same as Legal Name
	Perennial Holistic Wellness Center, Inc. / Sammar Humeid dba Perennial Holistic Wellness Center	TUO	Same	Same	Sammar Mustafa Humeid / Perennial Holistic Wellness Center	Same
		L050	Same	11706 Ventura 91604	Natural Remedies Inc	Same
94	Progressive Horizon dba: West Coast Collective	ICO	0002207198-0001-7	3133 San Fernando 90065	Progressive Horizon Inc	West Coast Collective
		TUO	Not Resubmitted per TUO	15902 Hallilburton Rd #222 91745	Same	Same
	Progressive Horizon dba: West Coast Collective	L050	0002207198-0001-7	3133 San Fernando 90065	Same	Same

PROPOSITION D: EXISTING MEDICAL MARIJUANA BUSINESSES
TIMELY REGISTERED UNDER ICO, TUO AND MEASURE M

#	ICO and TUO Name(s)		BTRC Number(s)	BTRC Address(es)	BTRC Name(s)	BTRC dba Name
95	Purelife Alternative Wellness Center	ICO	0002107775-0001-0	1649 LaCienega 90035	CYJA Inc / Purelife Alternative / Yamileth Bolanos	Same as Legal Name
	Same	TUO	0002107775-0001-0	Same	Same	Purelife Alternative Wellness Center
		L050	Same	Same	Same	
96	Purple Heart Compassion	ICO	0002207463-0001-8	5823 Pico 90019	Yong Jie Yu	Purple Heart Compassionate
	Purple Heart Compassion Inc	TUO	0002258885-0001-6	Same	Purple Heart Compassion Inc	Same as Legal Name
		L050	Same	Same	Pura Vida Tres Inc	Same
97	RDC Collective Corporation	ICO	0002238832-0001-1	6102 Reseda 91335	RDC Collective Corp	Same as Legal Name
	RDC Collective Corporation / Reseda Caregivers Collective	TUO	Same	Same	Same	Reseda Caregivers Collective
		L050	Same	18448 Oxnard 91356-1504	RDC Collective Corp / Reseda Caregivers Collective	Same as Legal Name
98	Red Moon Inc	ICO	0002239627-0001-1	14350 Oxnard 91401	Red Moon Inc	Same as Legal Name
	Same	TUO	Same	Same	Same	Same as Legal Name
		L050	Same	Same	Same	Same
99	Relief Corp dba Canna Care Relief	ICO	0002208428-0001-3	1716 Sepulveda 90025	Relief Corp	Same as Legal Name
	Same	TUO	Not Resubmitted per TUO	Same	Same	Same
		L050	0002208428-0001-3	Same	Relief Corp	Same
100	Resource Referral Services	ICO	0002178426-0001-3	5113 Pico 90019	Resource Referral Services Inc	Same
	Resource Referral Services Inc / Resource Referral Services	TUO	Not Resubmitted per TUO			
		L050	0002178426-0001-3	8940 National 90034-3308	Resource Referral Services Inc / HNC - Herbal Nutritional Center / One Love Herbal Collective	HNC - Herbal Nutritional Center / One Love Herbal Collective
101	Robertson Caregivers	ICO	0002034460-0002-9	2515 Robertson 90034	Steven W Prince / Robertson Caregivers Beverlywood	Robertson Caregivers Beverlywood
	Robertson Caregivers Beverlywood / Robertson Caregivers	TUO	Same	Same	Same	Same
		L050	Same	Same	Robertson Caregivers Beverlywood	Same
102	Safe Harbor Patients Collective Inc	ICO	0002230054-0001-9	5953 Hazeltine 91401	Safe Harbor Patient's Collective Inc	Same as Legal Name
		TUO	Same	Same	Same	Same as Legal Name
		L050	Same	Same	Same	Same
103	San Fernando Valley Discount Medical Supply Inc	ICO	0002265879-0001-5	6732 White Oak 91406 / 15005 Sherman #321 91405	San Fernando Valley Discount Medical Supply Inc	Same as Legal Name
	Same	TUO	Not Resubmitted per TUO	Same	Same	Same
		L050	0002265879-0001-5	13550 Roscoe 91402-5515	San Fernando Valley Discount Medical Supply Inc	Same
104	San Fernando Valley Patients Group	ICO	0002118901-0001-6	8805 Reseda 91324	John Watkins / San Fernando Valley Patients Group	San Fernando Valley Patients Group
	Same	TUO	Same	Same	Same	Same
		L050	Same	9716 Glenoaks 91352-1519	Same	Same
105	Sherman Oaks Collective Care	ICO	0002191730-0001-6	14200 Ventura 91423	Sherman Oaks Collective Care Inc	Same as Legal Name
	Same	TUO	Same	Same	Same	Same as Legal Name
		L050	Same	Same	Same	Same

PROPOSITION D: EXISTING MEDICAL MARIJUANA BUSINESSES
TIMELY REGISTERED UNDER ICO, TUO AND MEASURE M

	ICO and TUO Name(s)		BTRC Number(s)	BTRC Address(es)	BTRC Name(s)	BTRC dba Name
106	Sherman Oaks Holistic Oasis	ICO	0002349992-0001-2	13650 Burbank 91401	Luis Bobadilla	Same as Legal Name
	Same	TUO	Same	Same	Same	Same
		LO50	Same	Same	Sherman Oaks Holistic Oasis	Same
107	Silverlake Caregivers	ICO	0000410225-0002-1	2323 Beverly 90057	Tolabus Stein / Silverlake Caregivers Group	Silverlake Caregivers Group
	Silverlake Caregivers Group	TUO	Same	Same	Same	Same
		LO50	Same	Same	Same	Same
108	So Cal Coop Inc	ICO	0002219954-0001-1	19459 Ventura 91356	So Cal Co-op Inc	Same as Legal Name
	So Cal Co-op Inc	TUO	Same	Same	Same	Same
		LO50	Same	Same	Same	Same
109	Southern California Collective Inc	ICO	0002262211-0002-4	1121 Colorado 90041 / 501 N 1st St 91801	Southern California Collective / Southern California Caregivers	Colorado Collective
	Southern California Collective Inc / Colorado Collective	TUO	Not Resubmitted per TUO	Same	Same	Same
		LO50	0002262211-0002-4	521 Alvarado 90057-2903	Southern California Collective / Hua-Yuan Hsu / Colorado Collective	Same
110	Strain Balboa Caregivers Inc	ICO	0002112381-0001-2	7207 Balboa 91406	Shaun Lang	Same as Legal Name
	Strain Balboa Caregivers Inc / Strain Balboa Caregivers Collective	TUO	Same	Same	Strain Balboa Caregivers, Inc	Same
		LO50	Same	17523 Ventura 91316-3836	Same	Same
111	Studio City Caregivers	ICO	0002210774-0001-6	3625 Cahuenga 90068	Studio City Caregivers Co-op Inc	Same as Legal Name
	Studio City Caregivers Co-op Inc / Studio City Caregivers / SCC	TUO	Same	Same	Same	Same
		LO50	Same	Same	Same	Same
112	Sun Valley Caregivers	ICO	0002183557-0001-7	11000 Randall 91352	Sun Valley Caregivers Inc	Same as Legal Name
	Sun Valley Caregivers / SVC	TUO	Same	Same	Same	Same
		LO50	Same	Same	Same	Same
113	Sunrise Caregiver Foundation	ICO	0002246867-0001-7	1151 Pacific Coast 90710	Sunrise Caregiver Foundation Inc	Same as Legal Name
	Sunrise Caregiver Foundation Inc.	TUO	Same	Same	Same	Same
		LO50	Same	Same	Same	Same
114	Sunset Herbal Corner	ICO	0002255600-0001-6	7225 Sunset 90046	Sunset Herbal Corner Inc	Same as Legal Name
	Sunset Herbal Corner Inc / Sunset Herbal Corner	TUO	Same	Same	Same	Same
		LO50	Same	Same	Same	Same
115	Superior Herbal Health	ICO	0002184569-0001-7	1011 84th 90044	Superior Herbal Health LLC	Same as Legal Name
	Superior Herbal Health Inc / Superior Herbal Health / Superior Herbal Health, LLC	TUO	Not Resubmitted per TUO			Same
		LO50	0002184569-0001-7	Same	Superior Herbal Health LLC	Same
116	The Green Goddess Collective	ICO	0002101730-0002-7	5711 Figueroa 90042 / 1663 Waterloo 90026	Daniel J. Stein / Green Goddess Collective	Green Goddess Collective
	The Green Goddess Collective / Green Goddess Holistic Care Collective, LLC	TUO	Same	70 Windward 90291-4102	Same	Same
		LO50	Same	70 Windward 90291-4102	Same	Same

PROPOSITION D: EXISTING MEDICAL MARIJUANA BUSINESSES
TIMELY REGISTERED UNDER ICO, TUO AND MEASURE M

	ICO and TUO Name(s)		BTRC Number(s)	BTRC Address(es)	BTRC Name(s)	BTRC dba Name
117	The Healing Touch	ICO	0002243390-0001-6	4430 Santa Monica #105 90029	The Healing Touch Inc	Same as Legal Name
	Welcome The Healing Touch / The Healing Touch	TUO	Same	Same	Same	Same
		L050	Same	18013 Ventura 91336-3517	Same	Same
118	The Higher Path Holistic Care	ICO	0002163060-0001-5	2227 Sunset 90026	Daniel Stein / Nicole McLaughlin / The Higher Path Holistic Care	The Higher Path Holistic Care
	The Higher Path Holistic Care Collective	TUO	Same	Same	Same	Same
		L050	Same	1302 Sunset 90026-4425	Daniel Stein / The Higher Path Holistic Care	Same
119	The Little Cottage Caregivers LLC	ICO	0002104144-0003-0	8133 Foothill 91040	The Little Cottage Caregivers LLC / The Little Cottage Caregivers	The Brothers Caregivers Group / The Little Cottage Caregivers Inc.
	Same	TUO	Same	Same	Same	Same
		L050	Same	Same	Same	Same
120	The Relief Company	ICO	0002218073-0001-2	5669 Pico 90019	Randy Cruzado / The Relief Collective	The Relief Collective
	The Relief Collective / The Relief Company	TUO	Same	Same	Same	Same
		L050	Same	15127 Holiday 91342-5503	Same	Same
121	The Van Nuys Group LLC dba: The Green Easy	ICO	0002274496-0001-5	6741 Van Nuys 91405 / 3441 Cahuenga 90068	The Van Nuys Group LLC / The Green Easy	Same as Legal Name
	Same	TUO	Same	7947 3rd 90048-4305	Same	Same
		L050	Same	Same	Same	Same
122	The Wellness Earth Energy Dispensary	ICO	0002198991-0001-0	12021 Ventura 91604	The Wellness Earth Energy Dispensary LLC	Same as Legal Name
	The Wellness Earth Energy Dispensary Collective Inc. / The Wellness Earth Energy Dispensary, LLC	TUO	Not Resubmitted per TUO			
		L050	0002198991-0001-0	Same	Same	Same
123	United Medical Alliance Inc dba: Bluegate	ICO	0002112599-0001-9	3428 Whittier 90023 / 15840 Halliburton 91745	United Medical Alliance Inc	Circle of Hope Alliance
	United Medical Alliance dba: Bluegate	TUO	Not Resubmitted per TUO		Same	Same
		L050	0002112599-0001-9	3428 Whittier 90023	United Medical Alliance Inc / Circle of Hope Alliance	Same
124	Universal Herbal Center	ICO	0002174190-0001-8	3177 Cahuenga 90068	Universal Herbal Center LLC	Same as Legal Name
	Universal Herbal Center Inc	TUO	0002168897-0001-0	Same	Universal Herbal Clinic Inc	Same
		L050	0002174190-0001-8	Same	Universal Herbal Center LLC	Same
125	V Farm 1509 dba: The Farmacy	ICO	0002227550-0001-1	1509 Abbot Kinney 90291	VFarm1509	Same as Legal Name
	V Farm 1509 / The Farmacy Venice / The Farmacy	TUO	Same	Same	Same	Same
		L050	Same	Same	Same	Same
126	V.H.C. / Valley Health Center	ICO	0002248388-0002-1	19019 Parthenia 91324	Marc Benson Earl / Valley Health Center	North Hollywood Medical Center
	Valley Health Center	TUO	Same	Same	Same	Same
		L050	Same	7766 Burnet 91405-1007	Same	Same
127	Valley Herbal Center Inc	ICO	0002231006-0001-2	11675 Vanowen 91605	Valley Herbal Center Inc	Same as Legal Name
	Same	TUO	Same	6805 Hazeltine 91405-3218	Valley Herbal Center	Same
		L050	Same	Same	Same	Same

PROPOSITION D: EXISTING MEDICAL MARIJUANA BUSINESSES
TIMELY REGISTERED UNDER ICO, TUO AND MEASURE M

	ICO and TUO Name(s)		BTRC Number(s)	BTRC Address(es)	BTRC Name(s)	BTRC dba Name
128	Venice Beach Care Center	ICO	000218164-0001-9	410 Lincoln 90291	The Compassion Network LLC / Venice Beach Care Centers	Venice Beach Care Centers
	The Compassion Network LLC dba: Venice Beach Care Center	TUO	Same	Same	Same	Same
		L050	Same	Same	Same	Same
129	Venice Caregiver Foundation	ICO	000224571-0001-4	10887 Venice 90034 / 5561 Sultana 91780	Venice Caregiver Foundation Inc	Same as Legal Name
	Venice Caregiver Foundation / Culver City Collective	TUO	Not Resubmitted per TUO			
		L050	000224571-0001-4	10887 Venice 90034-7108	Venice Caregiver Foundation Inc	Same
130	Vermont Herbal Center Inc	ICO	000225414-0001-7	955 Vermont 90006	Vermont Herbal Center Inc	Vermont Herbal Center
	Same	TUO	Same	Same	Same	Same
		L050	Same	Same	Same	Same
131	W Farm 1045 dba: The Farmacy	ICO	000222445-0001-6	1035 Gayley 90024	WFarm1045	The Westwood Farmacy
	W Farm 1045 / The Farmacy Westwood / The Farmacy	TUO	Same	Same	Same	Same
		L050	Same	Same	WFarm1045 Inc / The Westwood Farmacy	Same
132	Wellness Caregivers	ICO	000221571-0001-4	18663 Ventura 91356 / 12923 Chandler 91401	Wellness Caregivers / Yana Janasi	Same as Legal Name
	Same	TUO	Same	Same	Same	Same
		L050	Same	6318 Van Nuys 91401	Same	Same
133	Tanis Industries dba West Valley Patients Group	ICO	000222545-0001-6	23043 Ventura 91364	James Tanis / West Valley Patients Group	West Valley Patients Group
	West Valley Patients Group, Inc. / Tanis Industries	TUO	Same	Same	West Valley Patient Group / West Valley Patients Group	Same
		L050	Same	Same	Tanis Industries LLC / West Valley Patients Group	Same
134	Westside Caregivers Club Inc	ICO	000218917-0001-4	22148 Ventura 91364	Westside Caregivers Club Inc / Westside Caregivers Club	Westside Caregivers Club
	Same	TUO	Same	Same	Same	Same
		L050	Same	Same	Same	Same

LA CITY ATTORNEY REPORT ON DISCONTINUING BTRCS

MICHAEL N. FEUER
CITY ATTORNEY

REPORT NO. R15-0318
DEC 1 4 2015

REPORT RE:

DISCONTINUING THE ISSUANCE OF BUSINESS TAX REGISTRATION CERTIFICATES TO MEDICAL MARIJUANA DISPENSARIES NOT IN COMPLIANCE WITH PROPOSITION D AND RELATED ACTIONS

The Honorable City Council
 of the City of Los Angeles
Room 395, City Hall
200 North Spring Street
Los Angeles, California 90012

Council File No. 14-0366-S2

Honorable Members:

Pursuant to your request, the Office of the City Attorney (City Attorney) and the Office of Finance (Finance) present this joint report responding to the City Council's actions taken on October 28, 2015, relating to medical marijuana dispensaries (MMDs) not in compliance with Proposition D.

Discontinuance of MMD BTRCs

The City Attorney has prepared and now transmits for your consideration the enclosed draft ordinance, approved as to form and legality, which would amend Subsection (b) of Section 21.50 of Article 1, Chapter II of the Los Angeles Municipal Code (LAMC) to: (1) limit taxation of medical marijuana collectives to those that attest to compliance with Proposition D; (2) prohibit the issuance of new business tax registration certificates (BTRCs) for MMDs; and (3) add Subsection (g) to Section 21.50 to require MMDs to attest to compliance with Proposition D when submitting their annual renewals. The draft ordinance provides that any person who makes a false statement or representation in the affidavit would be guilty of a misdemeanor.

Pursuant to Council Rule 38, a copy of this draft ordinance amendment was provided to Finance. Finance concurs with the draft amendment and recommends City Council approval. In anticipation of this proposed amendment, Finance has initiated necessary operational modifications to the various BTRC application and registration processes to effectuate Council's instruction and to support this legislative action. It should be noted that Finance's on-line E-registration and E-filing services will require programming changes, with assistance from ITA, to eliminate the ability for a MMD to apply for a BTRC or to file an annual business tax renewal via the Internet. Furthermore, operational changes are underway to alter the BTRC registration process and business tax renewal process at Finance's Public Counter locations, mail-in units and via the Department's Call Center.

We also have enclosed a sample affidavit to be attested to under penalty of law and remitted by each MMD claiming compliance with Proposition D with its annual renewal pursuant to the proposed draft ordinance. Per the draft ordinance, the final form of the affidavit would be subject to the Director of Finance's approval. The affidavit would be subject to public disclosure and may be released to law enforcement upon request.

Modification of BTRC

Finance has worked with the City Attorney to initiate the revision of current language on the face of the BTRC to more explicitly clarify that the issuance of a BTRC to a MMD does not indicate compliance with Proposition D, nor does it indicate permission by the City to operate a MMD business. In addition, Finance is in the process of altering the MMD BTRC to implement a distinct color scheme which will enable those viewing a displayed MMD BTRC to readily identify that the BTRC was issued to a MMD solely for tax compliance purposes.

Automatic Reporting Process

Effective October 1, 2015, Finance implemented a monthly reporting process which includes the reporting to the City Attorney, the Los Angeles Police Department, and the Building and Safety Department of all MMDs which have been issued a BTRC. This same data is also available on the City's Open Data website.

Displaying an Expired BTRC or a BTRC of a Different Classification

Further pursuant to your request, the enclosed draft ordinance would add a new Subsection (h) to Section 21.50 to make posting an expired or otherwise invalid BTRC a misdemeanor and similarly to prohibit any MMD from displaying a BTRC of a different classification, such as retail sales, for medical marijuana business activity. Pursuant to Council Rule 38, a copy of this draft ordinance was provided to the Los Angeles Police Department with a request that it provide any comments to the City Council or its Committees when this matter is considered.

Summary of State Medical Marijuana Legislation

Recently enacted State legislation, the Medical Marijuana Regulation and Safety Act (Act), creates a State regulatory and licensing system for commercial cannabis activities. State regulations will be comprehensive, and address matters to include health and safety, testing, security and worker protections. The Act requires that, once State regulations have been implemented, all commercial cultivation, manufacture, dispensing, distribution, testing and transportation of marijuana be licensed by the state and authorized by the local jurisdiction where the activity is to take place: "Upon the date of implementation of regulations by the licensing authority, no person shall engage in commercial cannabis activity without possessing both a state license and a local permit, license, or other authorization." Bus. & Prof. Code §19320(a). Engaging in commercial cannabis activities without a State license will be subject to both civil and criminal penalties. The Department of Consumer Affairs estimates that it will begin issuing State licenses in January 2018. The Act provides that deliveries of medical marijuana can only be made by a dispensary and in cities and counties that do not "explicitly prohibit" such deliveries by local ordinance. Additionally, cities that do not have an ordinance regulating or prohibiting marijuana cultivation by March 1, 2016, will lose the authority to regulate or ban cultivation within their city limits. In such jurisdictions, the State will become the sole licensing authority for cultivation.

The Act expressly preserves local regulatory authority and provides for continued enforcement of Proposition D by the City of Los Angeles: "Issuance of a state license or a determination of compliance with local law by the licensing authority shall in no way limit the ability of the City of Los Angeles to prosecute any person or entity for a violation of, or otherwise enforce, Proposition D...or the city's zoning laws. Nor may issuance of a license or determination of compliance with local law by the licensing authority be deemed to establish, or be relied upon, in determining satisfaction with the immunity requirements of Proposition D or local zoning law, in court or in any other context or forum." Bus. & Prof. Code §19321(d).

Because Proposition D, as currently written, does not provide for the issuance of permits or other authorization by the City of Los Angeles, medical marijuana businesses in the City will not be able to obtain a State license and, therefore, will not be able to comply with the Act. As such, when the State begins issuing licenses (projected to be January 2018), MMDs in the City will not be authorized under State law unless the Act is amended or the City establishes a permit or other authorization process.

The Act does not disturb local authority to levy fees and taxes. In fact, it expressly provides that "local jurisdictions retain the power to assess fees and taxes, as applicable, on facilities that are licensed pursuant to this chapter and the business activities of those licensees." Bus. & Prof. Code §19320(d). Therefore, the City's ability to tax medical marijuana businesses will remain intact, although the Council may be faced with the choice of whether to tax MMDs that are unlawful under State law. Again, whether any MMD could lawfully operate under the State law will depend on the City's establishment of a permit or comparable process for MMDs or an amendment to the Act.

If you have any questions regarding these matters, please contact Assistant City Attorney Beverly Cook at (213) 978-7760 or Ed Cabrera, Assistant Director of Finance at (213) 978-1516. They or other members of the City Attorney's Office and the Office of Finance will be present when you consider this matter to answer any questions you may have.

Very truly yours,

MICHAEL N. FEUER, City Attorney

By _____
DAVID MICHAELSON
Chief Assistant City Attorney

ANTOINETTE CHRISTOVALE,
Director of Finance

By _____
ED CABRERA
Assistant Director of Finance

DM/EC/PJ:pj
Transmittals

ORDINANCE NO. _____

An ordinance amending Subsection (b) of Section 21.50 of Article 1, Chapter II of the Los Angeles Municipal Code to limit taxation of medical marijuana collectives to those that attest to compliance with Proposition D; adding Subsection (g) to Section 21.50 to require medical marijuana collectives to attest to compliance with Proposition D when submitting their annual renewals; and adding Subsection (h) to Section 21.50 to make posting an invalid BTRC a misdemeanor and to similarly prohibit any medical marijuana collective from displaying a BTRC of a different classification.

**THE PEOPLE OF THE CITY OF LOS ANGELES
DO ORDAIN AS FOLLOWS:**

Section 1. Subsection (b) of Section 21.50 of Article 1, Chapter II of the Los Angeles Municipal Code is amended to read as follows:

(b) Every person engaged in operating or otherwise conducting a medical marijuana collective that attests under penalty of law to compliance with Proposition D and not otherwise specifically taxed by other business tax provisions of this Chapter, shall pay a business tax of $60.00 for each $1,000.00 of gross receipts or fractional part thereof. No new business tax registration certificates shall be issued for any medical marijuana collective business activity. Any medical marijuana collective that does not attest to compliance with Proposition D shall not be taxed under any Section of this Article for any medical marijuana collective business activity. It shall be the burden of the medical marijuana collective to determine and accurately represent to the Office of Finance whether it complies with Proposition D.

Sec. 2. A new Subsection (g) of Section 21.50 of Article 1, Chapter II of the Los Angeles Municipal Code is added to read as follows:

(g) Every medical marijuana collective taxed by this section shall remit with its annual renewal an affidavit in a form approved by the Director of Finance attesting to its compliance with Proposition D and such affidavit shall be subject to public disclosure. Any person who makes a false statement or representation in the affidavit is guilty of a misdemeanor.

Sec. 3. A new Subsection (h) to Section 21.50 of Article 1, Chapter II of the Los Angeles Municipal Code is added to read as follows:

(h) It shall be a misdemeanor for any person operating a medical marijuana collective as defined by Section 21.50(c) to maintain or display a business tax registration certificate for any classification other than that set forth in Section 21.50(b) for medical marijuana collective business activity or to maintain or display an expired, suspended or otherwise invalid business tax registration certificate.

Sec. 4. **Urgency Clause**. The City Council finds and declares that this ordinance is required for the immediate protection of the public peace, health and safety for the following reason: In order to protect the public from being misled by medical marijuana collectives that display City business tax registration certificates to give the impression to the public, and even to courts of law, that the City endorses their businesses or certifies that they are in compliance with Proposition D, as has been reported regarding many such businesses found not to be in compliance with Proposition D and prosecuted by the City Attorney.

Sec. 5. **Severability Clause.** If any provision of this ordinance is found to be unconstitutional or otherwise invalid by any court of competent jurisdiction, that invalidity shall not affect the remaining provisions of this ordinance which can be implemented without the invalid provisions, and to this end, the provisions of this ordinance are declared to be severable. The City Council hereby declares that it would have adopted this ordinance and each provision thereof irrespective of whether any one or more provisions are found invalid, unconstitutional or otherwise unenforceable.

Sec. 6. The City Clerk shall certify to the passage of this ordinance and have it published in accordance with Council policy, either in a daily newspaper circulated in the City of Los Angeles or by posting for ten days in three public places in the City of Los Angeles: one copy on the bulletin board located at the Main Street entrance to the Los Angeles City Hall; one copy on the bulletin board located at the Main Street entrance to the Los Angeles City Hall East; and one copy on the bulletin board located at the Temple Street entrance to the Los Angeles County Hall of Records.

I hereby certify that this ordinance was passed by the Council of the City of Los Angeles, **by a vote of not less than three-fourths** of all of its members, at its meeting of _____.

HOLLY L. WOLCOTT, City Clerk

By _____
Deputy

Approved _____

_____
Mayor

Approved as to Form and Legality

MICHAEL N. FEUER, City Attorney

By _(signature)_
DAVID MICHAELSON
Chief Assistant City Attorney

Date   DEC 1 4 2015

File No.   CF 14-0366-S2

m:\econ dev_pub finance\public finance\pj shemtoob\mmb\draft ordinance amending lamc 21.50 re btrc and mmbs (final).doc

MEDICAL MARIJUANA COLLECTIVE ANNUAL BUSINESS TAX AFFIDAVIT

(Los Angeles Municipal Code Section 21.50)

1. Legal name of person filing medical marijuana collective's annual Business Tax renewal: _____.
   (must hold one of the positions identified in number 3 below and provide a copy of government issued identification for verification purposes)

2. I am filing a renewal for Business Tax Registration Certificate ("BTRC") No. _____ for the medical marijuana collective ("MMC"): _____.

3. My position at the MMC is:

   ☐ Individual owner ☐ Manager of the LLC
   ☐ Member of the LLC ☐ Partner
   ☐ Officer of the corporation (specify office held: _____)

4. I have reviewed and am familiar with Proposition D and have personal knowledge of the history and operations of the MMC referenced in Answer 2. This MMC is qualified for limited immunity under Proposition D to establish and operate a medical marijuana collective in the City of Los Angeles. This MMC:

   ☐ Operates at only one location;
   ☐ Has a BTRC issued before November 14, 2007, No. _____;
   ☐ Registered with the City Clerk pursuant to Ordinance 179027;
   ☐ Filed an Intent to Register with the City Clerk pursuant to Ordinance 181069 as amended by Ordinance 181530;
   ☐ Did not cease operation as provided in LAMC 45.19.6.3. D;
   ☐ Obtained a 21.50 BTRC in 2011 or 2012 and renewed it as provided in LAMC § 45.19.6.3.E – BTRC No. _____;
   ☐ Paid all taxes as provided by LAMC § 45.19.6.3.F;
   ☐ Is open only between the hours of 10:00 a.m. and 8:00 p.m;
   ☐ Complies with the site requirements of LAMC § 45.19.6.3.L and O;
   ☐ Complies with operational requirements of LAMC § 45.19.6.3 H, J, K and M;
   ☐ Has identified the MMC managers to the City Clerk and had its managers complete Livescans, pursuant to LAMC § 45.19.6.3.M, annually since 2013;
   ☐ Has managers who are compliant with LAMC § 45.19.6.3.M.

   Note: The above generally summarizes immunity requirements. Please consult Proposition D for further details.

5. **I understand that this tax registration certificate is not a license to operate an MMC and its issuance does not indicate compliance with LAMC Section 45.19.6/Proposition D.**

6. **I understand that the MMC's business tax renewal and payment will not be accepted unless a fully completed and signed affidavit is submitted to the Office of Finance.**

   I declare, under penalty of LAMC Section 21.50(g), that to the best of my knowledge the foregoing is true, correct and complete.

   Executed this ____ day of _____, _____ at Los Angeles, California.

   Signed: _____

   SUBJECT TO PUBLIC DISCLOSURE

PROPOSITION M
MARCH, 2017

RESOLUTION

An ordinance amending the Los Angeles Municipal Code regarding the enforcement, taxation and regulation of cannabis related activity in the City of Los Angeles.

WHEREAS, the Compassionate Use Act (CUA), adopted by the voters in 1996, and the Medical Marijuana Program Act (MMPA), enacted by the State Legislature in 2003, provided California's qualified patients and their primary caregivers with limited immunities to specified criminal prosecutions under state law, including to ensure that qualified patients and their primary caregivers who obtain and use cannabis for medical purposes are not subject to state criminal prosecution;

WHEREAS, commencing in 2007, according to local media reports and neighborhood observations and complaints, hundreds of medical cannabis establishments, including self-named collectives, caregivers and dispensaries, (Businesses) opened, closed and reopened storefront shops in the City without land use approval under the Los Angeles Municipal Code (LAMC);

WHEREAS, the proliferation of cannabis Businesses led to increased crime and negative secondary impacts in neighborhoods, including but not limited to violent crimes, robberies, the distribution of tainted marijuana, and the diversion of marijuana;

WHEREAS, beginning in August 2007, the City enacted a series of ordinances designed to curb the rampant increase in cannabis dispensaries, which resulted in an explosion of lawsuits against the City;

WHEREAS, at the municipal election held on March 8, 2011, the voters of the City of Los Angeles passed Measure M and thereby enacted Los Angeles Municipal Code Section 21.50, which imposed a tax of $50 for every $1,000 of revenues generated by Medical Marijuana Collectives;

WHEREAS, on May 21, 2013, the voters of the City of Los Angeles passed Proposition D, adding Article 5.1 of Chapter IV of the Los Angeles Municipal Code, providing potential limited immunity from enforcement to approximately 135 cannabis dispensaries that had potentially complied with the City's 2007 Interim Control Ordinance, 2011 Temporary Urgency Ordinance and 2011 Measure M, and also met other specified requirements, and increasing the tax to $60 for every $1,000 of revenues generated by Medical Marijuana Collectives;

WHEREAS, since the passage of Proposition D, the City Attorney's Office has initiated over 1,700 criminal filings against individuals and entities regarding non-immunized cannabis Businesses and shut down over 800 non-immunized medical cannabis Businesses;

WHEREAS, despite this aggressive enforcement by the City Attorney's Office, with the passage of Proposition D, an unknown number of medical cannabis Businesses, including growers, delivery apps and delivery services continue to open, close, and reopen in Los Angeles, with no regulatory authorization from the City;

WHEREAS, because large profits can be earned by operating medical cannabis Businesses, it is necessary to have commensurate monetary penalties to prevent persons and entities from opening and operating non-immunized or illegal medical cannabis Businesses and to discourage property owners from renting to these kind of medical cannabis Businesses;

WHEREAS, medical cannabis Businesses require sustained police enforcement, because they are attractive targets for criminals as well as to individuals who buy cannabis and resell it to minors and others who cannot purchase it for themselves. These secondary sales further damage blighted areas of the City and are a drain on police resources. Large monetary sanctions are a rational way to discourage the proliferation of illegal businesses which generate these negative secondary impacts;

WHEREAS, in 2015, the Legislature and Governor enacted the Medical Cannabis Regulation and Safety Act ("MCRSA") consisting of three separate bills, creating a state licensing system for the commercial cultivation, manufacture, retail sale, transport, distribution, delivery, and testing of medical cannabis. Licenses under MCRSA are not expected to be available until 2018;

WHEREAS, on November 8, 2016, the voters of the State of California will be asked to vote on Proposition 64, an initiative also known as the Adult Use of Marijuana Act (AUMA). Under AUMA, personal possession of an ounce or less of cannabis and/or up to eight grams of concentrated cannabis would be legal. Retail sales of nonmedical cannabis may only take place pursuant to a state license, scheduled to become available in 2018;

WHEREAS, the potential approval of AUMA would impose new challenges for local governments to properly legislate the commercialization of nonmedical cannabis and medical cannabis, including their derivative products and services;

WHEREAS, it is the belief of the City that the circumstances in which cannabis activity should be allowed or not should be the subject of a robust, deliberative process that includes comprehensive public discussion and debate, and to that end, the City Council retains the legislative power and authority to determine the extent to which any such activity should be allowed in the City;

WHEREAS, in order to protect the public and consumers of medical and nonmedical cannabis, and reduce the negative secondary impacts on the City's communities, the City Council intends to receive public input, deliberate and then enact by ordinance a comprehensive regulatory and enforcement system related to medical and nonmedical cannabis activity; and that in order to enact a comprehensive regulatory and enforcement system, cannabis lawmaking authority must be retained by the City Council and Mayor;

WHEREAS, so that medical marijuana is available to patients in need of it, medical marijuana Businesses that have been operating in compliance with the limited immunity and tax provisions of Los Angeles Municipal Code Sections 45.19.6.3 and 21.50 at the one location identified in the Business's business tax registration certificate on file with the City should continue to operate until City licenses or permits are available, and, thereafter, priority in the processing of applications for a City license or permit should be given to those Businesses;

WHEREAS, the City also wishes to impose and obtain voter approval of a gross receipts tax regime of various rates on those who engage in the commercialization of nonmedical and medical cannabis, including their derivative products and services to the extent allowed by any comprehensive regulatory system established by the City; and

WHEREAS, the tax regime proposed would assist the City in raising revenue, improve access, measure the commercial growth of the cannabis industry and assess the need for further rules or regulations to prevent access by minors, improve access to those who are medically in need, and protect public safety, public health and the environment;

NOW, THEREFORE,

THE PEOPLE OF THE CITY OF LOS ANGELES
DO ORDAIN AS FOLLOWS:

Section 1. This ordinance shall be known and may be cited as the "Los Angeles Cannabis Enforcement, Taxation, and Regulation Act (CETRA)."

Sec. 2. A new section 21.51 is added to Article 1 of Chapter II the Los Angeles Municipal Code to read as follows:

SEC. 21.51. TAXATION OF CANNABIS.

Nothing in this Section shall be construed as requiring the City to allow, permit, license, authorize, or otherwise regulate cannabis, cannabis products or any business related to cannabis and/or cannabis products.

(a) For the purpose of this Section, the following words and phrases shall be defined as follows:

1. "Cannabis" shall mean all parts of the plant Cannabis sativa Linnaeus, Cannabis indica, or Cannabis ruderalis, whether growing or not; the seeds thereof; the resin, whether crude or purified, extracted from any part of the plant; and every compound, manufacture, salt, derivative, mixture, or preparation of the plant, its seeds, resin, separated resin, the mature stalks of the plant, fiber produced from the stalks, oil or cake made from the seeds of the plant, any other compound, manufacture, salt, derivative, mixture, or preparation of the

mature stalks (except the resin extracted therefrom), fiber, oil, or cake, or the sterilized seed of the plant which is incapable of germination, or industrial hemp, as defined by Section 11018.5 of the Health and Safety Code.

2. "Cannabis products" shall mean any product that includes cannabis that has undergone a process whereby the plant material has been transformed into a concentrate or such other form in order to enhance or deliver the cannabinoid active ingredient.

3. "Cultivating" shall mean to plant, grow, harvest, dry, cure, grade, or trim cannabis.

4. "Gross receipts" shall have the same meaning as set forth in Section 21.00(a) of this Article and shall include without limitation, membership dues, value of in kind contributions, reimbursements, the amount of any tax imposed by the state, county or rapid transit district whether imposed upon the retailer or the consumer, and any other property received by the business in its ordinary course.

5. "License" shall consist of (i) a state license issued under Division 10 of the California Business and Professions Code, Chapter 3.5 of Division 8 of the California Business and Professions Code, or such other applicable cannabis related provisions under state law, and (ii) any such other applicable City authorization, permit, or license (not including a business tax registration certificate which shall not be construed as a permit in any way).

6. "Manufacturing" shall mean to compound, blend, extract, infuse, or otherwise make, process, or prepare cannabis or cannabis products.

7. "Testing" shall mean to perform a test of cannabis and/or cannabis products in a testing laboratory that is accredited by an accrediting body that is independent from all other persons involved in commercial or medical cannabis, and registered with the State Department of Public Health.

8. "Testing laboratory" shall mean a facility, entity, or site in the City of Los Angeles that offers or performs testing.

9. "Transporting" shall mean to transfer cannabis and/or cannabis products from the location of one person with a license to the location of another person with a license.

(b) For purposes of this Section, the business tax to be imposed shall be as follows:

1. Every person with a license that is engaged in business of conducting the sale of cannabis and/or cannabis products shall pay a business tax of $100.00 for each $1,000.00 of gross receipts or fractional part thereof. The sale of medical cannabis shall be taxed as provided under Section 21.52 of this Article.

2. Every person with a license that is engaged in business of transporting cannabis and/or cannabis products shall pay a business tax of $10.00 for each $1,000.00 of gross receipts or fractional part thereof.

3. Every person with a license that is engaged in business of testing cannabis and/or cannabis products shall pay a business tax of $10.00 for each $1,000.00 of gross receipts or fractional part thereof.

4. Every person with a license that is engaged in business of researching cannabis and/or cannabis products shall pay a business tax of $10.00 for each $1,000.00 of gross receipts or fractional part thereof.

5. Every person with a license that is engaged in business of manufacturing or cultivating cannabis and/or cannabis products shall pay a business tax of $20.00 for each $1,000.00 of gross receipts or fractional part thereof.

6. Every person with a license that is engaged in business relating to the commercialization of cannabis and/or cannabis products not specifically taxed under this Section shall pay a business tax of $20.00 for each $1,000.00 of gross receipts or fractional part thereof.

(c) The Office of Finance shall file quarterly reports summarizing the amount of business taxes collected from the persons described in subsection (b) of this Section with the City Council, Mayor, Controller, and City Administrative Officer beginning April 1, 2018.

(d) All business taxes shall be due and payable quarterly as provided under Section 21.04(b) of this Article beginning July 1, 2018, which shall include any taxes owed from January 1, 2018, and then monthly as provided under Section 21.04(c) of this Article beginning July 1, 2019.

(e) The Office of Finance shall prescribe and implement a reasonable process, including set times and secure conditions, whereby every person subject to business tax under this Section is allowed to pay, in cash, the amount of business tax reported on their written statement, as prescribed under Section 21.14 of this Article.

(f) The Director of Finance may prescribe such additional requirements or conditions, as provided under Section 21.15(h) of this Article, when granting a business tax registration certificate under Section 21.08 of this Article with respect to a person subject to this Section, which may include an affidavit of compliance and/or proof of license. Any person who makes a false statement or misrepresentation in any required affidavit under this Section is guilty of a misdemeanor.

(g) It shall be a misdemeanor for any person operating a nonmedical cannabis business to maintain or display a business tax registration certificate for any classification other than that set forth herein for nonmedical cannabis business activity or to maintain or display an expired, suspended or otherwise invalid business tax registration certificate.

(h) No business tax registration certificate issued for purposes of this Section or the payment of any tax required under this Section shall be construed as authorizing the conduct or continuance of any illegal business or of a legal business in an illegal manner. Nothing in this Section implies or authorizes that any activity in connection with cannabis and/or cannabis products is legal unless otherwise authorized by federal and any other applicable law.

(i) Every person subject to this Section must pay the full tax imposed by this Section regardless of any rebate, exemption, incentive, or other reduction set forth elsewhere in the Municipal Code, except as required by state or federal law. No provision in the Municipal Code shall lower the tax rate set forth in this Section or otherwise reduce the amount of taxes paid hereunder unless the provision specifically states that the reduction applies.

(j) The City Council may impose the tax authorized by this Section at a lower rate and may establish exemptions, incentives or other reductions as otherwise allowed by the Charter and state law. No action by the Council under this paragraph shall prevent it from later increasing the tax or removing any exemption, incentive, or reduction and restoring up to the maximum tax specified in this Section.

(k) The provisions of this Section shall be effective January 1, 2018.

Sec. 3. A new Section 21.52 is added to Article 1 of Chapter II the Los Angeles Municipal Code to read as follows:

SEC. 21.52 TAXATION OF MEDICAL CANNABIS.

Nothing in this Section shall be construed as requiring the City to allow, permit, license, authorize, or otherwise regulate medical cannabis or any business related to medical cannabis.

(a) For the purpose of this Section, the following words and phrases shall be defined as follows:

1. "Cannabis" shall have the same meaning as set forth in Section 21.51(a)(1) of this Article.

2. "Cannabis products" shall have the same meaning as set forth in Section 21.51(a)(2) of this Article.

3. "Gross receipts" shall have the same meaning as set forth in Section 21.51(a)(4) of this Article.

4. "License" shall have the same meaning as set forth in Section 21.51(a)(5) of this Article.

5. "Medical cannabis" shall mean a product containing cannabis or cannabis products sold for use by medical cannabis patients in California pursuant to the Compassionate Use Act of 1996, found at Section 11362.5 of the California Health and Safety Code.

(b) For purposes of this Section, the business tax to be imposed shall be as follows:

1. Every person with a license engaged in business of conducting the sale of medical cannabis shall pay a business tax of $50.00 for each $1,000.00 of gross receipts or fractional part thereof.

(c) The Office of Finance shall file quarterly reports summarizing the amount of business taxes collected from the persons described in subsection (b) of this Section with the City Council, Mayor, Controller, and City Administrative Officer beginning April 1, 2018.

(d) All business taxes shall be due and payable quarterly as provided under Section 21.04(b) of this Article beginning July 1, 2018, which shall include any taxes owed from January 1, 2018, and then monthly as provided under Section 21.04(c) of this Article beginning July 1, 2019.

(e) The Office of Finance shall prescribe and implement a reasonable process, including set times and secure conditions, whereby every person subject to business tax under this Section is allowed to pay, in cash, the amount of business tax reported on their written statement, as prescribed under Section 21.04 of this Article.

(f) The Director of Finance may prescribe such additional requirements or conditions, as provided under Section 21.15(h), as may be necessary when granting a business tax registration certificate under Section 21.08 of this Article with respect to a business subject to this Section, which may include an affidavit of compliance and proof of License. Any person who makes a false statement or misrepresentation in any required affidavit under this Section is guilty of a misdemeanor.

(g) It shall be a misdemeanor for any person operating a medical cannabis business to maintain or display a business tax registration certificate for any classification other than that set forth herein for medical cannabis business activity or to maintain or display an expired, suspended or otherwise invalid business tax registration certificate.

(h) No business tax registration certificate issued for purposes of this Section or the payment of any tax required under this Section shall be construed as authorizing the conduct or continuance of any illegal business or of a legal business in an illegal manner. Nothing in this Section implies or authorizes that any activity in connection with cannabis and/or cannabis products is legal unless otherwise authorized by federal and any other applicable law.

(i) Every person subject to this Section must pay the full tax imposed by this Section regardless of any rebate, exemption, incentive, or other reduction set forth elsewhere in the Municipal Code, except as required by state or federal law. No provision in the Municipal Code shall lower the tax rate set forth in this Section or otherwise reduce the amount of taxes paid hereunder unless the provision specifically states that the reduction applies.

(j) The City Council may impose the tax authorized by this Section at a lower rate and may establish exemptions, incentives or other reductions as otherwise allowed by the Charter and state law. No action by the Council under this paragraph shall prevent it from later increasing the tax or removing any exemption, incentive, or reduction and restoring up to the maximum tax specified in this Section.

(k) The provisions of this Section shall be effective January 1, 2018, at which time the language of this Section shall govern in the event of any conflict between this Section and Section 21.50 regarding taxation of medical marijuana collectives.

Sec. 4. A new Article 5.2 is added to Chapter IV of the Los Angeles Municipal Code to read as follows:

ARTICLE 5.2

CANNABIS REGULATION AND ENFORCEMENT

SEC. 45.19.7.1. REPEAL OF PROPOSITION D (MEDICAL MARIJUANA).

The voters of the City of Los Angeles adopted Article 5.1 of Chapter IV of the Los Angeles Municipal Code regarding medical marijuana (Sections 45.19.6 through 45.19.6.9) as part of Proposition D, a referendum submitted to the voters by the City Council at the election held on May 21, 2013. The Council shall adopt an ordinance repealing these provisions of Proposition D (Sections 45.19.6 through 45.19.6.9) effective January 1, 2018, unless the Council adopts a Resolution, by majority vote, specifying another date for the repeal. The Council retains and possesses authority to amend, by ordinance, these provisions of Proposition D prior to its repeal.

SEC. 45.19.7.2. COUNCIL AUTHORITY TO REGULATE CANNABIS RELATED ACTIVITY AFTER PUBLIC HEARINGS AND PRIORITY OF DISPENSARIES COMPLIANT WITH PROPOSITION D.

A. **Council Authority.** The City retains and possesses complete authority to regulate all aspects of cannabis related activity, including, without limitation, the authority of the Council to adopt ordinances amending any of the provisions of this Article and/or any other provision of City law regarding cannabis related activity, other than taxation provisions to the extent that voter approval of any changes to taxation provisions is required under the State Constitution.

B. **Public Hearings.** The City intends to adopt a comprehensive regulatory process and structure for all cannabis related activity by September 30, 2017. Prior to the creation of a comprehensive regulatory process and structure for cultivation, processing, distribution, sale and other cannabis related activity, including enforcement of any licensing and related oversight (*i.e.*, the "commercialization" of cannabis), the Council shall convene public hearings in the City involving all stakeholders in the process of developing the rules, regulations and ordinances necessary to regulate the safe commercialization of cannabis, including, but not limited to, Neighborhood Councils, police officers, school officials, probation officers, civic and service organizations, chambers of commerce, cannabis related industries and others. The public hearings shall include consideration and attempted resolution of matters including:

1. Rules concerning who may qualify to operate in any of the phases of commercialization of cannabis;

2. Penalties, fines, and other enforcement tools needed to ensure strict compliance with licensing to avoid the unlawful conduct of cannabis related activities in the City;

3. Regulation of transportation of cannabis products within the City;

4. Siting of all buildings and facilities involved in all phases of commercialization of cannabis;

5. Preventing the over-concentration of businesses involved in commercialization of cannabis;

6. Determinations of any necessary land use requirements such as distances to schools, parks, libraries, residences, liquor stores, stores selling

candy to children, and other such matters affecting the locations of stores and facilities involved in commercialization of cannabis;

7. Constitutional and appropriate measures regarding advertising commercialization of cannabis in such a way as to prohibit exposure to anyone under the age of 21;

8. Updated training and protocols to enable police officers to enforce laws against driving while under the influence of cannabis;

9. Requirements for auto rental agencies, particularly at airports, to advise visitors to the City regarding the rules concerning driving while under the influence, and other cannabis regulations, of which visitors may not be aware;

10. Historical issues of social equity and social justice related to the commercialization of cannabis;

11. Issues regarding how the City addresses compliance, complaints, and civil or criminal proceedings related to Proposition D medical marijuana dispensaries; and

12. Any and all other issues that may arise regarding the commercialization of cannabis in the City.

C. **Priority of Proposition D Compliant Dispensaries.** An existing medical marijuana dispensary ("EMMD") that is operating in compliance with the limited immunity provisions (Los Angeles Municipal Code Section 45.19.6.3) and tax provisions (Los Angeles Municipal Code Section 21.50) of Proposition D, may continue to operate within the City at the one location identified in its original or amended business tax registration certificate until such time that the EMMD applies for and receives a final response to its application for a City permit or license for commercial cannabis activity being conducted at that location. The City's designated licensing or permitting agency shall give priority in processing applications of EMMDs that can demonstrate to the City's designated licensing or permitting agency that the EMMD has operated in compliance with the limited immunity and tax provisions of Proposition D. To avail itself of the terms of this Section, including the priority processing, an EMMD must apply for a City permit or license within sixty calendar days of the first date that applications are made available for commercial cannabis activity. If the City issues the EMMD a license or permit for commercial cannabis activity, the EMMD shall continue to operate at its location within the City in accordance with the rules and regulations set forth by the City.

SEC. 45.19.7.3. ENFORCEMENT, PENALTIES AND DISCONNECTION OF UTILITIES FOR UNLAWFUL CANNABIS RELATED ACTIVITY.

A. This Section is effective January 1, 2018 and applies to all entities and persons engaging in medical and/or nonmedical cannabis related activity, who are legally required to, but do not have, a City issued license, permit or authorization ("Establishment").

B. It is unlawful to: (1) Own, set up or operate an Establishment, (2) Participate as an employee, contractor, agent or volunteer or in any other capacity in an Establishment, (3) Use any portion or portion of any parcel of land as an Establishment, or to (4) Lease, rent to, or otherwise allow an Establishment to occupy any parcel or portion of parcel of land.

C. A violation of subsection B is a public nuisance and may be abated by the City or by the City Attorney, on behalf of the people of the State of California, as a nuisance by means of a restraining order, injunction or any other order or judgment in law or equity issued by a court of competent jurisdiction. The City or the City Attorney, on behalf of the people of the State of California, may seek injunctive relief to enjoin violations of, or to compel compliance with this Section or seek any other relief or remedy available at law or equity. Each day that a violation continues is deemed to be a new and separate offense and subject to a maximum civil penalty of $20,000 for each and every offense.

D. Any person violating subsection B shall be guilty of a misdemeanor punishable by a fine of not more than $1,000.00 or by imprisonment in the County Jail for a period of not more than six months, or by both a fine and imprisonment. Each day that a violation continues is deemed to be a new and separate offense.

E. The Department of Water and Power is authorized to disconnect utilities for Establishments. The circumstances and manner in which disconnection shall occur shall be specified by the City Council after receiving input from the Department of Water and Power.

F. The remedies specified in this Section are cumulative and in addition to any other remedies available under state or local law for a violation of this Code.

G. Nothing in this Section shall be construed as requiring the City to allow, permit, license, authorize or otherwise regulate medical or nonmedical cannabis, or as abridging the City's police power with respect to enforcement regarding medical or nonmedical cannabis.

Sec. 5. Nothing in this ordinance is intended to be in conflict with state law or to abrogate local police power and/or charter city authority derived from the California Constitution.

Sec. 6. Future Amendment. The City retains and possesses complete authority to regulate all aspects of cannabis related activity, including, without limitation, the authority of the Council to adopt ordinances amending any of the provisions of this ordinance, any of the provisions of Article 5.1 of Chapter IV of the Los Angeles Municipal Code regarding medical marijuana adopted by the voters as part of Proposition D at the election held on May 21, 2013 (Sections 45.19.6 through 45.19.6.9) prior to the repeal of those provisions, and/or any other provision of City law regarding cannabis related activity, other than taxation provisions to the extent that voter approval of any changes to taxation provisions is required under the State Constitution.

Sec. 7. Competing Measures. In the event that this measure and any other measure relating in any way to the regulation of cannabis in the City of Los Angeles are submitted to the voters of the City of Los Angeles on the same ballot, all of the provisions of the other measure shall be deemed to be in complete and total conflict with this measure. In the event that this measure receives a greater number of affirmative votes than the other measure, the provisions of this measure shall prevail in their entirety over all of the provisions of the other measure, and the other measure shall be null and void.

Sec. 8. Severability. If any section, subsection, subdivision, clause, sentence, phrase or portion of this measure is held unconstitutional or invalid or unenforceable by any court or tribunal of competent jurisdiction, the remaining sections, subsections, subdivisions, clauses, sentences, phrases or portions of this measure shall remain in full force and effect, and to this end the provisions of this measure are severable. In addition, the voters declare that they would have passed all sections, subsections, subdivisions, clauses, sentences, phrases or portions of this measure without the section, subsection, subdivision, clause, sentence, phrase or portion held unconstitutional or invalid.

Sec. B. The City Clerk is hereby authorized and directed to publish a notice containing the proposed ballot measure, specifying the date of March 7, 2017, as the date the measure is to be voted upon by the qualified voters of the City of Los Angeles. The notice shall be published once in a newspaper of general circulation in the City of Los Angeles, and in each edition thereof during that day of publication. The City Clerk is authorized and directed to prepare and keep in the City Clerk's office a sufficient supply of copies of the proposed ballot measure and to distribute the proposed ballot measure to any and all persons requesting a copy. Further, the City Clerk is authorized and directed to mail copies of the proposed ballot measure to each of the qualified voters of the City of Los Angeles.

Sec. C. The City Clerk is hereby authorized and directed to cause a notice to be published once in a newspaper of general circulation that copies of voter information pamphlets containing the proposed ballot measure may be obtained upon request in the City Clerk's office.

Sec. D. The City Clerk shall file a duly certified copy of this Resolution forthwith with the Board of Supervisors and with the Registrar-Recorder of the County of Los Angeles.

SIGNIFICANT LOCAL CASE LAW

SIGNIFICANT LOCAL CASE LAW

Local Police Powers - Preemption 9th and 10th Amendment

Kirby v. County of Fresno (Dec. 1, 2015, Case No. F070056) Cal.App.4th

Held: **Local Governments May Regulate and/or Ban Medical Cannabis Dispensaries and Cultivation, but Growing Medical Cannabis is Not a Crime.**

Recently, in December 2015, the California Court of Appeal followed the lead of several other courts in affirming the ability of local jurisdictions to regulate, and even ban, medical cannabis dispensaries and cultivation within their borders. In *Kirby*, the Court upheld a Fresno County ordinance banning dispensaries and prohibiting personal cultivation of medical cannabis. Specifically as to cultivation, the Court summarized that the right of any person to cultivate medical cannabis under state law "is subject to the authority of local government to hinder, inconvenience or ban the cultivation of medical cannabis through zoning and land use ordinances." The Court did find, however, that State law preempted the County's attempt to criminalize cultivation of medical cannabis, and the trial court erred in upholding the criminalization provisions of the County's ordinance. Given the trial court's error as to this limited issue, the Court reversed the trial court's dismissal of the action. Nonetheless, this case provides strong support for a local agency's ability to regulate medical cannabis cultivation and dispensaries under its land use regulatory authority.

Pack v. Long Beach (2011) 199 Cal.App.4th 1070

Held: **Federal Law Does Not Preempt Local Cities From Creating Restrictions For Dispensaries**

In 2011, the California Court of Appeal struck down a Long Beach medical cannabis dispensary licensing ordinance as being contrary to federal law. Ruling in favor of the plaintiffs, whose collective had been denied a permit under a city-sponsored lottery system, the court held that the Long Beach licensing law was invalid insofar as it positively permitted activities that conflict with the federal CSA. The *Pack* court distinguished between local ordinances that affirmatively "authorize" or "permit" conduct that is illegal under federal law (i.e., cannabis distribution, cultivation or possession) and those that merely "impose further limitations on medical cannabis collectives beyond those imposed under the MMPA ... [which] do not, in any way, permit or authorize activity prohibited by the federal CSA." In other words, ordinances framed in terms of *restrictions* on the location or manner of operation of dispensaries merely exist to show that their government tolerates those activities that are not prohibited. There, local ordinances are federally permissible.

Riverside v. Inland Empire Patients Health & Wellness (2013) 56 Cal.4th 729

Held: **Cities Have the Authority to Ban and/or Regulate Medical Cannabis Businesses**

This case held that the "CUA and MMP do not preempt a city's police power to prohibit the cultivation of all marijuana within [the] city." This means that a total permanent ban by the city does not conflict with CUA or MMP. Local governments have a traditional land use and police power to allow, restrict, limit, or exclude certain types of businesses. Thus, the court granted cities the authority to regulate, restrict, and/or ban medical cannabis business within the city.

Maral v. City of Live Oak (2013) 221 Cal.App.4th 975

Held: **Cities Have the Authority to Ban and/or Regulate Medical Cannabis Businesses and Cultivation**

The *Live Oak* case sits on the same grounds as the *Riverside* case above. In December 2011, the City of Live Oak adopted an ordinance that prohibited the cultivation of cannabis for any purpose within the city's jurisdiction. On the one hand, the City banned all cultivation of medical cannabis by individuals, so they could not cultivate their own medicine. On the other hand, the City banned all medical cannabis dispensaries within the City, so medical cannabis patients could not obtain their medicine from others. As in *Riverside,* the *Live Oak* court held that the local government has the authority and ability to completely ban cultivating medical cannabis. The court found that neither, CUA or MMPA, preempts a local government's ability to regulate or ban medical cannabis cultivation.

City of Lake Forest v. Moen, (Sep. 1, 2009, Orange Cnty. Super. Ct. No. 30-2009-298887)

Held: **Dispensaries Cannot Be Banned But Must Grow Cannabis On Site**

In March 2012, the court found that cities cannot shut down a medical cannabis dispensary that cultivates its own cannabis. Medical cannabis dispensaries can only sell cannabis from where it is cultivated. Thus, cannabis cannot be brought from somewhere else and dispensed at a store. Here, the city sought to shut down the cannabis dispensary because it was a nuisance in the community. It was ruled that a collective that includes a dispensary function — growing its own cannabis — does not constitute a nuisance. As a result, a city injunction stating that the city can shut down dispensaries as a wholesale nuisance, was struck down.

People v. West Valley Caregivers, Inc., (2015) 242 Cal. App. 4th Supp. 24

Held: **Dispensaries Have the Burden of Proof to Establish Affirmative Defense Under Proposition D**

In December 2015, the court held that a dispensary has the burden of proof under Proposition D to establish an affirmative defense that the business satisfied several enumerated requirements, which included registration under the ICO, continuous operation, and did not share managers with other such businesses. The dispensary's burden of proof is a preponderance of the evidence. The court also found that the availability of the affirmative defense under Proposition D "appears to have been intended for a purpose collateral to a defendant's guilt or innocence: to allow patients access to medical cannabis despite the deleterious impact of CBs on the community."

City of Los Angeles v. Nestdrop (January 26, 2016, Appellate Case No. B262174, Los Angeles Sup. Ct. No. BC565409)

Held: **A temporary injunction was granted against a Los Angeles-based phone app that allows people to order home delivery directly from a nearby dispensary.**

On December 2, 2014, the Los Angeles City Attorney's Office was granted a temporary injunction against Nestdrop, contending the company was violating Proposition D. However, Nestdrop does not actually operate a dispensary; rather Nestdrop is a phone app that merely provides a medium for medical cannabis patients and dispensaries to conduct transactions—no different from a phone or computer, other than being specifically tailored for medical cannabis delivery. As a result, the City Attorney has not alleged a specific unlawful delivery that Nestdrop aided and abetted, but rather has asserted that Prop. D bans all delivery of medical cannabis. To reach this result, the City Attorney relies on a hyper-technical, non-obvious reading of Prop. D in which the four words—"at the one location"—contained in the section of Prop. D that provides immunity to medical cannabis businesses registered with Los Angeles under its ICO. According to the City Attorney, the "at the one location" language means that Prop. D's immunity for pre-ICO medical cannabis businesses is confined to a particular parcel of land rather than the vehicles associated with the medical cannabis business. Nestdrop has filed an appeal which is now pending before the Court of Appeal.

City of Los Angeles v. Green Dot Medicinal Cannabis Patients' Group, (January 26, 2016, Appellate Case No. BR052212, Los Angeles Sup. Ct. No. 4CA14844)

Held: **Los Angeles Dispensaries Are Not Required to Show Proof of Insurance Dated on or Before 9/14/07 in Order to Qualify for Limited Immunity Under Proposition D**

In January 2016, the court found that the Green Dot dispensary was not required to submit proof that they had business insurance as of September 14, 2007, and that their submission of proof of insurance effective on November 13, 2007 – the registration filing deadline for the ICO – did not preclude the dispensary from asserting an affirmative defense under Proposition D. The plain language of the ICO required CB registrants to file their applications and supporting documents, including proof of insurance, by November 13, 2007, showing operation in compliance with state law as of September 14, 2007. The court found that there was no provision in the ICO requiring that insurance certificates be dated on or prior to September 14, 2007, and that there was no showing that insurance was necessary in order for the business to be operated in compliance with state law.

Safe Life Caregivers v. City of Los Angeles, (January 13, 2016, Appellate Case No. B257809 Los Angeles Sup. Ct. No. BC521581)

Held: **Proposition D Was a Properly Enacted Ordinance and is Not Preempted by the MCRSA**

In this case, nearly 20 dispensaries brought numerous challenges to the validity of Proposition D. The dispensaries' principle contention was that Proposition D was adopted in violation of Government Code § 65804, a section of the state Zoning Act, which imposes minimal procedural standards for city zoning hearings. The court held that any failure to follow the Zoning Act requirements for council-enacted ordinances had no effect on the validity of Proposition D. The dispensaries next argued that Proposition D was preempted by the MCRSA. The court, however, found that because

Proposition D was a municipal initiative on a wholly municipal matter, it was properly enacted without a planning commission hearing. Moreover, the MCRSA stated that nothing it its regulatory scheme "shall be interpreted to supersede or limit existing local authority for law enforcement activity, enforcement of local zoning requirements or local ordinance, or enforcement of local permit or licensing requirements." It also explicitly stated that issuance of a state medical cannabis license "shall in no way limit the ability of the city of Los Angeles to prosecute any person or entity for a violation of, or otherwise enforce, Proposition D." Accordingly, the court held that Proposition D was not preempted by the MCRSA and affirmed the trial court's dismissal of the dispensaries' claims, and denied leave to amend.

ENDNOTES

[1] https://www.whitehouse.gov/ondcp/state-laws-related-to-marijuana
[2] https://www.washingtonpost.com/news/post-politics/wp/2017/02/23/spicerfeds-could-step-up-anti-pot-enforcement-in-states-where-recreational-marijuana-is-legal/?utm_term=.a33c88805f28
[3] http://www.businessinsider.com/sessions-says-he-will-enforce-federal-weed-laws-2017-3
[4] http://www.politico.com/story/2017/03/jeff-sessions-marijuana-crackdown-senators-react-235616
[5] http://www.kgw.com/news/politics/pot-industry-pushes-ahead-despite-mixed-messages-from-trump/421477038
[6] http://www.politico.com/story/2017/03/jeff-sessions-marijuana-crackdown-senators-react-235616
[7] https://www.usnews.com/news/best-states/california/articles/2017-03-07/ap-interview-la-sheriff-thinks-feds-may-target-marijuana
[8] http://thehill.com/homenews/state-watch/321639-confusion-mounts-over-trump-administrations-stance-on-marijuana
[9] https://www.buzzfeed.com/alysonmartin/marijuana-industry-says-trump-cant-turn-back-the-clock-on-le?utm_term=.gx1VOP9Lk#.ed0Kw1QLR
[10] http://www.mercurynews.com/2017/02/17/6-new-things-we-learned-from-californias-cannabis-czar/
[11] http://www.mailtribune.com/apps/pbcs.dll/article?AID=/20080323/NEWS/803230336
[12] S. Dinan and B. Conery, "DEA pot raids go on; Obama opposes," Washington Times, February 5, 2009.
[13] See, Ogden, D., Memorandum for Selected United States Attorneys: Investigations and Prosecutions in States Authorizing the Medical Use of Marijuana, U.S. Dept. of Justice, Office of the Attorney General, October 19, 2009 [the "Ogden Memo"].
[14] Same.
[15] http://www.cnn.com/2010/POLITICS/10/15/holder.marijuana/
[16] California Proposition 19 was ultimately defeated, with 53.5% of California voters voting "No" to the legalization of marijuana.
[17] http://www.rollingstone.com/politics/news/obamas-war-on-pot-20120216?page=2
[18] See, Cole, J., Memorandum for United States Attorneys: Guidance Regarding the Ogden Memo in Jurisdictions Seeking to Authorize Marijuana for Medical Use, U.S. Dept. of Justice, Office of the Deputy Attorney General, June 29, 2011 [the "Cole Memo"].
[19] Same.
[20] Same.
[21] http://www.thedailychronic.net/2015/48319/rohrabacher-farr-amendment-prevents-feds-from-continuing-to-shut-down-california-dispensary/
[22] http://www.cannalawblog.com/breaking-judge-orders-feds-to-stop-enforcement-against-california-marijuana-dispensary/
[23] http://www.canbar.org/newsworthy/2015/11/5/case-update-us-v-marin-alliance-for-medical-marijuana
[24] Available here: http://blog.sfgate.com/smellthetruth/2015/10/19/major-victory-for-marijuana-dispensary-in-federal-court/
[25] http://www.huffingtonpost.com/entry/medical-marijuana-ruling_us_56265df9e4b08589ef48fee0
[26] Full text of opinion is available here: https://cdn.ca9.uscourts.gov/datastore/opinions/2016/08/16/15-10117.pdf
[27] Id.
[28] Id.
[29] https://www.brookings.edu/blog/fixgov/2016/08/19/mcintosh-decision-limits-doj-powers-but-medical-marijuana-advocates-should-worry/
[30] Id.
[31] Id.
[32] See discussion in "Chapter II: State Law," infra.
[33] Id.
[34] Id.
[35] https://www.merryjane.com/news/congress-could-decriminalize-marijuana-nationwide; The Amendment currently remains in effect through September 30, 2016 and must be renewed for inclusion in next year's federal spending plan. Renewal of the Amendment was approved by the Senate back in May but, as of the writing of this book, has yet to be voted on by the House. See: http://theleafonline.com/c/business/2016/08/court-blocks-federal-prosecutions/
[36] 84 Stat. 1236.

[37] 21 U.S.C. § 801-848.
[38] 21 U.S.C. § 811
[39] 21 U.S.C. § 801(1)-(6); see, Gonzales v. Raich (2005) 545 U.S. 1, 11-12.
[40] 21 U.S.C. §§ 811 and 812.
[41] 21 U.S.C. § 812(b)(1).
[42] 21 U.S.C. 812(c).
[43] See, 21 U.S.C. 812(c); Raich, supra, 545 U.S. at 14-15; United States v. Oakland Buyers' Cooperative (2001) 532 U.S. 483.
[44] Same.
[45] http://www.huffingtonpost.com/2015/01/26/pediatricians-call-on-dea_n_6550486.html
[46] http://www.newsweek.com/case-reclassify-grass-312845
[47] http://www.dea.gov/druginfo/ds.shtml
[48] Same.
[49] Same.
[50] http://www.newsweek.com/case-reclassify-grass-312845
[51] http://www.brookings.edu/blogs/fixgov/posts/2015/02/13-how-to-reschedule-marijuana-hudak-wallack
[52] Same.
[53] http://www.huffingtonpost.com/2014/04/04/eric-holder-reschedule-marijuana_n_5092010.html
[54] Same.
[55] http://www.huffingtonpost.com/2015/01/26/pediatricians-call-on-dea_n_6550486.html
[56] http://www.newsweek.com/case-reclassify-grass-312845
[57] Same.
[58] 2015 US Dist Lexis 51109
[59] https://thinkprogress.org/obama-administration-ignores-science-refuses-to-loosen-restrictions-on-marijuana-fa6cba6f725f#.tx1vsp3k5
[60] http://www.denverpost.com/2016/08/11/dea-not-rescheduling-marijuana/
[61] http://www.denverpost.com/2016/08/11/dea-not-rescheduling-marijuana/
[62] https://www.leafly.com/news/politics/outrage-follows-dea-refusal-to-reschedule-cannabis/
[63] https://fsrn.org/2016/08/dea-marijuana-stays-in-most-restricted-drug-class-despite-state-relaxation/
[64] https://fsrn.org/2016/08/dea-marijuana-stays-in-most-restricted-drug-class-despite-state-relaxation/
[65] http://www.inc.com/will-yakowicz/nightmare-of-schedule-ii-cannabis.html
[66] https://fsrn.org/2016/08/dea-marijuana-stays-in-most-restricted-drug-class-despite-state-relaxation/
[67] http://www.inc.com/will-yakowicz/nightmare-of-schedule-ii-cannabis.html
[68] http://www.fool.com/investing/2016/08/06/clinton-or-trump-find-out-which-candidate-the-mari.aspx; https://www.brookings.edu/blog/fixgov/2016/08/11/the-deas-marijuana-decision-is-more-important-than-rescheduling/; http://www.inc.com/will-yakowicz/nightmare-of-schedule-ii-cannabis.html.
[69] http://www.inc.com/will-yakowicz/nightmare-of-schedule-ii-cannabis.html
[70] http://www.inc.com/will-yakowicz/nightmare-of-schedule-ii-cannabis.html
[71] http://www.inc.com/will-yakowicz/nightmare-of-schedule-ii-cannabis.html
[72] https://www.brookings.edu/blog/fixgov/2016/08/11/the-deas-marijuana-decision-is-more-important-than-rescheduling/
[73] http://www.nnbw.com/news/23595334-113/dea-marijuana-remains-a-schedule-i-controlled-substance#
[74] https://www.brookings.edu/blog/fixgov/2016/08/11/the-deas-marijuana-decision-is-more-important-than-rescheduling/
[75] http://www.usnews.com/news/articles/2016-08-11/dea-ends-half-century-pot-monopoly-but-withholds-big-prize-for-reformers
[76] https://news.vice.com/article/medical-marijuana-researchers-are-tired-of-working-with-shitty-weed
[77] https://news.vice.com/article/medical-marijuana-researchers-are-tired-of-working-with-shitty-weed
[78] https://www.federalregister.gov/documents/2016/08/12/2016-17955/applications-to-become-registered-under-the-controlled-substances-act-to-manufacture-marijuana-to
[79] http://www.cannabisfn.com/dea-rejects-bid-to-reclassify-marijuana/
[80] http://www.inc.com/will-yakowicz/nightmare-of-schedule-ii-cannabis.html
[81] http://hightimes.com/culture/11-us-presidents-who-smoked-marijuana/
[82] http://herb.co/2015/11/27/whats-the-difference-between-hemp-and-cannabis/
[83] http://www.kyagr.com/marketing/industrial-hemp.html
[84] http://www.huffingtonpost.com/2015/06/04/ron-wyden-hemp-senate_n_7515424.html
[85] 333 F.3d 1082 (9th Cir. 2003)
[86] Id.

[87] https://www.gpo.gov/fdsys/pkg/FR-2016-08-12/pdf/2016-19146.pdf
[88] http://www.kyagr.com/marketing/industrial-hemp.html
[89] http://www.cannalawblog.com/think-you-are-selling-legal-cbd-oil-dea-says-think-again/
[90] https://hoban.law/blog/2017/2017-01/dea-cbd-marijuana-extract-not-hemp
[91] http://helenair.com/news/state-and-regional/medical-marijuana-providers-ask-federal-judge-to-throw-out-montana/article_967304ce-bdcf-5184-b7f9-11fa8d28980d.html
[92] H.R. 2578.
[93] http://www.fda.gov/NewsEvents/PublicHealthFocus/ucm421168.htm
[94] http://www.nutraingredients-usa.com/Regulation/Warning-letters-to-CBD-companies-hinge-on-disease-claims-sidestep-issue-of-ingredient-s-legality
[95] 21 U.S.C. 812
[96] See, F.R.C.P. 35(b); 18 U.S.C. § 3553(e).
[97] These dollar amounts indicate max fines if the defendant is an individual. If the defendant is not an individual, max fines are significantly higher. See, 21 U.S.C. §§ 841 and 844.
[98] If the marijuana was sold to a minor or within 1,000 feet of a school or other specified areas, the criminal penalties double. (See, 21 U.S.C. §§ 859 and 860.) Criminal penalties also increase for second and subsequent offenses. (See, 21 U.S.C. § 841.)
[99] Criminal penalties increase for second and subsequent offenses. (See, 21 U.S.C. § 841.)
[100] Holder, E., Memorandum for the Department of Justice Attorneys: Guidance Regarding Section 851 Enhancements in Plea Negotiations, U.S. Dept. of Justice, Office of the Attorney General, September 24, 2014.
[101] http://www.cnn.com/2015/02/17/politics/attorney-general-eric-holder-drug-sentencing-prosecutions/
[102] http://famm.org/ag-eric-holder-no-more-super-mandatory-minimums-to-punish-defendants-who-want-a-trial/
[103] http://www.cnn.com/2015/02/17/politics/attorney-general-eric-holder-drug-sentencing-prosecutions/
[104] Same.
[105] Holder, E., Memorandum for the Department of Justice Attorneys: Guidance Regarding Section 851 Enhancements in Plea Negotiations, U.S. Dept. of Justice, Office of the Attorney General, September 24, 2014.
[106] 21 U.S.C. § 903.
[107] See, County of San Diego v. NORML (2008) 165 Cal. App. 4th 798; Emerald Steel Fabricators, Inc. v. Bureau of Labor and Industries (2010) 348 Ore. 159.
[108] Same.
[109] Rice v. Santa Fe Elevator Corp. (1947) 331 U.S. 218, 230.
[110] See, Todd Garvey, "Medical Marijuana: The Supremacy Clause, Federalism and the Interplay Between State and Federal Laws," Congressional Research Service, November 9, 2012.
[111] (2011) 199 Cal.App.4th 1070.
[112] Proposition D, preamble.
[113] http://www.washingtonpost.com/blogs/post-politics/wp/2012/12/14/obama-ive-got-bigger-fish-to-fry-than-pot-smokers/
[114] http://www.cannalawblog.com/marijuana-at-the-border-customs-and-border-protection-misses-the-cole-memo-gets-sued/
[115] http://www.cannalawblog.com/marijuana-at-the-border-customs-and-border-protection-misses-the-cole-memo-gets-sued/
[116] http://www.cannalawblog.com/marijuana-at-the-border-customs-and-border-protection-misses-the-cole-memo-gets-sued/
[117] http://www.cannalawblog.com/marijuana-at-the-border-customs-and-border-protection-misses-the-cole-memo-gets-sued/
[118] http://www.cannalawblog.com/marijuana-at-the-border-customs-and-border-protection-misses-the-cole-memo-gets-sued/
[119] https://www.justice.gov/sites/default/files/tribal/pages/attachments/2014/12/11/policystatementregardingmarijuanaissuesinindiancountry2.pdf
[120] http://www.cannalawblog.com/is-tribal-cannabis-still-possible/
[121] https://www.justice.gov/sites/default/files/tribal/pages/attachments/2014/12/11/policystatementregardingmarijuanaissuesinindiancountry2.pdf
[122] Id.
[123] http://www.cannalawblog.com/is-tribal-cannabis-still-possible/
[124] http://archive.jsonline.com/news/wisconsin/federal-raids-cool-tribal-excitement-over-potential-marijuana-profits-b99632595z1-361687291.html

[125] http://archive.jsonline.com/news/wisconsin/federal-raids-cool-tribal-excitement-over-potential-marijuana-profits-b99632595z1-361687291.html
[126] http://fusion.net/story/212947/legal-weed-native-american-casino/
[127] http://archive.jsonline.com/news/wisconsin/federal-raids-cool-tribal-excitement-over-potential-marijuana-profits-b99632595z1-361687291.html
[128] http://www.mintpressnews.com/feds-seize-12000-marijuana-plants-from-two-small-native-american-tribes/207584/
[129] http://www.cbsnews.com/news/after-federal-raids-u-s-tribes-cautioned-about-marijuana/
[130] http://www.cannalawblog.com/is-tribal-cannabis-still-possible/
[131] http://abovethelaw.com/2015/11/mixed-smoke-signals-for-tribal-marijuana-from-doj/?rf=1
[132] http://indiancountrytodaymedianetwork.com/2015/10/06/santee-sioux-assert-tribal-sovereignty-open-first-marijuana-resort-161976
[133] http://www.cannalawblog.com/is-tribal-cannabis-still-possible/
[134] http://indiancountrytodaymedianetwork.com/2015/11/08/flandreau-santee-sioux-tribe-burns-crop-suspends-marijuana-operation-162363
[135] http://indiancountrytodaymedianetwork.com/2015/11/08/flandreau-santee-sioux-tribe-burns-crop-suspends-marijuana-operation-162363
[136] http://www.vice.com/read/south-dakota-tribe-burns-weed-crop-in-anticipation-of-a-federal-raid-119
[137] https://www.greenrushdaily.com/2016/09/13/native-american-tribes-can-legally-grow-sell-marijuana/
[138] https://www.merryjane.com/news/state-forces-santee-sioux-tribe-to-burn-1mm-worth-of-marijuana
[139] http://indiancountrytodaymedianetwork.com/2016/08/08/charges-filed-against-men-assisting-santee-sioux-marijuana-venture-165406
[140] http://indiancountrytodaymedianetwork.com/2016/08/08/charges-filed-against-men-assisting-santee-sioux-marijuana-venture-165406
[141] http://indiancountrytodaymedianetwork.com/2016/08/08/charges-filed-against-men-assisting-santee-sioux-marijuana-venture-165406
[142] http://www.cbsnews.com/news/after-federal-raids-u-s-tribes-cautioned-about-marijuana/
[143] http://www.cbsnews.com/news/after-federal-raids-u-s-tribes-cautioned-about-marijuana/
[144] http://www.cbsnews.com/news/after-federal-raids-u-s-tribes-cautioned-about-marijuana/
[145] http://niccdc.org/2015/12/warm-springs-tribes-approve-marijuana-sales-in-historic-vote/
[146] http://www.huffingtonpost.com/entry/pit-river-marijuana-raid_us_55a938cfe4b0f904bebfe52a
[147] http://www.vice.com/read/ultra-health-interview-weediquette-viceland
[148] http://time.com/4559278/marijuana-election-results-2016/
[149] Health & Safety Code § 11362.5(b)(1)(A).
[150] Health & Safety Code § 11362.5(b)(1)(B).
[151] Health & Safety Code § 11362.5(d).
[152] People v. Kelly (2010) 47 Cal.4th 1008, 1013; People v. Mower (2002) 28 Cal.4th 457, 474.
[153] People v. Trippet (1997) 56 Cal. App. 4th 1532, 1551.
[154] Mower, supra, 28 Cal.4th at 477; People v. Jackson (2012) 210 Cal. App. 4th 525, 529-553.
[155] Mower, supra, 28 Cal.4th at 467-469.
[156] Probable cause is defined as trustworthy facts sufficient enough that a reasonable person would believe the suspect committed or is planning to commit a crime or unlawful act.
[157] Same.
[158] People v. Urziceanu (2005) 132 Cal. App. 4th 747, 772-773.
[159] People v. Wright (2006) 40 Cal.4th 81, 85.
[160] Health & Safety Code § 11359.
[161] Health & Safety Code § 11360.
[162] Health & Safety Code § 11366.
[163] Health & Safety Code § 11366.5.
[164] Health & Safety Code § 11370; See, Health & Safety Code § 11362.775.
[165] See, S.B. 420, 2003 Leg., 2003-2004 Leg.
[166] At trial, the burden is on the defendant to generate a reasonable doubt as to whether a CUA defense applies; thereafter, the burden shifts to the prosecution to disprove that defense beyond a reasonable doubt. At a preliminary hearing, the question is one of probable cause. As noted in Mower, probable cause will not lie where, in light of all the circumstances, it appears that a defendant is entitled to a CUA defense. See, Mower, supra, 28 Cal.4th at 476-483.
[167] See, Mower, supra, 28 Cal.4th at 476-483.
[168] Urziceanu, supra, 132 Cal. App. 4th at 785.
[169] Stats. 2003, ch. 875, § 1, subds. (b)(3).
[170] Health & Safety Code § 11362.81(d).

[171] Full text of the A.G. Guidelines can be read online here: http://ag.ca.gov/cms_attachments/press/pdfs/n1601_medicalmarijuanaguidelines.pdf.
[172] People v. Hochanadel (2009) 176 Cal. App. 4th 997.
[173] Same. According to the A.G. Guidelines, the standard by which a cooperative or collective should be complying with the guidelines is one of "substantial compliance." (A.G. Guidelines at p. 6.) This means that if a collective or cooperative is not "substantially complying" with the A.G. Guidelines, it is "likely operating outside the protections of [the CUA] and the MMP."
[174] Health & Safety Code § 11362.71(f).
[175] Same.
[176] San Diego v. NORML (2008) 165 Cal. App. 4th 798.
[177] Health & Safety Code § 11362. 78; San Diego NORML, supra, 165 Cal. App. 4th at 830.
[178] A.G. Guidelines at p. 6.
[179] Health & Safety Code § 11362.77(a).
[180] Health & Safety Code § 11362.77(f).
[181] A.G. Guidelines at p. 10.
[182] Same.
[183] Kelly, supra, 47 Cal.4th at 1008.
[184] Kelly, supra, 47 Cal.4th at 1013; People v. Trippett (1997) 56 Cal. App. 4th 1532, 1549; Health & Safety Code § 11362.5(d).)
[185] People v. Hochanadel (2009) 176 Cal. App. 4th 997.
[186] Same. According to the A.G. Guidelines, the standard by which a cooperative or collective should be complying with the guidelines is one of "substantial compliance." (A.G. Guidelines at p. 6.) This means that if a collective or cooperative is not "substantially complying" with the A.G. Guidelines, it is "likely operating outside the protections of [the CUA] and the MMP."
[187] A.G. Guidelines at p. 4.
[188] Physicians may not prescribe marijuana because the federal Food and Drug Administration regulates prescription drugs and, under the CSA, marijuana is a Schedule I substance, meaning that it has no recognized medical use. Under California law, however, a physician cannot be "punished" or "denied any right or privilege" for issuing a verbal or written recommendation for medical marijuana. (Health & Safety Code § 11362.5(c).) (Health & Safety Code § 11362.5(d); A.G. Guidelines at p. 4.
[189] Health & Safety Code § 11262.5(b)(1)(A); A.G. Guidelines at p. 4.
[190] Health & Safety Code § 11262.5(e); A.G. Guidelines at p. 4.
[191] People ex rel. Lungren v. Peron (1997) 59 Cal.App.4th 1383, 1390, 1400.
[192] Health & Safety Code § 11362.7(d)(2); A.G. Guidelines at p. 4.) Primary caregivers also may receive certain compensation for their services. (Health & Safety Code § 11362.765(c); A.G. Guidelines at p. 4.
[193] Health & Safety Code § 11362.7(a).
[194] Corp. Code, § 12201, 12300.
[195] Id. at § 12311(b).
[196] Id. at § 12201.
[197] Ibid.
[198] See id. at § 12200, et seq.
[199] Food & Agric. Code, § 54033.
[200] See, e.g., id. at § 54002, et seq.
[201] A.G. Guidelines at p. 8.
[202] Random House Unabridged Dictionary; Random House, Inc. © 2006.
[203] A.G. Guidelines at p. 8
[204] Corporations Code § 12311(b).
[205] Corporations Code § 12201, 12300.
[206] Corporations Code § 12201
[207] A.G. Guidelines at p. 8.
[208] See, A.G. Guidelines at p. 4.
[209] A.G. Guidelines at p. 8.
[210] People v. Hochanadel (2009) 176 Cal. App. 4th 997; People v. Colvin (1981) 114 Cal. App. 3d 614.
[211] Peron, supra, 59 Cal. App. 4th at 1400.
[212] California Corporations Code section 12310.
[213] People v. Hochanadel (2009) 176 Cal. App. 4th 997.
[214] People v. Jackson (2012) 210 Cal. App. 4th 525, 529-530; A.G. Guidelines at p. 6, 9.
[215] A.G. Guidelines at p. 9; see also, Health & Safety Code § 11362.765(a).

[216] http://www.marijuanacontrollegalizationrevenueact.com/what/the-language-full-text/
[217] A.G. Guidelines at p. 10; see also, Health & Safety Code §§ 11362.765 and 111362.774.
[218] A.G. Guidelines at p. 10.
[219] Same.
[220] Same.
[221] Same.
[222] Colvin, supra, 114 Cal. App. 3d at 1041; Jackson, supra, 210 Cal. App. 4th at 530.
[223] http://www.boe.ca.gov/news/marijuana.htm
[224] See, Riverside, supra, 56 Cal.4th 729.
[225] People v. Mulcrevy (Dec. 2014) C075885.
[226] People v. Bergen (2008) 166 Cal. App. 4th 161.
[227] Health & Safety Code § 11379.6(a) provides in pertinent part: "Except as otherwise provided by law, every person who manufactures, compounds, converts, produces, derives, processes, or prepares, either directly or indirectly by chemical extraction or independently by means of chemical synthesis, any controlled substance specified in Section 11054, 11055, 11056, 11057, or 11058 shall be punished by imprisonment pursuant to subdivision (h) of Section 1170 of the Penal Code for three, five, or seven years and by a fine not exceeding fifty thousand dollars ($50,000)."
[228] Health & Safety Code § 11358 provides in pertinent part: "Every person who plants, cultivates, harvests, dries, or processes any marijuana or any part thereof, except as otherwise provided by law, shall be punished by imprisonment pursuant to subdivision (h) of Section 1170 of the Penal Code."
[229] Bergen, supra, 166 Cal. App. 4th 161.
[230] Bergen, supra, 166 Cal. App. 4th 161.
[231] http://www.cannalawblog.com/producing-cannabis-extracts-in-california-is-risky/
[232] http://www.cbs8.com/story/31086445/police-raid-kearny-mesa-business-suspected-of-illegally-producing-hash-oil
[233] On June 27, 2016, the California legislature passed SB 837 to amend certain areas of the MCRSA. SB 837 changed the name of the Medical Marijuana Regulation and Safety Act and the Bureau of Medical Marijuana Regulation to the Medical Cannabis Regulation and Safety Act and the Bureau of Medical Cannabis Regulation, and makes other changes. See: http://www.leginfo.ca.gov/pub/15-16/bill/sen/sb_0801-0850/sb_837_bill_20160627_chaptered.htm
[234] Hon. Steven K. Lubell, Memo re: Statewide Implementation of the Medical Marijuana Regulation and Safety Act, January 22, 2016
[235] Hon. Steven K. Lubell, Memo re: Statewide Implementation of the Medical Marijuana Regulation and Safety Act, January 22, 2016
[236] SB 837, § 30.
[237] SB 837, § 32.
[238] AB 243, 19332(g).
[239] SB 837, § 30.
[240] SB 837, § 30.
[241] SB 837, § 32.
[242] SB 837, § 30.
[243] SB 837, § 30.
[244] SB 837, § 30.
[245] AB 2516.
[246] SB 837, § 6.
[247] SB 837, § 30.
[248] SB 837, §§ 30, 32.
[249] AB 243, 19332(g).
[250] SB 837, § 30.
[251] SB 837, § 30.
[252] SB 837, § 30.
[253] SB 837, § 35
[254] People v. Bergen (2008) 166 Cal. App. 4th 161.
[255] See full text of AB 2679 here: http://leginfo.legislature.ca.gov/faces/billNavClient.xhtml?bill_id=201520160AB2679
[256] http://www.thedailychronic.net/2016/62743/california-governor-signs-standards-protections-medical-marijuana-manufacturers/
[257] SB 837, § 23.
[258] SB 837, § 30.
[259] SB 837, §§ 28, 30.
[260] SB 837, § 35.

[261] SB 837, § 35.
[262] SB 837, § 30.
[263] SB 837, §§ 28, 30.
[264] SB 837, §§ 28, 30.
[265] SB 837, § 30.
[266] SB 837, §§ 28, 30.
[267] SB 837, § 30.
[268] AUMA, § 3.
[269] AUMA, § 26061.
[270] AUMA, § 26062(d).
[271] AUMA, §2(J).
[272] AUMA, § 26070.
[273] AUMA, § 34011.
[274] AUMA, § 26062
[275] http://www.laweekly.com/news/how-recreational-marijuana-will-change-la-and-how-it-won-t-6815483
[276] AUMA, § 26062(d).
[277] AUMA, § 26055.
[278] AUMA, § 26057.
[279] AUMA, § 26054.1.
[280] AUMA, § 25064.
[281] Id.
[282] AUMA, § 26057.
[283] AUMA, § 26057.
[284] AUMA, § 11357.
[285] AUMA, § 11358.
[286] AUMA, § 11359.
[287] AUMA, § 11360.
[288] AUMA, § 11361.8.
[289] AUMA, § 26200.
[290] AB 266, § 19321.
[291] AUMA, § 26054.2(a).
[292] AUMA, § 26054.2(b).
[293] http://www.cannalawblog.com/californias-auma-initiative-why-has-everyone-stopped-caring-about-priority-licensing-status/
[294] AB 243, 19332(g).
[295] http://www.cannalawblog.com/californias-auma-initiative-why-has-everyone-stopped-caring-about-priority-licensing-status/
[296] AB 266, 19328.
[297] AB 266, 19328.
[298] Id.
[299] Id.
[300] Food & Agricultural Code § 81006.
[301] Id.
[302] https://www.gpo.gov/fdsys/pkg/FR-2016-08-12/pdf/2016-19146.pdf
[303] 333 F.3d 1082 (9th Cir. 2003)
[304] Id.
[305] http://www.cannalawblog.com/think-you-are-selling-legal-cbd-oil-dea-says-think-again/
[306] https://hoban.law/blog/2017/2017-01/dea-cbd-marijuana-extract-not-hemp
[307] http://helenair.com/news/state-and-regional/medical-marijuana-providers-ask-federal-judge-to-throw-out-montana/article_967304ce-bdcf-5184-b7f9-11fa8d28980d.html
[308] H.R. 2578.
[309] B&P §§ 19300, 19320.
[310] B&P § 26055(e).
[311] B&P § 26054.1.
[312] B&P § 26054.1.
[313] http://mjbizdaily.com/crafting-industry-qa-california-cannabis-czar-lori-ajax/
[314] http://www.sandiegouniontribune.com/business/sd-me-pot-banking-20170210-story.html
[315] http://leginfo.legislature.ca.gov/faces/billNavClient.xhtml?bill_id=201720180AB64

[316] http://leginfo.legislature.ca.gov/faces/billNavClient.xhtml?bill_id=201720180AB64
[317] B&P § 19321.
[318] http://www.cannalawblog.com/eight-unknowns-about-californias-mcrsa-and-proposition-64/
[319] http://mjbizdaily.com/crafting-industry-qa-california-cannabis-czar-lori-ajax/
[320] http://www.cannalawblog.com/california-marijuana-licensing-new-doubts-on-meeting-2018-deadline/
[321] AB 266, 19328.
[322] http://www.canorml.org/news/A_SUMMARY_OF_THE_MEDICAL_MARIJUANA_REGULATION_AND_SAFETY_ACT
[323] AUMA, § 26070.
[324] http://mjbizdaily.com/crafting-industry-qa-california-cannabis-czar-lori-ajax/
[325] B&P § 19321.
[326] B&P § 26054.2(a).
[327] See, S.B. 420, 2003 Leg., 2003-2004 Leg.
[328] At trial, the burden is on the defendant to generate a reasonable doubt as to whether a CUA defense applies; thereafter, the burden shifts to the prosecution to disprove that defense beyond a reasonable doubt. At a preliminary hearing, the question is one of probable cause. As noted in Mower, probable cause will not lie where, in light of all the circumstances, it appears that a defendant is entitled to a CUA defense. See, Mower, supra, 28 Cal.4th at 476-483.
[329] See, Mower, supra, 28 Cal.4th at 476-483.
[330] While verbal recommendations are technically permitted under the MMP, it is recommended that patients obtain and carry written proof of their physician's recommendation to help them avoid arrest. (A.G. Guidelines at p. 5.) This is because "[o]fficers are not obligated to accept a person's claim of having a verbal physician's recommendation that cannot be readily verified with the physician at the time of detention." (A.G. Guidelines at p. 7.) (Health & Safety Code § 1136.5(d); Attorney General Guidelines at p. 5.
[331] A sample of a written designation of primary caregiver can be found online here: http://www.safeaccessnow.net/pdf/caregiver.pdf.
[332] Urziceanu, supra, 132 Cal. App. 4th at 772-773; Peron, supra, 59 Cal. App. 4th at 14000; People v. Mentch (2008) 45 Cal.4th 274.
[333] AB 243, § 11362.777(g) and SB 643, § 19319.
[334] SB 643, § 2220.05.
[335] http://www.latimes.com/local/political/la-me-pc-police-would-have-to-reimburse-for-return-seized-pot-20140514-story.html
[336] Same.
[337] People v. Lamonte, 53 Cal.App.4th 544, 552 (4th Dist. 1997).
[338] 8 U.S.C. § 1227(a)(2)(B).
[339] See, Moncrieffe v. Holder (2013) 569 U.S.
[340] https://www.ilrc.org/sites/default/files/resources/report_prop64_final.pdf
[341] Article 4, Section 19321 of AB 266.
[342] AB 266 provides that "[a] licensee shall not commence activity under the authority of a state license until the applicant obtained, in addition to the state license, a license or permit from the local jurisdiction in which he or she proposes to operate, following the requirements of the applicable local ordinance."
[343] B&P § 26055(e).
[344] Article 4, Section 19321 of AB 266.
[345] See, Nordyke v. King (2002) 27 Cal.4th 875, 883-884; People v. Commons (1944) 64 Cal. App. 2d Supp. 925, 929-939.
[346] Riverside v. Inland Empire Patients Health & Wellness Center, Inc. (2013) 56 Cal.4th 729, 748.
[347] A.G. Guidelines at p. 9.
[348] http://clkrep.lacity.org/onlinedocs/2017/17-1100-S2_misc_11-8-16.pdf
[349] http://mjbizdaily.com/l-a-cannabis-businesses-face-regulations-uncertainty-with-new-ballot-measures/
[350] https://www.leafly.com/news/politics/las-prop-m-passes-today-heres-will-change
[351] http://www.nbcsandiego.com/news/politics/Bill-Bans-Pot-Stores-Near-Schools--95554994.html
[352] Health & Safety Code § 1136.768(f).
[353] Widener, Michael N. "Medical Marijuana Premises Leasing and Property Lawyer Dilemmas in Statutorily Altered States." (2012).
[354] United States v. Tamez, 941 F.2d 770, 774 (9th Cir.1991).
[355] Widener, Michael N. "Medical Marijuana Premises Leasing and Property Lawyer Dilemmas in Statutorily Altered States." (2012).
[356] Marijuana At The Crossroads: Article: Marijuana at the Crossroads: Keynote Address, 89 Denv. U.L. Rev. 977, 988.

[357] Widener, Michael N. "Medical Marijuana Premises Leasing and Property Lawyer Dilemmas in Statutorily Altered States." (2012).
[358] Same.
[359] United States v. 1840 Embarcadero, 932 F. Supp. 2d 1064 (N.D. Cal. 2013).
[360] Symposium: The Road To Legitimizing Marijuana: What Benefit At What Cost?: Medical Marijuana and Federal Narcotics Enforcement in the Eastern District of California, 43 McGeorge L. Rev. 109, 118.
[361] City of Oakland v Lynch (9th Cir, Aug. 20, 2015, No. 13-15391,
[362] Same.
[363] Widener, Michael N. "Medical Marijuana Premises Leasing and Property Lawyer Dilemmas in Statutorily Altered States." (2012).
[364] http://www.reuters.com/article/2013/01/08/us-usa-marijuana-oakland-idUSBRE90704P20130108
[365] Same.
[366] Garvey, Todd, and Brian T. Yeh. "State Legalization of Recreational Marijuana: Selected Legal Issues." Congressional Research Service Report for Congress. 2013, pg 32.
[367] http://www.forbes.com/sites/jacobsullum/2014/06/03/would-the-rohrabacher-farr-amendment-actually-stop-medical-marijuana-raids/
[368] Qualified Patients Assn. v. City of Anaheim, No. G046417 (Cal. Ct. App. Jan. 15, 2014); Auto Equity Sales, Inc. v. Superior Court (1962) 57 Cal.2d 450, 455 (Auto Equity).
[369] City of Riverside v. Inland Empire Patients Health & Wellness Center, Inc. (2013) 56 Cal.4th 729.
[370] People v. Superior Court of Los Angeles County, No. B257222 (Cal. Ct. App. Mar. 9, 2015).
[371] http://humboldtrelief.org/2013/06/23/pre-ico-dispensaries-list-2013-mmj-patient-information/
[372] Pot Banking 2016: More State Ballots But Continued Unease, By Douglas Fischer and Jodi Avergun http://www.americanbanker.com/bankthink/pot-banking-2016-more-state-ballots-but-continued-unease-1079125-1.html?zkPrintable=true
[373] 21 U.S.C. 812(c).
374 http://www.forbes.com/sites/jacobsullum/2014/09/18/local-banks-terrified-by-friendly-neighborhood-cannabis-merchants/
375 http://www.nytimes.com/2014/02/15/us/us-issues-marijuana-guidelines-for-banks.html?_r=0
376 26 U.S.C. § 280E.
377 See, Edmondson v. Commission (1981) 42 T.C.M. 1533.
378 http://www.forbes.com/sites/anthonynitti/2015/01/24/irs-futher-limits-deductions-for-state-legal-cannabis-facilities/
379 http://www.usatoday.com/story/news/nation/2014/11/03/irs-limits-profits-cannabis-businesses/18165033/
380 Same.
[381] https://ww2.kqed.org/news/2017/01/12/branding-bud-marijuana-companies-want-california-to-issue-trademarks-for-pot/
[382] http://www.huffingtonpost.com/2014/06/07/hershey-marijuana-sues-weed_n_5462886.html
[383] http://www.denverpost.com/business/ci_26741590/colo-springs-edibles-firm-settles-suit-over-hershey
[384] 35 U.S.C. § 161.
[385] Article I, Section 8 of the US Constitution
[386] H&S § 11364.5(12)
[387] State v. Smoke Signals Pipe & Tobacco Shop, LLC, 922 A.2d 634, 642 (N.H. 2007)
[388] Opinion of the Justices, 121 N.H. at 545.
[389] Mid-Atlantic Accessories Trade Ass'n v. Maryland, 500 F. Supp. 834, 844 (D. Md. 1980) (holding that the term "intended for use" in a similar statute applies to the accused).
[390] Health & Safety Code § 11364; see Health & Safety Code § 11374
[391] 21 USC Subchapter I, Control And Enforcement Part D §863
[392] B&P §§ 26151-26154.
[393] (Conant v. Walters (9th Cir. 2002) 309 F.3d 269.)
[394] (Id.)
[395] (People v. Mower (2002) 28 Cal.4th 457.)
[396] (Id.)
[397] (Id.)
[398] (People v. Konow (2004) 32 Cal.4th 995.)
[399] (Id. at 1024-1026.)
[400] (People v. Mentch (2008) 45 Cal.4th 274.)
[401] http://www.examiner.com/article/medical-marijuana-and-caregivers
[402] (People v. Mitchell (2014) 225 Cal.App.4th 1189.)

[403] (People v. Anderson (Jan. 9, 2015, F066737) _ Cal.App.5th _.)
[404] (City of Garden Grove v. Superior Court of Orange County, Felix Kha (2008) 157 Cal.App. 4th 355.)

Made in the USA
Middletown, DE
26 July 2020